Living Without Jim is an incredible account of a woman's journey after the death of her husband. It's an amazing story of God's sustaining power and supernatural strength that carried her during her time of overwhelming grief and loss. This book is a must-read for anyone that has lost someone they love!

—**Martha Munizzi,** international praise and worship recording artist

Sue Keddy gives the reader an intimate, heartfelt look into the life experiences that brought her closer to the presence of the Lord. By overcoming incredible tragedy, she has found the strength and determination to embrace the calling God has on her life. *Living Without Jim* will break your heart, awaken your mind, and breathe new life into your soul. Overflowing with emotion and inspiration, it is an amazing testament of the resiliency of the human spirit. I recommend this book to anyone who has lost hope or is feeling stagnant, so that they may surge forward with renewed faith and a greater understanding of God's purpose.

—**Pastor Matthew Barnett,** co-founder of the Dream Center

Sue Keddy's perfect world came crashing down in a few agonizing seconds when the love of her life was snatched away. With disarming candidness, Sue allows us a glimpse of some of her most intimate moments of heartache and comfort, discouragement and hope, struggle and triumph. The account, however, reads like a love story, a modern-day Song of Songs—but one in which the beloved, separated from and pining for her lover, finds her healing, comfort, and strength in the very Jesus whose love had captured them both and bound them so closely together through life. Engagingly honest, beautiful in its simplicity and captivating in its appeal, *Living Without Jim* is a rich blend of priceless biblical reflection and devotional depth. The radiance of Jesus shines brilliantly through this moving testimony of a courageous woman's journey of faith. But be warned: you will have moments when you want to take your shoes off as you feel the breath of angels, a gentle breeze parts the curtain of heaven...and you find yourself staring into the face of eternity!

—**Dr. Ivan Satyavrata,** leader of the Assemblies of God church and its network of ministries in Kolkata, India; author of *The Holy Spirit: Lord and Life-Giver*

Here you will find raw emotion, deep sadness, living hope, and a transparency that is rarely expressed by Christian authors. You will come to know an exceptional person, a great missionary, an amazing wife, a devoted mother, and a passionate Christ-follower. More than that, if you read this amazing journal, you will be confronted by an authentic faith and challenged to serve Christ more. So be prepared. We are certain this book will find a unique place in Christian literature; it's a valuable addition to our understanding of time, space, eternity, and grief.

—Drs. Paul and Carol Alexander, missionary educators and motivators. Paul serves as president and Carol as director of post-graduate studies at Trinity Bible College, Ellendale, ND

LIVING WITHOUT
Jim

SUE KEDDY

Deep River BOOKS

Dedication

During one of my trips to Pakistan, a lady came to the door of the home where I was staying. She said she had been told there was a widow visiting from abroad and that she wanted to meet her. We were escorted to a small room, and as the door shut behind us she told me her story. Her husband had died a violent death, and she had suddenly found herself completely alone. The pain was so great, she prayed every night for God to take her in her sleep. But each morning she woke up to the agony of loneliness. With tears streaming down her cheeks she asked me, "How do you live?"

A broken heart often results in just existing, living out a *Groundhog Day* kind of drudgery, until it's finally over.

I told my unexpected guest that when you have Jesus, it's possible to truly *live.* His companionship, His wisdom, His grace, His mercy and His indescribable love—love that is constant no matter how I feel, or what I do or don't do—enables me to wake up with purpose and *live* with joyful abandon and childlike wonder.

This book is dedicated to every crushed spirit who has ever asked her question.

This book was written for you.

CONTENTS

Foreword

It's hard to be human and not have those moments when you imagine the possibility of tragedy in your life and find yourself gripped with fear. I've had those moments more than I'd like to admit. Whether it was the loss of health, possessions, or a loved one, it's easy to wonder whether life could ever go back to being "good" again. We can remind ourselves of God's promises to never leave us and to work all things together for our good, but in the end will that really be enough? Can peace and joy ever truly be recovered?

I met Sue Keddy after a women's conference at my church. I had just finished speaking, when she suddenly approached me on the side of the platform. The service was concluding and she sensed that we only had seconds to talk. With the most inviting smile and sincere excitement, she asked me to be a part of an event she was hosting in Canada. We quickly exchanged information and, before I knew it, she was gone. How is it you can know someone is unusually special in just forty-five seconds? I'm not sure, but as Sue made her way back to her seat, I thought *That's a woman who really knows Jesus . . . and I'd love to know her better.* God gave me that privilege when I travelled to Canada to speak at her women's conference the following year.

When I arrived at the venue, I was taken into a room where Sue was to meet with me before the service. She walked in, wearing her infectious smile, and we exchanged a little small talk. Then I seized the moment to finally learn more about her. "So . . . tell me about you," I asked. I wasn't expecting the story that would follow. Within minutes, I was doing my best to hold back tears as she shared with me about the road of loss and sorrow she had traveled over recent years. The more she talked, the more I became aware of how amazing Jesus is. All I could see was the incredible contrast of a story filled with pain and a storyteller who radiated a supernatural peace and joy. When she told me the Lord was leading her to write a book, I was thrilled. I had no doubt that God had given her a message that needs to be shared, to encourage the rest of us who have also experienced suffering—or who simply fear it. A friendship began that day, which has led to me receiving the honor of writing this foreword.

In *Living Without Jim*, Sue graciously allows us to journey with her through the first year following the greatest tragedy of her life. As I read, I felt as though I had entered her world. I cried with her. I grieved with her. And because it's Sue, I even laughed with her at times. And yet, the true purpose of this book goes way beyond empathizing with the writer. The challenge for the reader is in Sue's response to her suffering. Her ultimate prayer continues to be, "Not my will, Lord, but yours be done." And, as she submits to God plan, we are given front-row seats to watch His incredible faithfulness take over. With each passing day, we witness God's power to comfort, provide, and bring victory to a person whose trust is in Him.

Are God's promises enough to bring us through pain and suffering? Can real peace and joy ever truly be recovered? Sue's life and testimony remind us that the answer is still just what we'd hoped it would be: Yes. Jesus really is enough.

Susan Cymbala Pettrey
Brooklyn Tabernacle,
Brooklyn, New York

Preface

We sat in the brand-new burgundy 1975 Cutlass Supreme. He asked me to slide closer. His arm slipped around me as he whispered in my ear, "It's nice to know we'll be together forever . . ."

We lived an adventure covering three continents. We raised two incredible sons and gained a beautiful daughter-in-law. We rode horses through rivers in the Dominican Republic, cooked lamb on a mountaintop in the North-West Frontier Province of Pakistan, and braved the South China Sea in a junk during a typhoon.

We began every morning reading from God's Word and then giving the day to Him. Tuesday morning, January 25th, 2005 was no different. We read about how God's strength is made perfect in our weakness. As I reached out to hold his hand, I heard a strange gurgle in his breathing.

His eyes were bright and looking at something I couldn't see.

His hands were open.

My hands were empty.

I screamed his name. I shook him. I begged Jesus to give him life. The ambulance came, and everyone did their best. The doctors worked on him for another hour in the emergency ward, but God had another plan.

My best friend was in heaven. And I was still on earth.

My heart was full of thanksgiving for the years we had been given, but I had no idea how I would continue to live without him.

Ten days before, Jim had suffered a serious heart attack. The main artery to his heart was completely shut, but the doctors had inserted a stent and blood flow was restored. They promised we were on the road to recovery. As I left the hospital the morning after his attack, the words, "He gives and takes away . . . blessed be the name of the Lord..." (Job 1:21) filled my thoughts. I was overjoyed that the Lord had given Jim back to me. He had chosen to spare his life, and I couldn't stop smiling.

The days just prior to his heart attack, I was overcome by an urgency to pray. As I moved around our home laying my hands on photos of our family and friends, I interceded with moans and groans and tears. I sat at my piano singing, surrendering those I loved into the Lord's keeping.

I had no idea what was coming.

But God knew.

In fact, God planned it. And therein lies my only comfort, and, I believe, yours.

This is a glimpse into the pages of my journal. It is a record of the first year of my ordained journey without Jim. It is God's grace on paper. It is the manna that God provided for me in my wilderness, manna that still continues to fall for me daily.

My prayer is that it will inspire you to look at the sky in anticipation of when the real journey will finally begin.

January 30, 2005. Day 6.

My Jimbies is in heaven.

I can't believe I'm writing those words. It's so unreal, yet my nausea tells me otherwise. While Curtis accompanied his father's body home across the ocean, I was at the funeral home choosing cement casing for the casket to slip into. This afternoon I sat trembling in a dressing room while my sisters-in-law handed me funeral outfits. I'm numb. I don't even remember what I bought.

I know Jim is fine, and even happy because he's with Jesus. I know for him it will be but a blink of an eye until we're together again, *but I'm still here,* so I'm not fine and I'm definitely not happy. I don't even know how I'm breathing.

My best friend is gone. *How am I supposed to live without him?*

I asked my family that question tonight, and the answer I got was pained stares. Instead of Jim's hand in mine, I was holding photos. I sat in the middle of the floor, surrounded by people who love me but never having felt more alone. In the agonizing silence, Kathy, Jim's eldest sister, began to sing: "When peace like a river, attendeth my way, when sorrows like sea billows roll; whatever my lot, thou hast taught me to say, it is well, it is well, with my soul."

Initially I couldn't sing. I wasn't even sure I wanted to. But just like in the emergency room when the doctor told me Jim was gone, I knew I had a choice: I could embrace God's sovereignty, or I could resent Him for allowing this nightmare.

The doctor's words left me crumpled on the cold tile floor. As my son lifted me up and put me in a chair, I felt Jesus stand up in me, and I began to pray a prayer of thanksgiving. I had no saliva in my mouth and no strength to stand, yet in those moments I proved true what Jim and I had just talked about: When we are weak, He is strong. The grace that was given to me that morning enabled me to walk away from Jim's lifeless frame believing that God had a plan that I could trust.

So tonight, with my family, I chose to sing. My voice got louder. The photos dropped to my lap as I raised my hands in surrender to my God. Together we proclaimed that although we had no answers, it was well with our souls, and in His grace, *we would live.*

In those moments I realized that the hope we have because of Jesus is just as real as our loss.

> Who, O God, is like you? Though you have made me see troubles, many and bitter, you will restore my life again; from the depths of the earth you will again bring me up. You will increase my honor and comfort me once again. (Psalm 71:19–21)

January 31. Day 7.

Today is my forty-seventh birthday. Jim had made reservations for dinner and booked a room for a romantic getaway.

Me standing at his casket wasn't in his plan.

The line was endless. Hundreds were turned away after the first visitation and told to come back in the evening. It was an overwhelming outpouring of love. I couldn't deny God's strength. I know every breath was from Him.

I rarely took my hand off the coffin, telling myself Jim was not there, yet taking comfort that somehow he was. Many commented about how he was in a better place and how we would never wish him back, *but oh . . . how I wish him back.* The resurrection of Lazarus brought glory to Jesus, so wouldn't Jim's resurrection do the same?

As people inched their way closer to our family, they watched a beautiful video montage of our life together set to a recording of one of my favorite hymns:

> I don't know about tomorrow; I just live from day to day.
> I don't borrow from its sunshine, for its skies may turn to grey.
> I don't worry o'er the future, for I know what Jesus said.
> And today I'll walk beside Him, for He knows what is ahead.
> Many things about tomorrow, I don't seem to understand . . .
> But I know who holds tomorrow and I know who holds my hand.
> (I Know Who Holds Tomorrow, Forrest Stamphill)

In the middle of so much not knowing, *this* is all I know: *When tomorrow comes, Jesus will be there—and this life is not all there is.*

February 1. Day 8.

Jim's funeral was today.

Nearly eight hundred people raised their voices and sang the song Job sang first: "He gives and takes away . . . blessed be the name of the Lord!"

Choosing to do this is the only way I can continue to live.

The service was a beautiful testimony of how precious Jesus was to Jim and how precious Jim was to us. It was a story of God's love and faithfulness. Jim would have been so proud of his boys! Curtis led the service and the worship from the piano, and CJ wrote and sang a ballad that opened the windows of heaven, filling the sanctuary with angels:

> I hope today when I look up, he looks down over the ledge of heaven at me, so small now; without my father standing with me, I don't know how, I don't know how.
>
> You dry my tears when I look up; you look down and over the ledge of heaven on me and your love pours out.
>
> Your arms have always been around me and though I feel broken . . . quiet and weak, your love falls down; your love falls down . . .
>
> My father would carry us around on his shoulders, but Jesus will not let us down, and He'll always hold us,
>
> And His hands wipe away all of our tears and His glory warms us . . .
>
> In Him we have nothing to fear, He'll always hold us . . . He'll always hold us . . . He'll *always* hold us.
>
> My father would carry me around on his shoulders . . .
>
> But Jesus will not let me down . . .
>
> (CJ Keddy, 2005)

Just like their Dad, my sons are turning my eyes to Jesus. I am the most blessed mom on the planet. I was the most blessed wife on the planet.

And now . . . I am the most blessed widow on the planet.

February 5. Day 12.

I crawled under the covers last night holding my Bible to my chest, whispering over and over, "He will heal the broken-hearted," and somehow I slept until 7:30 this morning without feeling Jim's heart pound beside me.

I miss him so much I physically hurt. I ache to tell him everything and to hear his voice reassuring me that everything will be okay. I miss his long hugs. I miss feeling the warmth of his hand in mine. I miss his calming smile.

I'm determined to dwell on the good, like the miracle of being able to sleep without Jim snuggled next to me and the growing number of people who have come to know Jesus because of Jim's death. I am thankful that one second he laughed, and the next he was with Jesus. He died happy. He had no regrets.

I am clinging fiercely to God's sovereignty and trying hard not to think about tomorrow, and I'm finding out *it's a second-by-second discipline.*

This loneliness is the most intense emotion I've ever felt, and I can't fathom learning to live without him. I've been remembering our good-byes during his first two years of Bible College. We loved our monthly rendezvous, but dreaded the agonizing G-word. We would hang on to each other until the very last moment. It felt like forever while I waited for his call to let me know he'd arrived safely back to his dorm.

On the rare occasions we found ourselves apart after we got married, we gave each other letters to open at bedtime. This time, there are no letters, and there is no specific date set for a reunion, yet I believe a day is coming when Jesus will eliminate words like *good-bye, sorrow,* and *pain,* and I will see Jim again. I can't circle the day on my calendar, but I'm convinced heaven is real.

In the meantime, while I wait for my faith to become sight, I want to reflect on Jesus and His amazing power in this extremely weak and frail jar of clay so that others will see and want The One I have.

> Have mercy on me, O God, have mercy on me, for in You my soul takes refuge. I will take refuge in the shadow of Your wings until this disaster has passed. I cry out to God Most High, to God, who *will fulfill His purpose for me!"* (Psalm 57:1–2)

Keep me up above the despair.

Help me bear out this pain.
I entrust my broken heart to You.

February 6. Day 13.

Thirteen days since Jim whispered he loved me.
Thirteen days since he's called me Subies.
The loneliness is heavy and always there.
I wish he could call me from heaven and let me know how he's doing, who he's seen, and who he's talked to.
I just want to be together.

> Because you are my help, I *choose* to sing in the shadow of your wings. My soul *chooses* to cling to you. Your right hand upholds me." (Psalm 63:7–8)

I will remind my soul to choose *all day long.*

February 7. Day 14.

I have moved into 71 Nelson Street.
In the fall of 1999 we were blessed to have two Bible college interns from Canada come and live with us in Hong Kong. It was extra special because we had watched this couple grow up when we were pastoring in Canada. We were honored to have them and will be forever bound with memories that make us laugh and cry. Now I am living with them and their two adorable toddlers, Gracie and Caleb. It is healing to change diapers, read stories, and build forts out of blankets. *How can I wallow in sadness when I'm pretending to be a cow?*
It's true. *God sets the lonely in families* (Psalm 68).

February 8. Day 15.

Today is the anniversary of when I told Jim I loved him for the very first time. He declared his love for me on my eighteenth birthday, and I spent a week in a deliriously wonderful stupor before I could reciprocate. We said those three words to each other many times every day since. They were the first words out of our mouths each morning and the last words spoken before we went to sleep each night.

Thank You, Sovereign God, for the love Jim loved me with. It was a reflection of Your love. I am so blessed to have been loved like that.

May everyone You send my way feel as loved as I felt.

February 9. Day 16.

Another day. Another miracle.

I've been thinking about how Jim and I professed to love Jesus more than we loved each other. Our friends from Asia would often ask me how I could trust Jim, because after all, *he was a man*. Many of their husbands had mistresses, so they couldn't understand why Jim didn't. My answer was always the same: "Jim loves Jesus more than he loves me."

I always believed I loved Jesus more than Jim, and in theory *maybe* that was true, but I'm realizing now that when I was freaking out and needed reassurance, it was Jim I ran to, not Jesus. We were a dynamic duo joined at the hip on a most incredible adventure that took us literally around the world.

On the first night without Jim, Curtis reminded me of the dream God gave me just before we left Canada. In the fall of 1988, Jim told me he felt God wanted us to resign from our pastorate in Fort Erie so that we could be ready for what was coming. I explained to him that we had two young sons and a car payment and that it just wasn't wise to resign without a place to go. He gently urged me to pray about it, so I prayed that God would show Jim that this was not His voice he was hearing! I went to sleep worrying about my husband, who had clearly lost touch with reality. It's a wonder God didn't smite me with leprosy for my attitude, but just like Moses needed a burning bush to get his attention, I needed a dream.

I was standing on top of a massively tall mountain shrouded in mist. As I peeked over the edge, my whole body tingled. Jesus called me by name and asked me to look down at my feet. I looked down and saw a very simple rectangular mat, just big enough to sit on, which is exactly what Jesus asked me to do.

"Susan, I want you to get on the mat and go down the mountain."

The mountain was huge and the mat was flimsy, so I refused. Jesus asked me again, this time telling me that all He was asking me to do was to get on the mat and go down the mountain, which by the way, both belonged to Him.

This was another leprosy moment, because even after finding out that the mat and the mountain were His, I still tried to strike a deal.

"Okay, there are a few things You need to do. Soup up the mat. Make it sturdier. Build in a brake device. If the ride gets too fast, I want to be able to slow it down, or if it becomes too scary, I want to be able to stop the thing and get off. *If I can control the mat, I will do what You ask.*"

"Susan, just get on *My* mat and go down *My* mountain. It is going to be fun!" The fun is what finally convinced me.

As soon as I sat down, Jesus held me, and I felt completely safe. Instantly we were flying through the air, and it was so exhilarating I began to laugh! For as long as I live, I will never forget what happened next.

Jesus began to laugh too!

As He held me close to His chest, the two of us laughed together. He whispered in my ear, "See? I told you it would be fun!"

I woke up, rolled over into Jim's arms, and blurted out my dream. Since then we lived to hear His laughter and were continuously wowed by where that mat took us.

"Mom," Curtis said, "I want to remind you that Dad wasn't on that mat. Jesus was, *and still is.* So Mom, the ride will continue!"

It actually had bothered me for years that Jim wasn't on the mat. Jim's explanation was that God knew I was the one who needed theatrics to be persuaded. Although that always made me smile, the question still nagged at my heart.

Why was it just me?

I know now that even then, my Sovereign God was preparing me for what was to be.

I want to love and need Jesus the most.

I want my longing for Jesus to be more than my longing for Jim.

I need to feel His arms around me and hear His laughter.

February 10. Day 17.

There are two verses in the book of Daniel that give my soul hope:

> The people who know their God will display strength and take action. Those who have insight among the people will give understanding to many. (Daniel 11:32–33)

That means that whatever God shows me about Himself will not only strengthen me, but everyone He brings into my day. How powerful is that?

Oh Lord, give me Your grace to believe it.

Please use this pain to point others to Your love.

February 11. Day 18.

Today I took two-year-old Gracie out for lunch. As she squirmed on my lap, she began to play with Jim's ring, which now hangs on a golden chain around my neck.

"Auntie Sue, what's that?"

I told her it was Uncle Jim's ring. Then she started to play with my locket that dangles next to Jim's ring. Her little fingers were struggling with the clasp, so I opened it for her. She looked closely at the two faded pictures inside and asked, "Who's that?"

I sighed and told her that it was Uncle Jim and Auntie Sue. As I thought back to when it was always "JimnSue" and how it was now "just Sue," emotions collided and tears began to roll down my cheeks. Gracie smiled up at me as if she could read my heart and emphatically declared, *"And Jesus!"*

I have no doubt that God filled my little friend's mouth. His words brought instant comfort, a renewed hope and joy into my brokenness. I closed my locket and repeated the words with a regained conviction.

"Yes, Gracie, *and Jesus!*"

Tonight as we were playing tag, my God used Gracie yet again. When she gets excited, she clenches her hands into a fist and bounces up and down with a super-infectious smile. I told her that when Uncle Jim got excited he would always say, "Hokey toot!" Immediately Gracie started running around the living room enthusiastically shouting, "Hokey toot!" Dizzy with delight, she collapsed into a heap, looked up at me, and said, "Auntie Sue, where is Uncle Jim?"

Catching my breath I said, "Gracie, Uncle Jim's in heaven. He's not with Auntie Sue anymore. *He's with Jesus.*"

Beaming from ear to ear, Gracie leapt up, grabbed my hands, and pulled me into a dance while chanting, "Hokey-toot! Uncle Jim's in heaven! Uncle Jim's in heaven!"

I couldn't help but think how perfect her perception is.

A childlike faith is what the Lord asks of us. A faith that says "Hokey-toot!"

when we hear someone has gone to heaven . . . a faith that exclaims "And Jesus!" when we hear ache and despair in someone's voice.

Sovereign God, please give me a dose of Gracie's faith.

February 12. Day 19.

I feel like the Israelites must have felt in the wilderness when they came out of their tents to collect the manna that God daily dropped from the sky. They were told to get only enough for that day. Those that tried to hoard it away quickly found out it spoiled. It had to be a daily gathering.

I really do feel like the Israelites.

Psalm 18 reminds me that God can turn darkness into light and that with His help I can advance against a troop and scale a wall; that His way is perfect and that His Word is flawless. Therefore, I can trust Him to be an impenetrable shield all around me and constant place of refuge.

I have been persuaded that there is no one like my God and that daily He will arm me with strength. He will make my feet secure to this new path so that I can fearlessly stand on the heights and fight against the Enemy who lives to destroy me. God's own hand will sustain me and will broaden the ordained path beneath me so that my ankles will not turn.

I'm going to be okay, because God says so.

I spent a good chunk of today with my family. We ate lunch at one of our favorite restaurants. Jim would always buy a case of his beloved hot sauce from this place to bring back with us. We'd pack it in our shoes and socks, and somehow, year after year, it made it across the ocean unscathed. After lunch we walked over to a yummy dessert place before going to a movie. The last time I was at any of these places was with Jim.

It is horrible torture walking alone where we used to walk hand in hand. Everyone is inclusive and loving, yet I am so lonely. I miss my best friend. I miss our private jokes. I miss his expressions. I miss his dry wit. I miss his insights. I miss his kisses. I miss his touch. *I miss it all.* It is so painful knowing that our romance has come to an end. We'll never go out on a date ever again. We'll never light a candle. We'll never make love ever again.

I know it's useless to ask God to take this pain away, so I'm begging for His endurance to walk through it. I am depending completely on His grace so that I can keep choosing to trust like Gracie. David writes:

Blessed are those whose strength is in You. Blessed are those who have set their hearts on pilgrimage. When they walk through the valley of weeping it will become a place of springs where pools of blessing and refreshing collect after rains. They will grow constantly in strength. (Psalm 84:5–7, *The Living Bible*)

Sovereign God, I accept the invitation to meet with You, for it is only when I meet with You that my strength will be renewed.

February 13. Day 20.

Psalm 20 filled my basket this morning.

"He will answer me when I am in distress."

"The name of my God will protect me. He will send me help from the sanctuary. He grants me support."

He is my covering, my security, the lifter of my head, and He has sent His family to surround me.

When we walked out of the church following Jim's casket, two hundred fellow pastors formed an honor guard that stretched all the way to the hearse. One man, whom I have yet to meet, generously paid for Jim's funeral expenses. The funeral home had never in all their years had someone outside of the family call them to settle the bill. As I stood at the casket, my two sons stood on my left, my three sisters-in-law stood on my right, and in the far corners of the room were two close buddies. They placed themselves there like sentries in a palace. Neither of them took their eyes off me as they tried to anticipate my every need.

"He gives me the desires of my heart and makes all my plans succeed."

The deepest desire of my heart is for Jesus to look good. I want the hope He gives to be seen in my life.

My soul has been strengthened to live another day!

February 14. Day 21.

Help me to be abandoned to Your will, continuously accepting Your plan for my life, even on this day of chocolates and roses. The pain in my heart is not because it's Valentine's Day. *The pain is because Jim is never coming home.*

O Captain of the mighty host of heaven, I pledge to You my allegiance. With

Your help I embrace widowhood. I offer up to You my loneliness and all the tomorrows without roses. I trust You to make something beautiful out of the ugly.

Because Your love is better than life, my lips will glorify You! (Psalm 63:3)

February 15. Day 22.

Psalm 23 has become brand-new to me. When Jesus becomes your absolute everything, every verse of scripture is intensely personalized. I don't think it's possible to comprehend the depth of love and care God has for His children until you find yourself on a path of sorrow and read His words through eyes of pain.

"The Lord is my shepherd. I shall not want." He rubs oil in my wounds. He pens me in at night and lays Himself down across the threshold to protect me from danger. And then He wakes me up in the morning and does it all over again. *How could I want anything else?*

"He makes me lie down in green pastures." He gives me a peace that is unmatched.

"He leads me beside still waters." These still waters are the "pools of refreshing" in the valley of weeping. I can't get there on my own, so He takes me there.

"He restores my soul." I've never fully understood this statement until now. He is not just sustaining me, He is reviving me. *He is restoring my soul. I want to live.*

"He guides me in the paths of righteousness, for His Name's sake." He helps me to do the right thing, all for the sake of His name. *It is all about His glory, not my situation.*

"Even though I walk through the valley of the shadow of death—I will fear no evil, for You are with me!" I am in a valley that is absent of fear because His presence has chased it away.

"Your rod and Your staff, they comfort me!" The rod is used to protect, and the staff is used to rescue and guide. I couldn't be safer.

"You prepare a table before me in the presence of my enemies. You anoint my head with oil. My cup overflows." When I choose to focus on His feast, my enemies are rendered powerless!

"Surely goodness and mercy will follow me all the days of my life, and I will dwell in the house of the Lord forever!" My Shepherd's love and mercy will pursue me all the way to heaven.

I'm ready to face Day 22.

February 16. Day 23.

I woke up singing! *How can a widow wake up with a song in her heart?* As I rolled over amazed at the joy I was feeling, my eyes focused on a flip calendar propped up on the bedside table beside me. Under today's date was written the reason for my joy:

> It is God who arms me with strength and makes my way perfect.
> (2 Samuel 22:33)

I lay there wondering how God does what He does. His care is so intimate that I feel like I am the only one He's looking after on this big old earth! As I soaked in His love, it suddenly dawned on me that Jim and I were in the same place! *We were both dwelling in God's presence!*

I never want to be anywhere else.

February 17. Day 24.

This morning I woke up sad, without a song, without a Scripture, and feeling sorry for every argument and stressed moment between Jim and me. I know in my head that those dynamics are part of marriage, but I still want to hold him and apologize for every cross word ever spoken. I asked Jesus to forgive me for my selfishness and to tell Jim how sorry I am. Whenever we 'told each other we were sorry, it was like a tag team. We went back and forth with the "I'm sorry" or the "I was selfish" ball. Then there were a lot of "Are you okay?" hugs.

I need to talk to him. I need to pray with him this morning. I need to make his coffee, and I need him to make me my tea. I need to watch the news together. I need to see him smiling. I need a spontaneous cuddle time. *I have a reservoir of memories to draw from, but all I want to do is make new memories.*

Everyone wants to help, but quite frankly, there is nothing anyone can do or say. It's hard to breathe, and today is just a tsunami of a day. The tears won't stop. Being without him is the cruelest of tortures.

I tell my soul to trust the Lord and accept His will, but my heart feels like it's in a vice. The dreadful realization that he's never coming back is devastating. I'd say unbearable, but I've always believed that the Lord only gives us what we can bear, although my heart is wondering now if that's true.

Our landlord from Hong Kong just called, interrupting my thoughts and heaping more pain on what I thought was already unspeakable hurt. He knew Jim had died, and—like a lot of people—just didn't know what to say. He did however want to know if I was going to continue renting his apartment. I've been praying about this, and it wasn't until the words came out of my mouth that I knew the answer. I gave notice and promised I would be out by the end of March.

Death is so terribly permanent.

Jesus, help me to genuinely rejoice that Jim is with You.

Help me to rejoice with him that he is finally home.

Help me to remember that even when I don't wake up with a song on my lips, I can still choose to sing.

February 18. Day 25.

Though he brings grief, he will show compassion. His unfailing love is just that great! (Lamentations 3:32)

The Lord is my strength and my shield. My heart *chooses* to trust in Him and I am helped. My heart leaps for joy, and I will give thanks to Him in song. (Psalm 28:7)

It's hard to imagine my heart ever leaping for joy again, but God's Word says it will, *if I choose to trust Him.*

My Sovereign also declares that He sits enthroned over the flood of uncertainties that threaten to destroy me and that He will carry me. (Psalm 29:10)

I do believe my heart just fluttered.

February 19. Day 26.

And we know, that in all things, God works for the good of those who love Him, who have been called according to His purpose. (Romans 8:28)

I'm grappling with how becoming a widow at forty-six and turning forty-seven on the day of the visitation could be even remotely good, but the remainder of Romans 8 explains that God often uses suffering to make us like Jesus.

Whenever Jim talked about the purpose of suffering, he would liken it to going to the dentist. We willingly climb into that chair knowing it's not going to be fun. We open our mouths so that instruments can intrude, apply pressure, inflict pain, and even extract something that has been attached to us for most of our lives. We allow our senses to be assaulted and altered because germs have accumulated, causing decay that if allowed to fester will send poison throughout our entire body—resulting in a nasty infection or possibly worse. We trust our dentist, knowing that his goal is to make things right. He doesn't yank and pull on our jaws for his own pleasure. He puts his hands in our messed-up, sometimes grossly neglected mouths to root out the bad, bringing healing and restoration.

It's the same with God. When I willingly submit myself to Him, accepting everything from His hand and trusting Him no matter what He allows, I will come through whole and transformed.

I have to believe that this sorrow will not overcome me, it will change me.

I'm ready to face the world.

February 20. Day 27.

I woke up with Psalm 46:10 on my lips: "Be still and know that I am God." I love being in the presence of God. It's never His presence that comes and goes, it's me. When I'm trusting, there is peace. When I'm not . . . there isn't.

11:00 p.m.

Both of my parents have come down with pneumonia. My initial reaction was to go and help them; the second was panic. Since I've come back, the farthest I've gone inside their home is the front hall. My legs just won't take me where my heart wishes it could go.

A crumpled, dried-out corsage bound together with a faded bow that Jim pinned on my dress at our high school grad; a tearstained letter he wrote on behalf of Curtis thanking me for the pain I endured to give him life; an empty jar of Moondrops perfume, Jim's favorite scent; my journal of year one of our married life: they are all neatly tucked away in my cedar chest in my parent's home.

It's a strange blend of comfort and pain; wanting to remember, mixed with the sadness of how our romance is over.

As I hung up the phone after receiving the news, I thought about the unfailing love of my Sovereign Lord who fights for me and beckons me to hide in His strength. I felt that familiar nudge and asked a friend to take me to their home.

When I walked in, Mom threw her arms around me, confessing she had been praying that I'd come. I paused the grief button and sprang into action. I focused on the need at hand and made them a big batch of homemade chicken noodle soup. We watched *Wheel of Fortune* and *Jeopardy*. When I knew they were comfortable for the night, I went home and promised I'd be back in the morning.

I'm learning that when my legs won't take me where He wants me to be, He'll carry me there, if I let Him.

February 21. Day 28.

But the plans of the Lord *stand firm forever* and *the purposes of His heart stand firm* through all generations. So, we wait in hope for the Lord. He is our help and shield. In Him our hearts rejoice for we trust in His holy name. May Your unfailing love rest upon us, O Lord as we put our hope in You. (Psalm 33:11, 22)

Sovereign God, I wait for You.
Prove to me that You have a purpose for this pain.
Protect me from hopelessness and overtake me with Your love.

February 22. Day 29.

My first thought this morning was that it has been twenty-nine long, lonely days since Jim died. I lay in bed feeling the pangs of separation and finding no words to describe the pain of not seeing his face, hearing his voice, or feeling his touch. I trudged to the computer to check my e-mail, and there it was.

My manna had arrived via Google. Via my son Curtis.

His words instantly changed my perception. The despair lifted, and hope jump-started my heart as I read: "Mom, Dad is not dead! Dad is very much alive! It is those of us that are left behind who haven't started to live yet!"

Wow. Jim has been alive in heaven for twenty-nine days!

How can I not be happy for him?

Heaven was one of his favorite things to talk about. He preached about going there every chance he got. Just two weeks before he died, he leaned into the congregation and told them that when God opened the door to eternity for him, he wanted to go with his eyes and hands wide open. He couldn't wait to see what God had been preparing for him since the foundations of the world were laid. His eyes filled with tears as he spoke of the longing in his heart just to be home.

Sovereign God, help me to remember that if I choose to, it is actually possible to see things the way You do.

February 23. Day 30.

The king is not saved by a mighty army; a warrior is not delivered by great strength. *Behold, the eye of the Lord is on those who fear Him, on those who hope for His loving-kindness, to deliver their soul from death.* (Psalm 33:16–19)

The Lord is watching me big-time, because without His loving-kindness I'd be dying in the pit of despair. His love enables me to commit my way to the Lord and keeps me on my guard against self-pity. The Kay Translation writes Psalm 37:5-6 like this: "Roll thy way upon the Lord; *then rest and assure thyself in Him and He Himself will work!*"

I love this! The image of rolling is perfect, because oftentimes lifting it all up to Him seems impossible, but *rolling* is doable! It's freeing to realize that after I roll my sorrow His way, *I can rest,* knowing that Jesus will do amazing things.

When I can't lift, I can always roll.

I like that.

February 24. Day 31.

The Israelites would hammer God's words above their doors so His law was always in their sights. Over the past month, my Sovereign God has given me helps for this journey. Today I tack these truths over the door of my heart so that I too will constantly be reminded to do what He says to me:

• Embrace My sovereignty.

• Lift up your loneliness as a sacrifice of worship, trusting that I have a purpose, and will use it for My glory.

> • Your suffering has eternal worth. It is making you more like Jesus and pointing others to Him.
> • It is possible to see things the way I do.
> • When you spend yourself for others, the loneliness is pushed back.

Midnight.

CJ picked me up for dinner and reminded me that it was exactly one month ago that I called to tell him Jim had died. I called him twice. The first time was to tell him that Jim was not breathing but they were trying to resuscitate him. CJ was at church and immediately told his pastor, who stopped the worship service to have everyone pray. They surrounded CJ and cried out for God to intervene. As everyone was saying "Amen," I called again.

He walked outside without his coat and stood in the freezing cold. He was in snow up to his ankles when he heard me say, "Dad's with Jesus." Within seconds of hanging up, Ali was by his side. They went to the home of the amazing family he stayed with when he returned to Canada for schooling, and friends came from far and wide to offer their love and support.

At the same time, Curtis was already beginning to wade through the endless red tape that goes along with dying in a country that is not your own. He had to go to several institutions in order to get the proper authorizations and signatures, each time being forced to identify his dad's lifeless frame. His good buddy Chris went with him.

I was eventually taken back to our home, where I mechanically changed out of my pajamas into my jeans. The police were there taking pictures because it's Hong Kong policy to investigate the scene if someone dies at home. The house was a disaster from the chaotic attempts to revive Jim just hours before. Our empty cereal bowls were still on the table. Our bed was still unmade.

Curtis arranged for me to go to his pastor's home, which is where I stayed until it became so overrun with our friends that they were forced to move me to a hotel where the crowds could be accommodated. As CJ and I remembered these events, we were in awe at how God's arms held each of us on both sides of the globe.

I know that as I crawl into bed tonight, those arms will never let me go.

February 25. Day 32.

What is more, I consider everything a loss because of the surpassing worth of knowing Christ Jesus my Lord, for whose sake I have lost all things. I consider them garbage that I may gain Christ. (Philippians 3:8)

This verse has never meant so much to me as it does now. I found a piano today and felt like I'd been reunited with an old friend. I played an old chorus over and over until my soul was convinced: *"He is all I need . . . He is all I need . . . Jesus is all I need . . ."*

My mind went back in time to when we were standing on the balcony of the Brooklyn Tabernacle in New York City. Pastor Jim Cymbala encouraged every married couple in the house to find each other's hand and declare this song together. I realize now that I had no idea what I was declaring, until yesterday as I sang that song *without* Jim's hand in mine.

Jesus, I'm sorry that it took Jim's going to be with You for me to want to know You more.

Midnight.

Lori and Ruth have taken me on a road trip to visit my brother Dwight. He's been struggling for the past four years with cancer. He wasn't able to be at Jim's funeral due to his own pain.

Just five months ago, our family all came together for CJ and Ali's wedding. Every time the camera flashed, we were keenly aware that these would likely be the last photos with Dwight. In our wildest imaginations, none of us knew that they would be the last photos with Jim. *It feels so strange. Dwight is across the parking lot, and Jim is unreachable.* When I walk through his door, it won't just be the reality of Jim's loss that will hit him, but also the uncertainty of his own life that hangs in the air.

I recently read how a group of monks used to put small candles between their toes as they traveled through a dark tunnel to a monastery. The light from the candles illuminated just enough of the path for them to take the next step.

I like that visual.

What looks dark tonight will be lit up tomorrow, one step at a time.

February 26. Day 33.

I woke up feeling those candles between my toes, with a song on my lips and Psalm 44 in my heart.

> You are my King and my God who decrees victories! Through you we push back our enemies; through Your Name we trample our foes! I do not trust in my bow or my sword. They do not bring me victory! *You* give me victory over my enemies! *You* put my adversaries to shame!

Self-pity and despair are crouching at the door of my heart, waiting to swallow me up and rob me of my song, but today *I choose to call on Your name and watch You fight for me!*

Oh! Jesus, I love You so much!

Let's go see Dwight!

February 27. Day 34.

When we saw each other, we both started to cry. There were no words, just a very long hug. As we walked through downtown Philly breathing in the aromas of the Italian delis and cannoli shops, Dwight and I talked about dying and God's sovereignty. He and I view things so differently. He allows himself to ask why, and I do not. Just like when we were kids, we both think we're right, which resulted in some loud and passionate arguments at the supper table. Now we just sigh and shake our heads in resignation, appreciating our differences and celebrate the things we agree on.

Both of us offer up our pain as a sacrifice of worship and beg God to make something beautiful out of the ugliness we find ourselves existing in.

Both of us are desperate and rely completely on the courage and strength that comes from heaven.

Both of us feel those candles between our toes as the darkness is illuminated one step at a time.

February 28. Day 35.

My son describes his sadness as like wearing a wet sweater, uncomfortable and heavy. As I read his words, I thought about God's promise to exchange our mourning for a 'garment of praise.' All we need to do is reach our arms up to Him and let Him do the rest.

Ah . . . that feels better.

March 1. Day 36.

I can't believe it's been thirty-six days. It feels like a lifetime and one minute ago all at the same time.

My mind won't stop replaying our last seconds. I hear Jim laugh; then I hear air leaving his body. I relive the panic, the screaming of his name, my son's name, and the name of Jesus. I can hear my son begging his dad not to leave us. I can see him pushing on Jim's chest, administering CPR. I can see Jim's wide-open mouth, his limp body, and his eyes. They were so bright I could see my reflection.

This morning I choose to surrender rather than protest.

Thank You, Sovereign God, that You know everything! You have perfect knowledge of the past, the present, and the future. You knew that Jim would laugh one second and take his last breath the next.

Thank You, Sovereign God, that You are everywhere! Jim and I are both in Your presence right now. We are both safe in Your hands.

Thank You, Sovereign God, that You have no beginning and no ending! You always were and You always will be.

Every moment of our lives has been already written.

I trust You.

March 2. Day 37.

Sovereign God, I praise You for being perfect and holy in all Your ways. I know that I can fully trust You today and in every tomorrow.

Psalm 51 is David's plea for a new heart and a renewed spirit. He longs for the joy of his salvation to be restored! He cries out: "My sacrifice O God, is a broken spirit; a broken and contrite heart that You, oh God, will not despise."

I'm so thankful I serve the same God as David.

I'm thankful that when I offer my brokenness up to Him, He accepts it.

I'm thankful for words like *renew* and *restore,* because they make another day of living possible.

March 3. Day 38.

I'm trying to choose a marker for Jim's grave. Some are advising me to just buy the basic marker, that Jim wouldn't want something lavish and that I need to be careful with my money because I am alone now.

I just need everyone to stop telling me what to do.

I run into Your arms Jesus. Please show me what You want.

Later.

I've made a decision. I'm doing what Jim would do for me, which is to give him the best. Even when I put up a fight, Jim won every single time. His generosity toward me was lavish and endless, so I'm going to take huge pleasure in ordering the marker that I think he'd love.

Jim is with Jesus. I know only his shell is under the earth, but that plot of land will be beautifully identified so that our grandchildren can come and honor his memory. One day we will stand there together and look up at the sky in anticipation of that day when we'll be reunited in heaven.

11:30 p.m.

I've booked my flight to go home on March 23.

When we lived in the Dominican Republic, Jim and the boys became experts at riding the waves. While they were laughing and waiting for the next crash, I stood on the shore praying for their safety. Jim somehow convinced me to join them by telling me that all I had to do was run and jump headfirst into the oncoming wave! He promised me that after those first harrowing seconds, I would surface in the swells and love it.

He took my hand and said we would do it together.

I took a deep breath, and we ran into the water. He was yelling one of those man-type yells, and I was screaming in horror as the towering wave slammed against our bodies. The force of the water separated us, and I was sure I was dying. My body flopped around like a rag doll. The pressure was intense, but Jim was right: after a few scary seconds, I'd found my new favorite playground.

Going back to Hong Kong will be like running into a twenty-foot wave.

Just thinking about it makes me shiver. I can't picture myself living there without Jim, but I know it's where Jesus wants me to be.

Sovereign God, help me not to be afraid.

I am so used to having Jim hold my hand.

I choose to place my hand in Yours and jump head-on into the terror.

March 4. Day 39.

Real faith is choosing to believe in what we do not see, *especially when we don't feel like it.*

Jim didn't keep his sermons, so I felt like I had stumbled upon a treasure when I found a copy of a message he preached less than a year ago tucked in between the cover and the binding of his Bible. I reverently opened his notes and with tears streaming down my face, read them over and over again.

> You have heard it said that faith in God is a crutch. I say, that for me, having known the Lord through some very bad things and some very good things, that I believe Him to not be a crutch, but rather, my two legs. In the darkest valley, when any sense of His presence has long vanished, there are two legs of faith that I stand on and actually move forward on. One leg is the hold He has upon me. The other is His preeminence in all things!

Jim cried as he spoke those words. It was the best message of his life. *And he preached it for me.*

Hold me, Sovereign God. Move my legs forward.

Midnight.

Jim and I were blessed to run a summer program for the kids at our church camp. One of those kids, now all grown up and married, sat across the table from me tonight and thanked me for the impact we had on her life. It is so strange, because I am painfully aware of how far I am from where God wants me to be, but moments like tonight encourage me to keep going. I pray that twenty years from now, another generation will tell me that how I walked this ordained path led them to Jesus.

March 5. Day 40.

In God's Word, the number forty is significant. After God shut the door of Noah's ark, it rained forty days and nights. The Israelites wandered around in the wilderness for forty years. Jesus was tempted by Satan in the desert for forty days.

All of these events were riddled with stress, discouragement, and fear, but there was also deliverance, victory, and the miraculous! In each of these occasions God's servants had to submit to God's sovereignty, totally depending on Him for everything, *and He never let them down.* God sustained, supported, and enabled them to bear up under all the strain and obstacles.

Forty days.

This is my flood, my wilderness, my desert.

I need not fear, because I have the same God they had.

March 6. Day 41.

Have mercy on me, O God! I will take refuge in the shadow of Your wings until the disaster has passed. I cry out to God Most High, to God, who fulfills *His purpose* for me. He sends His love and faithfulness from heaven and saves me from those who hotly hunt me down. (Psalm 57:1–3)

I can hear the emphatic inflections in David's voice. He gives his soul an emotionally charged pep talk, and I guess that's why I relate to it so much. I love the picture of God's love and faithfulness coming down into our tiny lives and saving us from the enemies that never tire of attacking us.

David goes on to write that he "is in the midst of lions and ravenous beasts." That's exactly how I feel. The Enemy hisses and tells me that when the shock wears off I'm going to crash and burn. He hurls accusations: *"You should have acted quicker. You should have insisted the doctor do a bypass instead of the angioplasty. It's your fault!"* But like David, I cry out for mercy, and *instantly*, Gods love and faithfulness come swooping in and the voice of the Enemy is silenced!

Oh! How can I not praise you? For great is Your love! It reaches to the heavens and Your faithfulness reaches to the skies! Be exalted, O God above the heavens. Let Your glory be over all the earth! (Psalm 57:10–11)

11:30 p.m.

I went to church today for the first time since Jim went to heaven. As CJ led us in genuine worship, my eyes were turned to the Lover of my soul, who will never let me go and who fills me with new hope each day.

That makes Day 42 worth waking up to.

March 7. Day 42.

Oh my Strength, I watch for You. You are my fortress and my loving God. You will go before me. I will sing of Your strength. In the morning, I will sing of Your love; for You are my fortress and my refuge in times of trouble. O my Strength, I will sing praise to You. (Psalm 59:9–10, 16–17)

David wrote this just for me.

Dearest Strength,
I run to You! I hide in You and cling!
I will watch for You every second of this day.
With all my heart,
Susan

March 8. Day 43.

I'm so thankful that God's mercies are new with each sunrise and coupled with an endless supply of grace and courage.

I recently heard a story about a sixteen-year-old Scottish boy back in the nineteenth century who, because of his faith in Jesus, was sentenced to death. He was taken to the center of the town and put on display until the time of his execution. While he waited for the guillotine to drop, he yelled to the gawking onlookers:

"Good news! Good news! I am within sight of The Kingdom!"

I want to live with this kind of perspective and die with this kind of courage.

March 9. Day 44.

You answer us by giving us victory, and You do wonderful things to save us. People all over the world and across the distant seas trust in You. You calm the roar of the seas and the noise of the waves. The whole world stands in awe of the great things that You have done. Your deeds bring shouts of joy from one end of the earth to the other! (Psalm 65:5, 7–8, Good News Bible)

What right do I have to complain or to ask why?

The God who calms the sea and silences the crash of the waves is fighting for me.

March 10. Day 45.

Praise our God! Let the sound of His praise be heard! *He has preserved our lives and kept our feet from slipping.* Sing to God, *sing praises to His name and rejoice before Him!* (Psalm 66:9, Psalm 68:4)

I am living in a miracle.
My heart is crushed, yet I can sing.
I feel dead inside, yet never more alive.
What else can I do, except rejoice before Him?

March 11. Day 46.

My days have been filled with visits and conversation about heaven. I still don't have any appetite, and my clothes are now two sizes too big, but my spirit is continuously being nourished. It's like what Paul says: "Outwardly we are wasting away, but inwardly we are being renewed day by day" (2 Corinthians 4:16).

Between all the cups of tea, I have been learning to drive again. I got my driver's license when I was seventeen and drove right up until we left Canada. After we moved to Asia we didn't have a car, and whenever we visited this side of the pond Jim did all the driving, so when Gracie's dad threw me the keys to his truck, panic doesn't begin to describe how I felt. After a pep talk, I found myself putting the keys in the ignition. With my Brooklyn Tabernacle

Choir music blaring, I ventured out onto the highway and found the mall. The saleslady felt like she'd hit the jackpot when she saw the heap of clothes in my hand. She commented that my husband must be a real nice guy to let me buy a brand new wardrobe. I told her that he was for sure the best husband in the world. She asked me if I'd lost a lot of weight and was impressed when I told her I had, in fact, lost twenty pounds.

"Wow! No wonder your husband is letting you blow the budget!"

The room filled with angels as Strength came to my rescue. In the next few moments I watched as God gave eternal worth to my pain. I told her everything. I told her how Jim had died and how Jesus has never left my side. She cried as I spoke and struggled to know what to say when I was finished. I got the feeling that hearing my story was the beginning of hers. There is no greater joy than to be able to share the hope we have because of all Jesus has done.

On my way home I decided that if conversations like that happen every day, I will survive this journey.

March 12. Day 47.

But as for me, I will always have hope. I will praise You more and more. My mouth will tell of Your righteous deeds and Your saving acts *all day long.* (Psalm 71:14, 15)

You are *hope. You* were *hope. You* always will *be hope.*

Hope is another precious name for my Sovereign God!

I picked up a much worn book today written by another widow. The first line on page 1 made me weak. She wrote: "On the grey morning of January 25th, 1949, my world caved in. At 8:15 a.m. my husband's tired and damaged heart stopped beating."

It was like reading my own journal.

Fifty-six years ago, on the same day, at the same time, another forty-six-year-old wife experienced the same shock, same heartbreak, and same nausea. She loved and served the same God, and in those moments she felt the same strong arms holding her, and she heard the same words of comfort and assurance.

I've stepped onto a very crowded path. There are many ahead of me and others who are just beginning as I write these words.

Hope and Strength will forever do the miraculous.

March 13. Day 48.

I wonder if Jim knows I've lost twenty pounds. I can't imagine he'd be too interested in anything on earth, now that he's in heaven. How could he miss holding my hand when he's with Jesus? I will never forget the first time that happened. We were sitting in Cleary Auditorium on our first date. Act 1 of *Damn Yankees* was over, and Act 2 was about to begin. As the lights dimmed, Jim leaned over to me and asked, "Is it against your religion to hold hands?" Back in those days, *everything* was against our religion, even square dancing in a PE lesson! It still makes me laugh.

I whispered in the darkness, "Nope!"

Our fingers intertwined, and I tingled from head to toe.

To this day I don't even remember how the musical ended. For the rest of our lives, no matter where we were or what we were doing, our hands always found each other. When the doctor told me to come and see Jim's body one last time, I held and kissed his face, thanking him for his love and friendship, but the last thing I did was hold his hand. I choose to look at this separation as the first act of the play. I am anxiously waiting for this intermission to be over, for the lights to go down, and for Jim's voice to whisper, "Is it against your religion to hold hands?"

This time I'll never let it go.

March 14. Day 49.

Sovereign God, *You hold my hand.* You guide me with Your counsel and afterwards You will take me into glory. Who have I in heaven but You? *There is nothing on earth I desire besides You. My flesh and my heart may fail, but God is the strength of my heart and my portion forever.* (Psalm 73: 23–26)

When I read those verses this morning, I could hardly believe it! I went to bed thinking about how empty my hand felt, and I woke up to the promise of God holding my hand. My hand will never be empty.

10:30 p.m.

I am exhausted from crying. *I need Jim.* My brain is so full of things I want to tell him; decisions I wish he could weigh in on. It's pure, unadulterated anguish being without him.

Oh Jesus! Please hold me. Quiet my heart with Your love.

Ten minutes later

Only God could do what just happened.

I felt drawn to a shoebox full of love letters. I opened an envelope, removing a card Jim gave me to open at bedtime when I went to Pakistan by myself to visit a friend. On the outside of the card was a verse from Zephaniah 3:17: "The Lord your God is with you. He is mighty to save. He will take great delight in you. *He will quiet you with His love,* He will rejoice over you with singing."

Inside the card, Jim had written that the verse on the card was *just for me.* He said I was a strong girl and that Jesus was pleased with me. He expressed how much he loved and missed me and assured me that we'd be together soon. He signed the letter with:

"See you in minutes . . ."

Jim always knew just what to say, and he did it again tonight.

March 15. Day 50.

Today would have marked the end of the eight weeks recovery period from his angioplastate and the day that normalcy would have begun. We joked about how this would be "date night." (When the boys were young, we would refer to making love as having a date, and it stuck.) The Sunday morning before Jim died he told me he'd started a countdown to March 15th. He made this purring kind of a sound in the back of his throat that always made me grin.

Take me to my manna.

The last verses we read together were from 2 Corinthians 12:9–10 where Jesus says to Paul:

> My grace is sufficient for you, for My power is made perfect in weakness. Therefore, I will boast all the more gladly about my weaknesses *so that Christ's power may rest on me.* That is why, for Christ's sake, I delight in weaknesses, in insults, in hardships, in persecutions and in difficulties. *For when I am weak, then I am strong.*

Thank You, Sovereign God, for reminding me of this truth seconds before You took Jim home. You lovingly prepared my soul for that moment of absolute heartbreak.

You are stronger than strong.
Your grace makes this journey not only possible, but glorifying to You.

March 16. Day 51.

I have an appointment at the cemetery. I'm desperate for my manna.

> We will tell the next generation the praiseworthy deeds of the Lord. We will tell them about His power and the wonders He has done . . . The next generation will put their trust in God and will not forget His deeds and they will keep His commands. (Psalm 78:4, 6–7)

The theme of this Psalm is *remembering*. The Israelites kept forgetting about their awesome Deliverer and Provider. And when they forgot, they sinned. *I never want to forget God's tender mercies.* I want my grandchildren to grow up hearing their Nanny remember. I will tell the next generation the praiseworthy deeds of the Lord. I will tell the next generation about His power and miracles. I will tell them how God gave me manna every day and how He led me through the wilderness of my aloneness.

I will put my journals in their hands and let them read the stories, and they too will put their trust in God.

Jim and I were deeply moved when we walked through the cemetery where the first missionaries to China are buried. Also in that sacred place are the graves of three small children from one family, who all died in the same year. The third child's marker had the words of Job emblazoned on its surface: "Shall not the judge of all the earth do right?" We silently walked away longing to know and trust Jesus like those parents did.

That's how I want people to feel when they stand at our grave.

Thank You, Sovereign God! You have turned something sorrowful into a joyful mission!

11:00 p.m.

Mission accomplished.

I stood shivering at Jim's snow-covered grave. For a moment my eyes were fixed on the ground until my heart heard Jim speak: *"Hey, Subies! You're looking in the wrong direction! Look up here!"* I lifted my head to the sky and felt the warmth of the sun. Jim's youngest sister, Nancy, and her husband, Bob, stood on either side of me. The three of us linked arms and started to sing.

> What a day that will be, when my Jesus I will see!
> When I look upon His face, the one who saved me by His grace;
> When he takes me by the hand, and leads me to the Promised Land;
> What a day, glorious day that will be! (What a day that will be. Jim Hill)

We prayed for the generations to follow and then walked through the snow back to the car full of joy because of the unexplainable hope in our hearts!

The kind of hope that makes it possible to walk out of a cemetery smiling.

March 17. Day 52.

Amidst the intense loneliness and desperate longing for my best friend, *Jesus has come near.*

He does not remove the pain.

He holds me steady and walks me through it one step at a time.

This journey is teaching me that God's thoughts are not consumed with what we call "now." He has eternity on His agenda, and suffering makes us ready to rule and reign with Him. Our time here is mere preparation for what is ahead.

It reminds me again of what Jim preached just a few weeks before he died. He said with a twinkle in his eye and a crack in his voice, "I don't belong here. We don't belong here. We are citizens of heaven. We are merely on a journey to glorious, unbelievable heaven. We are waiting for that door to open so that we can go home. But while we wait, we must bring as many souls as we can with us, all the while submitting to His will as He makes us just like Jesus."

It has been fifty-two days of the Holy Spirit revealing secrets to my broken heart and leading me to my heavenly manna. What Jim and I had was as beautiful as you could ever hope for on this earth, but it was flawed because we're human and sometimes had selfish hearts. *But the love of God is perfect and forever.*

Would I trade this intimacy with Jesus for a chance to turn back the clock? Never.

Who would have ever guessed?

March 18. Day 53.

For the Lord God is a sun and shield; the Lord bestows favor and honor; no good thing does He withhold from those whose walk is blameless. O Lord Almighty, blessed is the man who trusts in You! (Psalm 84:11–12)

I love that the Lord is referred to as "a sun." It's already miraculous that I felt joy at Jim's grave, but realizing that the warmth I felt was *the Lord shining down on me* leaves me speechless.

Midnight.

My friend Ruth has taken me to Arnprior. As we drove past the hospital, my mind went back to the birth of our sons. Curtis was born here at 3:31 p.m. The Catholic school next door had just dismissed for the day, so the sidewalks were filled with happy kids. CJ was born at 1:00 a.m. The streets were dark and quiet. The only sound was in the maternity ward.

I can't believe it's been twenty-five years.

This afternoon I went back to the first church we pastored. Jim was the assistant pastor, and I was his pregnant wife for the entire time we lived here. I went downstairs to the basement, and all I could see was Curtis taking his first steps. When I blinked, there were thirty of our old friends around me in a group hug. We only lived in Arnprior for two short years, but the bonds that developed were for life.

Today's gathering began with a dear friend reading a newspaper article that Jim wrote for the local newspaper when we were moving to Cambridge. You know it's a small town when our departure makes the front page! He wrote about the elastic effect Arnprior had on us, saying that as time went by the elastic would stretch, so no matter where we ended up, our hearts would always be attached to Arnprior. He was right.

Thank You, my Sovereign God, for elastics.

March 19. Day 54.

O Lord God Almighty, who is like you? You are mighty O Lord and your faithfulness surrounds me! (Psalm 89:8)

Ruth and I left Arnprior and drove three hours to our very first haven in Peterborough, Ontario. We lived amidst a hodgepodge of unmatched furniture and inherited bright orange curtains, but it was home and we loved it. This was the place where we began to learn about God's faithfulness. Curtis was conceived within those walls, and it was a rough pregnancy. Jim was finishing his last year of Bible College, and I was working as a Red Cross homemaker, but due to severe morning sickness that lasted all day, I was forced to resign.

That's when I began to keep a journal.

We chose not to tell anyone about our financial struggles. Jim always said, "If we've told God, then why should we have to tell anyone else?" This became a deeply imbedded principle by which we governed our lives. We began to live in the miraculous. We'd wake up to boxes of groceries outside our door. Money would show up in our mailbox just in time to pay the rent. A church about an hour's drive up the road asked us to come and help them on the weekends. Without fail, every Sunday night when we would get in our car to drive back home, our backseat would be laden with fresh preserves, home-grown vegetables, and frozen roasts wrapped in brown paper.

Today, nearly three decades later, I stood looking at our little back door and our tiny windows wondering where the time has gone. With tears blinding my eyes I thought back over our wild adventure, convinced without a doubt that God will remain faithful in all the days ahead.

March 20. Day 55.

I have to say good-bye to my parents today. I couldn't have waded through the endless legalities connected to death without my Dad's expertise. I can feel a gigantic surge of emotion even as I write. Holy Spirit, take me to my manna.

> Love and faithfulness go before you! *Blessed are those who have learned to acclaim You and who walk in the light of Your presence, O Lord. They rejoice in Your name, all day long. They exalt in Your righteousness, all day long.* For You, O Lord, are *their glory and strength.* (Psalm 89:14–17)

Yes! Sovereign God, Your love and faithfulness have gone before me, and the light of Your presence will guide me! You are my strength! You are holding my hand! Your arm is around me! I will rejoice in this, *all day long.*

I'm ready.

Midnight.

The three of us hung on to each other and wept. Mom and Dad prayed, entrusting me into my Sovereign God's hands like they have done countless times before, and then walked out the door.

March 21. Day 56.

> You are my Father! You are my God. You are the Rock, *my rock.* You are my Savior! You are my refuge and my fortress. I put my trust in You. (Psalm 89:26 and Psalm 91:2)

I am clinging. I am leaning. I am trusting.

Midnight.

Dwight drove up from Philadelphia today to finalize details for our parent's fiftieth wedding anniversary party in May. We met for breakfast and then had our good-bye. He wrapped me in a bear hug and then wondered out loud what we both were thinking.

Would this be the last time we saw each other on earth?

Neither of us answered.

Both of us cried.

March 22. Day 57.

Last summer, Jim and I went to visit a dear friend. She was finishing the first draft of her latest piece of art. The work in progress was of a lady standing at the side of a river gazing into the sky. Her hands were raised in total submission. There was a deer taking a drink from the water and an eagle in the distance soaring through the clouds. Marg told us she felt as though she was doing this particular painting for a specific person. We had no idea that it would be my wall it would hang on, serving as a constant reminder to surrender everything over to my Sovereign God.

Lord, when doubts fill my mind, when my heart is in turmoil, quiet me and help me to be still and know that You are God. In Your strength I toss self-pity back to hell where it belongs. I look at the sky and lift my hands up to You, giving You my pain and loneliness, trusting You to use it for Your glory.

March 23. Day 58.

In a few hours, I will board the plane back to Hong Kong. Myrna, one of Jim's sisters, is taking an unpaid leave from her job to help settle me in, and this is something neither I nor the Lord will ever forget.

I am leaving behind one son and being reunited with another. When CJ hugged me good-bye tonight, he assured me everything would be fine and not to worry about anything. He told me he loved me and made me promise to call him anytime. I'm afraid both my guys have put aside their own grief to comfort me. It breaks my heart because they too must learn how to live without their best friend.

Take me to my manna.

> *He guards the lives of his faithful ones.* Light is shed upon the righteous and joy on the upright in heart for He is our God and we are the people of His pasture. *We are the flock under His care.* (Psalm 97:10, 11 and Psalm 95:7)

What a wonderful truth to hang on to.
God is looking after my family.
We are His flock under His care.
Okay, it's time to go home . . .

March 24. Day 59.

As the plane took off from Toronto, we couldn't believe our ears. "Sit back, get cozy, and enjoy the magic carpet ride!"

Over the years I have heard pilots thank their passengers for choosing to fly their airline, but I have never heard one refer to his flight as a carpet ride! I'm sure when he clicked off his microphone he wondered what on earth he'd just said, but Myrna and I knew exactly where those words came from!

I've been back less than a day, and I've already signed a contract for a new apartment. I offered to pay much less than what the landlord asked and was stunned when she refused my offer and then said she had changed her mind and wanted even *less* than what I'd suggested! That never happens, especially in Hong Kong! What's even more mind-blowing is where I'll be living and how I got there.

Just before Christmas I stumbled upon a new apartment complex while visiting one of my friends. I was impressed with its beauty and location. It towered over the little spot in Hong Kong which had become our stomping grounds for over a decade. When I came home that evening, I told Jim all about it, and he told me that we should make an appointment to go and check it out after the Christmas busyness. We had been wanting a change because the building we lived in was under constant construction. Jim commented on how fun it would be to live in a place that overlooked our beloved Kowloon City, and said that even without seeing it, he felt we should move there!

Yesterday, within hours of touching down, we began the search for my new home. In Hong Kong this process involves going to real estate offices to look at listings, then having an agent accompany you to an available property. I went directly to the office that Jim and I have always used, but they didn't have anything in my price bracket. However, within seconds of walking out of the office, a stranger tapped me on the shoulder and asked me if I was looking for an apartment. She was an agent from another company and had noticed me leaving her competition. We followed her as she zigzagged through the crowded streets and ended up standing at the entrance of the new complex I had discovered back in December! I didn't even need to look at the apartment to know it already had my name on it. I remembered Jim's words and smiled up at the sky.

I haven't been back to our home yet. That happens tomorrow. I feel like I should be boarding up the windows of my heart for the hurricane that is about to hit, but I don't know how to do that.

All I can do is rest in the knowledge that wherever His ride takes me, His arms are around me.

March 25. Day 60.

Even though I saw you leave and have actually lived sixty days without you living and breathing beside me, part of me still expects you to be waiting for me when I walk into our home this morning.

I was thinking about our last Thursday together when you were recovering in the hospital. It was the only night there were no visitors, and you asked me to crawl into bed with you. That was so fun. At first my one foot hung down over the side of the bed, but you convinced me to bring it up and stick it right under the covers! You had your arm around me. My head rested on your shoulder, and we giggled and talked for three hours like we were all alone. You told me I was your best friend, and we both had teary eyes when visiting hours were over. I looked back as I was leaving, and your smile melted my heart. I was so thankful that you were alive. God in His mercy had spared your life. *If I had known what was about to happen, I would have found you a new heart.*

Thirty years was too short. Seventy years would not have been enough.

I know what I must do.

> Look to the Lord and His strength. See His face always. Remember the wonders He has done. Remember His miracles. (Psalm 105:4–5)

It's time to go to our haven. I'm counting on another miracle.

9:00 p.m.

I knelt beside our sofa, placed my head on the spot where Jim died, and came apart. After a few hours I went into our bedroom. I held Jim's clothes and clung to his pillow, drinking in his remaining fragrance.

I was frozen with grief.

I left, wondering if coming back was a mistake.

A few hours later we had dinner with a few of my friends. The names Jim and Jesus have become inseparable. *Jim is in heaven, and I'm still breathing only because of Jesus.* The comment was made that Jim had a good place in heaven because of how godly, kind, and generous he was. I agreed that Jim was all that and more, but that when God looked at Jim on the morning of January 25, he saw the righteousness of Jesus. That alone gained Jim entrance into eternity with God.

In those moments I knew why I had returned.

March 26. Day 61.

I'm going back to our home one last time to pack everything up. *Jesus, help me.*

Psalm 105 tells me that God's care for His people is constant.

They asked and He brought. They asked and He satisfied. They asked and He opened.

They asked and He remembered. They asked and He gave them joy. They asked and He gave them a home.

Sovereign God, I'm asking. Please come to my rescue.

11:43 p.m.

It's been a long, exhausting day of packing up our life. I found the invoice for the last negligee Jim bought me. I want to run away, but there's no escaping this pain. I spent twelve hours in our bedroom. I sorted through the closet, filling two bags to send to Jim's aunt so she can stitch me a quilt made from his clothes. I held his worn, stretched-out pullover sweater and remembered how I insisted that we go shopping so that he could replace it. He had been asked to teach part-time at one of Hong Kong's universities, and that disgusting sweater just wouldn't be appropriate, I said.

Now, that ratty old thing is what I want to wrap myself in forever.

I held each candle and thought about how they transformed every bedroom we shared into paradise. I held our last empty wine bottle with a candle already placed in it, deeply understanding that it was the last candle we would ever light. I held every CD, reliving the memories each of the melodies invoked. With heaving sobs, I put everything in a box, coming to grips with the fact that he will never hold me again.

Oh, I don't know what to do.

March 27. Day 62.

Last night all I could do was cry. It felt like sixty-two days ago. The pain was excruciating. I couldn't breathe and wasn't sure if I even wanted to. If I hadn't just signed a new lease, I would have pulled a Jonah and boarded a plane back to Canada.

Since coming back I've been able to share the hope of Jesus with so many, *but yesterday there were no moments like that.* I felt empty and desperately sad until 4:00 a.m. this morning, when thankfully my heart was stilled as verse after verse filled my thoughts about how God is my fortress and my hiding place. Sleep came, and I woke up a few hours later with a fierce determination to once again fix my eyes on Jesus.

What would I do without Him?

He is my life.

On this Easter Sunday, I *choose* to trust and follow my risen Lord, who by conquering death gave me an indestructible hope.

Midnight.

> He sent forth His Word and healed them. He rescued them from the grave! (Psalm 107:20)

Somewhere between the old traditional hymns "Up from the Grave He Arose" and "He Lives" my heart was infused with the resurrection power of my Savior. *"He stilled the storm to a whisper; the waves of the sea were hushed. I was glad when it grew calm, and He guided me to my desired haven"* (Psalm 107:29–30 paraphrased).

Sovereign God, my desired haven is that place where I'm completely abandoned to Your will and glorifying You on this ordained path of suffering.

March 28. Day 63.

> My heart is steadfast, O God; I will sing and make music with all my soul. *For great is Your love. It is higher than the heavens and Your faithfulness reaches to the skies.* Be exalted, O God above the heavens and let Your glory be over all the earth. *Save us and help us with Your right hand."* (Psalm 108:1, 4–6)

God's Word drives out panic and hopelessness, leaving behind a supernatural anticipation for the days ahead. I don't ever want to grow accustomed to this miraculous transaction.

Today we painted the new apartment, and it looks beautiful. I'm still trying to get my mind and heart around the fact that it's *my* apartment and that I will be there alone. As Myrna and I have come and gone, lugging cans of paint, bags of brushes, and rolls of plastic, the security guards are starting to call me by name.

It's strange that no one at Sky Tower will ever know Jim.

For sure they have missed out on something huge.

March 29. Day 64.

> I love the Lord, for He heard my voice cry for mercy. Because He turned His ear to me, I will call on Him as long as I live. *The cords of death entangled me and the anguish of the grave came upon me. I was overcome by trouble and sorrow, but then I called on the name of the Lord,*

"O Lord! Save me!" The Lord is gracious and righteous. Our God is full of compassion. The Lord protects the simple hearted. When I was in great need, He saved me. Be at rest, *once more*, O my soul, for the Lord has been good to you! (Psalm 116:1–6)

Jesus! Thank You for the assurance that every time there is a *once more . . .* You will be there.

I know that without the Lord's intervention, I'd be in a very dark place. It's so easy to entertain self-pity and live in the hollows of despair, so I'm thankful that when I call, *He comes.* I picture Him coming to my rescue like a shepherd saves a sheep that is being threatened by a wolf. In the cinema of my mind, He grabs the wolf by the back of his furry neck and hurls him into oblivion. I've had that wolf breathing into my face more times than I can count, but in those moments I've gasped out the name of Jesus and instantly found myself scooped up into my Shepherd's arms, nestled in that place of safety between His neck and shoulder.

There is a name that is above all names that everyone needs to know.

Their lives depend upon it.

March 30. Day 65.

There are unpacked bags and disassembled furniture in every room of my new apartment. There is so much to be done, but I know in time, a home will be made.

This mirrors my life right now.

Everything has been taken apart, and I don't quite know how it is all going to go back together. When I look at it all at once the job seems impossible, but if I separate it into small projects, it's more doable. *I know strength will be given for each task, and little by little the clutter will lessen and beauty will emerge.*

My manna today was from Psalm 118:23–24: "The Lord has done this, and it is marvelous in my eyes! This is the day that the Lord has made. I will rejoice and be glad in it!"

Psalm 118 would have been the last hymn Jesus and His disciples sang together at the conclusion of the Last Supper. Jesus was about to take upon Himself the sins of the entire world, so it's astounding to me that this was the song on His lips as He left to accomplish His Father's will.

Jesus rejoiced in His death because the outcome of His obedience to His Father would be eternal life for us!

This is the second time the Holy Spirit has taken me to these verses in the past two months. The first time was early in the morning on January 25. I read them in the context of rejoicing in a victory. Jim had survived a heart attack because God had spared his life. Less than two hours later, Jim was lying lifeless on our living room floor while paramedics tried to jump-start his heart with a defibrillator.

But if we do like Jesus did, we don't save those words for when God provides or does the miraculous.

We proclaim those words even as we walk into immense suffering, because we live to obey our God and trust that His purpose will bring forth life.

March 31. Day 66.

My soul is weary with sorrow. Strengthen me according to Your word. (Psalm 119:28)

Every day a little bit more gets done. The kitchen is now set up. The only way I can envision myself cooking is if I have guests at every meal, because the thought of cooking for just me is way too sad. My soul is hugely weary with sorrow, and if it weren't for the nearness of Jesus, I'd never get out of bed.

I took Myrna to our favorite Thai restaurant, and when the owner saw me she wondered where Jim was. *It's a strange comfort to watch God use the sorrow He has entrusted me with to draw a heart to Jesus.* Every time it happens, I am thankful that this pain is being given eternal value.

I just wish there could have been another way.

April 1. Day 67.

My comfort in my suffering is this; your promise preserves my life. (Psalm 119:50)

My most Sovereign God, You've *promised* me *Your strength, Your unfailing love,* and *Your constant presence,* which is why this verse is so true.

Your promises really do preserve my life.

April 2. Day 68.

Psalm 121 is a feast.

My help comes from the Lord, the Maker of heaven and earth!

The Lord will not let my foot slip. When I'm teetering on that precipice of despair, the Lord will steady me.

The Lord never ever sleeps. In the midnight hours when no one else is awake, Jesus is.

The Lord gives me exactly what I need. He has surrounded me with His presence and His people.

The Lord protects me from harm. That nasty wolf doesn't stand a chance!

The Lord's eye watches over my coming and going both now and forever. Nothing comes into my life that He hasn't allowed. For the rest of my days, the Creator of the universe—the One who holds everything together and knows all things—will be helping *me*.

I have absolutely nothing to worry about.

April 3. Day 69.

Today is Jim's Hong Kong memorial service.

The day before Jim went to heaven, we had a spontaneous cuddle time. With our arms wrapped around each other, we thanked God that He had spared Jim's life. We kissed and spoke about how fun the next twenty-five years would be. I asked him if during the past nine days since his heart attack he'd felt like he was going to die. He held me closer and told me he hadn't. *I desperately needed to hear him tell me that he was going to live forever, and that's exactly what he did.*

After a few deep sighs, our conversation shifted to the what-if scenarios. I asked him, if something *had* happened, where he would've wanted to be buried and who he would've wanted to speak and sing at his funeral. He said that Munsang College would be the perfect place for a Hong Kong memorial service. (Munsang is a well-established secondary school where Jim gave ten years of his life teaching about Jesus to thousands of students. On top of his classes, he felt incredibly honored to speak to the entire student body at weekly mandatory assemblies.) We stopped talking about what could have been, squeezed each other, and promised we'd die together.

This afternoon, Jim's memorial service will be in the same hall where Jim made Jesus famous week after week.

My prayer is that as we gather today, Jesus will be made famous one more time. May everyone leave knowing, "If Jesus had not been on my side when sorrow and grief and loneliness began to drown me, they would have swallowed me alive; the flood would have engulfed me, the torrent would have swept over me, and the raging waters would have swept me away. But praise be to Jesus who has not let me be torn by their teeth. I have escaped like a bird out of the fowler's snare. The snare has been broken and I have escaped! My help is in the name of the Lord!" (Psalm 124, paraphrased)

11:30 p.m.

Every seat was filled as over a thousand friends sat and experienced the presence of God today. Our little world was there, all in one place. As I walked into the hall, I saw Jim on two large screens on either side of the auditorium. Unbeknown to us, the last Christian Fellowship meeting had been recorded, and so there he was with his eyes heavenward, smiling and singing a song about longing to be with Jesus.

I had to sit down.

Precious friends from all over the world shared memories that made us laugh and cry. Everyone talked about Jim's kindness and love for them and his God. Curtis's voice cracked as he shared about his friendship with his dad. We all sang "Great Is Thy Faithfulness."

Before I closed the service with a few thoughts, we played a video clip of Jim being interviewed by some of his students. At the conclusion of the interview, his students asked him if there was anything more he wanted to say. Jim looked right into the lens and compelled those who were still undecided to *choose now* to give their lives to Jesus. Then he encouraged those who were followers of Christ to keep going, reminding them that if they ever faltered along the way, never to hide but *always to run into the arms of Jesus.* The students asked him to draw a picture, and Jim drew a helpless lamb in the Shepherd's arms. He smiled and said, *"That's how Jesus holds us."*

The technicians were supposed to stop the video, but it kept playing, so as I was walking to the podium I heard Jim's voice call out, "Sue," and for a split second I honestly thought he was there.

My heart pounded and the room began to spin.

I whispered "Jesus", and instantly His strength was mine.

I stood looking out on this world that the Lord grafted us into and began to talk about the *living hope* that is ours in Christ. I was able to thank our Muslim family for adopting us and loving us like they do. I thanked our students, our friends, and my family. *And I thanked Jesus for willingly being the final sacrifice for our sins, for being our risen Savior, and for the promise of His return.* I looked up and told Jim I would see him in minutes and then walked off the stage knowing that until that day comes, every second will be a miracle and a chance to make Jesus famous.

April 4. Day 70.

I will never forget the gratitude I felt as I looked out over the crowd yesterday. When we arrived in Hong Kong with our few suitcases and two young sons, we had no idea of who God would send us to. We spent the first two years telling the story of Jesus in Chinese school assemblies. One of us would relay the story, and Jim would bring it to life by drawing it on huge pads of paper. Thousands came to know Jesus, and we never got used to it.

In year three, Jim began his time at Munsang, and I taught at a kindergarten a few blocks away. Both of us had complete freedom to share the gospel, and we often pinched ourselves because it was just too good to be true. We also became part of a Filipino church that blessed us more than we could ever bless them. Most of the congregation was made up of domestic helpers, and from their lives we learned what servitude, perseverance, and joy really mean. Jim used to call them the best group of saints in the whole world. And then there is our Muslim family from Pakistan. What began with two families who lived next door to us in our first flat in the city grew into a community that truly adopted us as one of their own.

When I looked out at our world, I couldn't help but think of how faithful my God has been. I thought back to when He asked us to leave our country and family and realized how much we would have missed if we had disobeyed His call. When Jim was in the hospital, he told me that we had lived a hundred lifetimes in one. He said there was nothing that he had left unsaid, nor was there anything more that he wanted to do. With his trademark grin, he looked into my eyes and said he had absolutely no regrets. He also told me that if anything ever happened to him, I'd be surrounded by people and by God's own presence.

He was right.

April 5. Day 71.

Today is the Ching Ming festival, which means that every family in Hong Kong will make their way to the graves of their dead relatives. The mountainsides will be thick with smoke from the incense that stings your eyes and burns your throat. Everyone will bring food for the dead, as well as burn paper cars, houses, money, and even maids so that their loved ones will be well taken care of in the afterlife.

I sometimes wonder why I was born into a family that followed Jesus when there are millions right outside my door who don't know Him.

Comfort those who mourn today, my Sovereign. Open the eyes of those who do not know You—and those who do—to the Truth, so that we can all see You through the veil of smoke and despair and not become distracted by the pain and forget Your nearness.

> Give thanks to the Lord, for He is good. Give thanks to him who divided the Red Sea and who led his people through the desert. Give thanks to the One who remembered us in our low estate. *His love endures forever.* (excerpts from Psalm 136)

The same God who rescued His people from their enemy also led them through the desert for a very long time. This was not the quickest route to their final destination, but it was God's route. The wilderness was a difficult, lonely, desolate, depressing place, but it was God's wilderness, and His love was there.

John the Baptist was thrown into a prison cell for preaching about Jesus. He wasn't seeing the blind eyes being opened or the dead being raised to life. *All he saw was darkness.* He wasn't there when the disciples collected twelve baskets full of leftover bread and fish. *His hands were empty and wringing with confusion.* His soul was discouraged, so he sent a few of his friends to ask Jesus if He was 'the one'. *John knew better than anyone that Jesus was indeed the Messiah – 'the One' – but deserts and prison cells, good-byes and graves can shroud the truth and make a heart desperate for reassurance.* Jesus answered the question with a statement:

"Blessed are those who are not offended by what I do."

John's reaction to this statement is not found within the pages of God's Word, so we are left with an unfinished story and a challenge. When we are being led through a desert or find ourselves imprisoned, are we offended by what God has done or do we entrust to Him every step . . . believing that it's all preparation for the final destination?

I choose to believe that no matter what, it's going to be okay.

April 6. Day 72.

I had a dream that Jim was sleeping beside me. It was horrible to wake up and feel the crush of reality, but the words of an old song pushed away my sadness:

> Jesus is the sweetest name I know
> And He's just the same, as His lovely name
> And that's the reason, why I love Him so
> For Jesus is the sweetest name I know.

I am so thankful for my heritage. I have strong memories of sitting in a pew singing songs like the one that comforted me this morning. My father is a preacher, so I was one of those notorious preachers' kids. Being a PK had its drawbacks, but it also gave me a front-row seat to the power of God.

> O Lord, You know when I sit and when I rise. You hem me in. If I go up to the heavens, You are there. *If I make my bed in the depths, You are there.* If I say, "Surely the darkness will hide me and the light will become night around me," *even the darkness will not be dark to You . . . even the night will shine like the day, for darkness is as light to You! All the days ordained for me were written in Your book before one of them came to be.* (excerpts from Psalm 139)

11:00 p.m.

I'm lying in a new bed, in a new home, and I feel like a guest. I've been unpacking, finding the perfect spot for the tea bags, organizing books on the bookshelves, and the whole time I have felt as though I was getting the place ready for someone else. It wasn't until I crawled under the covers that it became real.

I live here, alone. I don't have a husband. Jim will never stand on my balcony and be wowed by the city lights.

The realization of all of this makes me weak.

I put up our Keddy wall of fame. Over the years it grew until it eventually covered an entire wall. This little apartment now looks like us. Curtis says that no matter where we lived it always looked the same, which he added was a good thing. We did that purposefully so that although we lacked a homestead, our sons would always feel at home no matter where in this big wide world we found ourselves.

The only thing left to do is to hook up the TV to the VCR and set up the computer, neither of which I know anything about. Jim did that stuff and even managed to hide all the wires. There is so much to learn. Even getting around the city is a challenge. I've been hanging on to Jim's hand for the past sixteen years, so I've never needed to pay attention to where I was going. I'm completely overwhelmed, and I keep hoping that if I miss Jim hard enough, he'll suddenly appear to take me out of my misery.

It's still impossible for me to believe that he is gone, even after two funerals.

But the manna that fell for me this morning is holding me steady tonight.

When I feel like the light is dark and closing in around me, I must tell my soul that even the darkness is not dark to my Sovereign God.

April 7. Day 73.

I'm so thankful for David and his heart. His Psalms have been perfect prayers these past seventy-three days.

"My eyes are fixed on you, O Sovereign Lord. In You I take refuge . . . I cry aloud to You for mercy . . . I pour out my troubles before You . . . When my spirit grows faint within me, it is You that knows my way." *When I feel so lost in this city, when I am taken over by frustration and loneliness, it is You who knows my way and listens to my cry.*

"I say, You alone are my refuge . . . You alone are my portion in the land of the living. Please, in Your faithfulness and righteousness come to my relief. I remember the days of long ago and consider what Your hands have done." *You have been nothing but faithful. My mind and my heart remember and stand amazed.*

"I spread out my hands to You. My soul thirsts for You like a parched land. Answer me quickly, O Lord because my spirit faints with longing." *Fill me with Your grace and endurance, one more time.*

"Let this morning bring me word of Your unfailing love, for I have chosen to put my trust in You. Show me the way I should go, for to You, I lift up my soul." *I'm desperate for You to lead me.*

"Rescue me from my enemies, O Lord, for I hide myself in You." *Don't let me give in, even a little, to self-pity.*

"Teach me to do Your will, for You are my God. May Your good Spirit lead me on level ground. For Your name's sake, O Lord, preserve my life!" *Let everyone see that You are enough!* (Psalm 141:1–2, 8; Psalm 142:1–3, 5–6; Psalm 143:1, 5–11)

11:30 p.m.

I spent the afternoon with one of my Muslim friends, and we had a beautiful conversation about how God has all our days written down. *There is huge comfort in this because it gives pain eternal worth.* With tears, she told me how much everyone misses Jim. He was everyone's brother and encourager. If curtains needed hanging or computers needed fixing, it was Jim who saved the day. There are so many who miss him. Don't let me forget that others are suffering too. *Please help me to comfort them with the comfort You are comforting me with.*

April 8. Day 74.

Psalm 144 tells me that my Sovereign God loves me, protects me, defends me, delivers me, hides me, and thinks about me! He reaches down, parts the heavens, and shoots arrows at self-pity, then lifts me up and out into a safe place!

I cannot allow myself to live in the depths of despair.

I must tell my soul that I am eternal, that this life is fleeting and that this journey is simply preparation for the real life in heaven.

I must focus on the unseen and simply trust.

Then, and only then, will I live above the despair and anticipate the future instead of longing for the past.

April 9. Day 75.

I have programmed my CD player to wake me up with a song every morning. The first words I heard today were telling me to hold tightly to God's hand because although weeping may last for the night, there is joy coming in the morning. I reached for my Bible and opened it to Psalm 145:

> Every day I will praise You and extol Your name forever and ever. Great are You Lord and most worthy of praise. Your greatness no one can fathom. I will meditate on Your wonderful works *all day long.*

The same CD was playing the morning Jim went to heaven. As I prepared breakfast, songs about heaven filled our living room. When I returned in March, I hit play, and as soon as I heard the opening score, I knew the song. It talks about pressing on through our weariness and how when we have given all we have to give, Jesus is there to give us His strength to keep going.

Jim's home-going was perfectly scripted. God knew that Jim had accomplished his work on earth and that his death would produce eternal fruit that could not have been harvested otherwise. It would be arrogant for me to ask the Author and Finisher of my faith, the Creator of the universe who orchestrates every detail of our lives even down to the songs that are being played in the background, 'Why'?

Instead, I choose to extol You, to hold on to You, and to press on in Your name, for Your name's sake!

April 10. Day 76.

There is just so much I want to tell Jim. He understood me the best, and what each of us lacked we gained from each other. Somehow, I have to learn how to live without that, and to love living again, because right now, nothing is fun. I'm the most comfortable when I'm writing all my thoughts down or when I'm talking about Jesus. In every other situation I feel awkward and just wish I was with Jim. It's weird to say *I* after saying *we* for over thirty years. I loved being married, and I don't know how to do single. I have no idea who I am without him.

Jesus, I lift up my aloneness to You. My soul is empty. I need my manna.

The Lord upholds the cause of the oppressed and gives food to the hungry. The Lord sets the prisoners free. The Lord gives sight to the blind. The Lord lifts up those that are bowed down. The Lord loves the righteous. The Lord watches over the alien and sustains the fatherless and the widow. The Lord reigns forever. (Psalm 146: 7–10)

Your Word tells me that You will uphold me, give me sight to see things the way You do, lift me up, love me forever, watch me always, sustain my sons, sustain me, and reign forever!

I'm ready to face Day 76.

April 11. Day 77.

Psalm 147 shows me yet again that I don't have to be strong. *It has nothing to do with what I can do.* My Lord delights in those who fear Him and put their hope in His unfailing love.

He heals the broken-hearted and binds up their wounds. He determines the number of the stars and calls them each by name! Great is our Lord and mighty in power. His understanding has no limit. (Psalm 147:3–5)

As I spend the afternoon with my Muslim sisters, give me moments to declare Your goodness and Your intimate care over my life. Open up all of our hearts to understand that not only have You named the stars, but You have also determined everything about our lives and long for us to trust You.

April 12. Day 78.

Since Day 6 of this journey, my manna has come from the Psalms. Today I have moved on to Philippians, my favorite book in the New Testament, and I look forward to reading it through my new eyes.

Philippians 1:21 says, "For to me to live is Christ and to die is gain." I am just beginning to fully understand the first half of this verse, and Jim is actually experiencing the second. *Jesus is the reason I live and my joy in the midst of sorrow.*

Paul, the author of Philippians, was not a stranger to suffering. He was beaten, imprisoned, shipwrecked, and mocked. He went without food, sleep, and shelter, yet he was able to write verses like, "I want you to know that what has happened to me has really served to advance the gospel" (Philippians 1:12) and For it has been granted to you on behalf of Christ not only to believe on Him, but also to suffer *for* Him" (Philippians 1:29).

There is a genuine, unmistakable fellowship with our Lord when we hurt. That fellowship is a rich blessing and the source of *real* joy. Only our Sovereign God could link words like *suffering* and *joy* together and have it make perfect, eternal sense, making it a catalyst to advance the gospel.

10:30 p.m.

I spoke to a group of college students tonight who are about to head into China as Christ's ambassadors. I really missed Jim. We were a team, and the Holy Spirit anointed our unity. I don't think I will ever get used to being just Sue. Part of me has died, and the element that remains is so broken. I feel incomplete, yet I must remember that although half of me is in heaven, I *am* complete in Jesus.

As I talked about the purpose of suffering, I wondered what was ahead for everyone in that room.

I pray that they will come to understand that only in weakness will God's strength be realized.

April 13. Day 79.

I tried to memorize Philippians 2 when Jim was memorizing the book of Ephesians. It's still incredible to me that he could recite so much of God's Word. He kept a well-worn Bible in his back pocket. Jim truly hid God's Word in his heart (*and in that back pocket!*) and it kept him steady and pure. I miss our long talks when we would dissect Scripture to figure out what God was really saying.

This morning, the more I read, the more I wrestled with my selfishness and the clearer the voice of the Lord became. *Jesus chose to be like He was, and God's Word tells me that my attitude should be just like His.*

Jesus made Himself nothing.

Jesus became a servant.

Jesus obeyed, even to the point of death.

Paul writes that we should "do everything without complaining or arguing so that we may become blameless and pure, children of God, without fault in a crooked and depraved generation, in which we will shine like stars in the universe, as we hold out the word of life"(Philippians 2:14–16).

I really want to live this new life without complaining or arguing with my God. I never want to grumble about the path God has put me on, not even to myself.

I want to outwardly and *inwardly embrace this appointed aloneness.*
Only then can I hold out the word of life and shine like the stars.

April 14. Day 80.

I consider everything rubbish, that I may gain Christ. (Philippians 3:7–11)

What an amazing pursuit Paul was on! He says for Christ's sake he has lost everything, including his name, position, reputation, friends, and job, yet he regards what he once had as rubbish compared to knowing Jesus!

I too want to know Jesus and *the power of His resurrection, but this is not possible until I share in the fellowship of His sufferings and die to self.*

It's encouraging to know that Jesus Himself wondered if there was another way, but then said, "Nevertheless, not My will but Your will be done;" and it's good to remember that while hanging on that cross, Jesus wondered why God had forsaken Him, *but ultimately surrendered His spirit into His father's hands.*

The words Jesus spoke from the cross show us that He truly understands every emotion we feel on our individual, carved-out paths. He has suffered far beyond what any of us will ever experience, and He now fills us with His endurance so that we too can finish the task given to us.

When I get to heaven, Jesus will be the only thing that matters.

April 15. Day 81.

My son says this journey is separated into three days. Day 1 was the day Jim went to heaven. Day 2 began when I returned to Hong Kong. And Day 3 begins today, after Myrna leaves. I'm confident that Jesus, who was with me throughout Day 1 and Day 2, will not leave me to face Day 3 alone.

I am a citizen of heaven on my way home!

This suffering is making me ready for eternity!

I must press on to win the prize!

I can always rejoice in the Lord!

The Lord is always near, so there is no need to ever be worried!

It's possible to embrace this path of loneliness with the strength that comes from Jesus.

(Philippians 3 and 4)

Midnight.

On my way up the elevator I looked down at the key chain that one of my Muslim sisters gave me a few years ago. On one side there is a picture of praying hands with the inscription, "Nothing is impossible." When you turn it over, there is an etched cross. I turned the key, opened the door, and walked right into the arms of Jesus.

It's gonna be okay.

April 16. Day 82.

Lord, I ask that You would fill me with the knowledge of Your will, through all spiritual wisdom and understanding, so that I will live a life worthy of You and may please You in every way, bearing fruit in every good work, growing in the knowledge of God. Strengthen me with all power according to Your glorious might so that I will have great endurance. Help me to proclaim You to my friends so that I may present those You have put into my life perfect in Christ. This is my work, and I can only do it because Christ's mighty energy is at work within me!

(borrowed from Colossians 1)

11:30 p.m.

I attended a Grief Share group today with my son. He said that his grief was like a gaping hole that will never be filled, not even by God. He explained that God was chiseling him into what he was destined to become and that this hole was part of God's plan for his life. *This hole will enable him to help others one day.*

He's right.

We are safe in God's hand, even when it holds a hammer.

April 17. Day 83.

Paul tells us in Colossians 3 that the secret to *real living* is to be crucified with Christ. *When we put our flesh to death, Jesus truly lives in us, and His reactions to this hurting world become ours.*

Jesus was famous for His mercy, kindness, acceptance, grace, and extravagant, unconditional love. His patient endurance and humility are the blueprint for all of us to follow.

I choose to be dead so that Jesus can be represented well.

April 18. Day 84.

There's something magical about waking up to sunshine, which is why I love to wake up to the Brooklyn Tabernacle Choir every day! This morning their voices reminded me that "every day with Jesus is sweeter than the day before." That is so true, because each day that passes brings us closer to the day when Jesus will take us home, and while we wait, He's given us clear instructions on how to live through every season of life.

Paul writes in Colossians 4:2, "Devote yourselves to prayer, being watchful and thankful." Devotion doesn't *suggest* that we pray, it *demands* that we pray. *If we are devoted to* something, *no matter what our eyes see or our hearts feel, we keep doing whatever we have to do even if we die doing it, because the end result is worth the persistence.*

We should pray that we will live a life worthy of the Lord and please Him in every way. We should pray that we will clearly proclaim the mystery of Christ *even when we are in chains.* We should pray that we will make the most out of every opportunity given to us and that we will stand firm in His will. We should be watchful of hollow, deceptive philosophies that turn our eyes away from the prize. We should be watchful of what our hearts are set on and what our minds are filled with. *We should be watchful for the day of His return* and *be thankful that His power fills us with His endurance.*

Sovereign God, whether I wake up to dreariness or sunshine, I ask that You would remind me daily to *devote* myself to prayer, being watchful and thankful.

April 19. Day 85.

We do not want you to be ignorant about those who fall asleep, or to grieve like the rest of men, who have no hope. We believe that Jesus died and rose again and so we believe that God will bring with Jesus those who have fallen asleep in Him. According to the Lord's own word, He will come down from heaven with a loud command; and with the trumpet call of God, and the dead in Christ will rise first! After that, we who are still alive will be caught up together with them in the clouds to meet the Lord in the air! And so we will be with the Lord forever! *Therefore encourage each other with these words!* (1 Thessalonians 4:13–18)

I think every sympathy card should have these words written in them, because this is the *only* sentiment that lessens the pain for those of us who have said a good-bye. While we wait for *that day,* Paul says we must put on faith and love as a breastplate and the hope of salvation as a helmet (1 Thessalonians 5:8). *Our God knows how easy it is to get distracted while we wait for heaven, and He knows without His armor, we won't survive.*

I remember the first and last time I played paintball. We took our kids to China for the weekend and spent an afternoon on a very authentic looking battlefield. We were given khakis, guns, and bags of ammunition. We were told the rules, separated into teams, and then sent out to destroy our opponents. *The only thing we weren't given was armor.* I stepped into battle and found myself under immediate fire. The sting of those paintballs exploding onto my flesh felt suicidal, so I opted to be the nurse on the sidelines. I felt like a deserter, but I must admit that I was a happy deserter who still believes that it's just foolish to go into war unprotected!

Our Commander in Chief never sends us into battle without armor!

He gives us exactly what we need so we can win the war.

Yup, put that on a sympathy card!

April 20. Day 86.

This is the first time in my life that I am solely responsible to pay the bills, do the grocery shopping, and make all the decisions. I feel like I'm stuck on one of those horrible spinning rides at the fair, and I know if Jim was here, he'd find a way to make it all stop. There were only two things he said he couldn't do: kill a spider and live without me.

It comforts me to know that I was chosen to bear this grief so that Jim could be spared. Paul encourages the church in Thessalonica that lasting relief from sorrow will be ours when Jesus returns, but until He comes we are to rejoice, both in the hope of that day and in our sufferings. He tells the church in Rome that suffering produces perseverance; perseverance, character, and character, hope – *a hope that will never disappoint us because God's love has been poured into our hearts* (Romans 5:2–5).

I am in a terrifying place, but I have to believe that God will enable me to persevere with His courage until lasting relief is given to me when He finally comes to take me home.

April 21. Day 87.

May our Lord Jesus Christ Himself and God our Father, who loved us and by His grace gave us *eternal encouragement and good hope,* encourage your hearts and strengthen you in every good deed and word. (2 Thessalonians 2:16–17)

After the funeral, normal life resumes for everyone except the one who's been left alone. It's no one's fault. It's just the way it is. That's why this verse tucked away in Thessalonians is a lifeline, reminding me that *God's encouragement is never going to end.* He is constantly directing my heart into His love and into Christ's perseverance and giving me peace at all times and in every way (2 Thessalonians 3: 3, 5, 16).

Maybe I should start creating sympathy cards.

April 22. Day 88.

Through Jesus and for His name's sake, we have received grace. (Romans 1:5)

God's grace, like God's encouragement, is eternal.

The poet Annie Johnson Flint was orphaned when she was six. My mom was abandoned by her alcoholic father when she was eight and found her mom dead on the floor when she was twenty. Annie's dream of becoming a pianist was shattered when arthritis crippled her fingers, so she became a poet. When I was a little girl sitting in the pew, it embarrassed me that my mother's voice would crack whenever she sang Annie Flint's famous poem, which was eventually put to music by Hubert Mitchell.

Forty years later, I understand.

> He giveth more grace when the burdens grow greater;
> He sendeth more strength when the labors increase;
> To added affliction, He addeth His mercy;
> To multiplied trials, His multiplied peace.
>
> When we have exhausted our store of endurance;
> When our strength has failed and the day is half done;
> When we've reached the end of our hoarded resources;
> Our Father's full giving is only begun.
>
> *His love has no limits, His grace has no measure,*
> *And His power has no boundary known unto men;*
> *For out of His infinite riches in Jesus,*
> *He giveth, and giveth, and giveth again.*

God's grace persuades us to believe that no matter what it looks like, God will use everything for His name's sake and for our eternal good.

God's grace is greater than our doubt, deeper than our hurts, and strong enough to carry us through anything.

April 23. Day 89.

I can't stop thinking about how we are the recipients of God's eternal encouragement and His limitless supply of grace. We also have the assurance of God's peace that is simply unexplainable. "We have peace with God through our Lord Jesus Christ" (Romans 5:1).

If that was all I knew, it would be enough.

My friend Mandy is in her thirties and was born and raised in China. She came to Hong Kong in the early nineties and was invited by a stranger to come to church. Thinking that it might be a good way to meet new people, she accepted the invitation. She told me later that after the first visit to the church she felt dirty. For some reason unknown to her, she went back and felt even dirtier. On her third visit, Mandy told me, *"Jesus cleaned me."*

Those three little words are why we have peace with God.

I love that we have a God who pursues us, cleans us up, and then walks us home, giving us whatever He feels we need for the journey. The closer we walk with Him, the more we begin to see what He sees, and the easier it is to follow.

Mandy's six-year-old son was born with a severe heart defect. He had open heart surgery after he was born, with the promise of more extensive surgery when he got older. I was with her when the doctor called to tell her that the surgery had been scheduled. That night as she was tucking Ivan into bed, she explained to him that after the operation one of two things would happen: he would wake up and see his family, or he would wake up and see Jesus.

Mandy told him that God would do whatever He thought was best. Every night leading up to the surgery, they talked about heaven. Just before she kissed him good-bye, she told him that if he felt afraid, just to talk to Jesus. Ivan told us later that as he was being rolled into the operating theater he felt very afraid, so he did exactly what his mom had said, and *Jesus whispered in his ear not to worry because He was going to be with him until it was over.*

Mandy and Ivan's story is a perfect picture of God's indescribable peace. When God's peace rules our hearts, it's possible to pray "Your will be done" and then trust Him no matter what the outcome. Mandy thanked me recently for showing her that she didn't need to fear death. Heaven had become more real to her than earth, and for that she was thankful. She told me that she had been watching me on my new path and was convinced that Jesus would be to her what He has become for me.

That is truly all I want.

I want everyone to become desperate for what Mandy, Ivan, and I have been given: a repaired heart, governed by a Sovereign God.

April 24. Day 90.

If we are God's children, then we are heirs of God and co-heirs with Christ, *if we share in His sufferings* . . . only then we will also share in His glory. (Romans 8:17)

We don't like to talk about suffering, let alone actually suffer, yet it is *God's prerequisite* to making us ready for eternity. *The sooner we accept this, the quicker we'll learn to trust Him.* Paul writes,

> I consider that our present sufferings are not worth comparing with the glory that will be revealed in us . . . and while we wait for that day of days to come, the Spirit himself helps us. He moans and groans and intercedes for us *in accordance with God's will.* So we know that in *all* things God works for the good of those who love Him who have been called according to *His* purpose . . .
>
> What then shall we say in response to this? If God be for us, who can be against us? What shall separate us from the love of Christ? Will trouble, hardship, persecution, famine, nakedness, danger or the sword? *I am convinced that* absolutely nothing *will be able to separate us from the love of God that is in Christ Jesus our Lord!* (Romans 8:18, 26–28, 31, 35, and 38, paraphrased)

Seal this in my soul forever!

April 25. Day 91.

Three months today. It feels like many lifetimes ago. It feels like it was just this morning.

Here's what I know.

Even when I'm wallowing in self-pity, *He reaches out to me with His eternal encouragement.*

I love the story Jesus told about the prodigal son. When the son finally comes to his senses and begins the trek home, what he doesn't realize is that his father, *full of compassion,* has *never stopped watching and waiting* for him to return! When the father catches a glimpse of him he runs to meet him, throws his arms around him, and welcomes him home! The son apologizes, and instant forgiveness chases away the shame as a celebration begins! Our God is just like the father in this story. He's waiting for us to fall into His arms.

My prayer is that anyone whose feeling condemned will have their eyes opened to see His outstretched hands, because that changes everything.

It did for me.

April 26. Day 92.

Have you ever seen anything quite like this extravagant generosity of God, this deep, deep wisdom? It's way over our heads. We'll never figure it out! *Is there anyone around who can explain God? Anyone smart enough to tell Him what to do? Anyone who has done Him such a huge favor that God has to ask his advice?* Everything comes from Him; everything happens through Him; everything ends up with Him! (Romans 11:33–35, *The Message*)

Paul reasons that a reasonable response to God's amazing care over our lives is to offer ourselves to Him as a *living sacrifice.*

I agree.

The world tells me that it's okay for me to be angry. In fact, the world has even broken down the process of grief into stages. There is denial and isolation, then anger, followed by bargaining, depression, and finally acceptance.

I am a widow who has chosen to bypass the first four stages and go right to the acceptance part, because that's what I believe God tells me to do.

When the doctor told me Jim had died, my flesh and spirit were instantly at war. Anger and acceptance stood face-to-face. In those first moments when I made a conscious decision to accept Jim's death as God's will, the war was over. Some may think that I'm in denial or pushing my anger into a corner. My response to that is: *I cannot be angry at my only source of comfort and strength. I have never felt so sad in all my life, but I'm convinced that the only way to heal is to give myself to the One who knows me best, and to believe with everything within me that He will use this pain for His glory.*

April 27. Day 93.

One Christmas, Jim and I unknowingly gave each other the same gift: a photo of a man and woman in each other's arms at a train station. Our hearts were both drawn to this print because we said many good-byes and hellos at train stations during his Bible school years. I now keep this picture beside my bed as a constant reminder of the reunion to come. As I looked at it this morning, my heart began to palpitate with excitement as I imagined Jesus coming back to take me to that reunion in the skies!

I picked up my Bible and turned to Romans 13, where Paul writes about how we are supposed to reflect Jesus in all that we say and do. He reviews a few of the commandments, emphasizing that love is the greatest. Then he explains why it is so important to live the way God commands.

> The hour has come for you to wake up from your slumber because our salvation is nearer now than when we first believed. *The night is nearly over! The day is almost here.* (Romans 13:11–12)

Oh, how I long for that final reunion, but until it happens *I must live right and represent Him well.*

April 28. Day 94.

I honestly can't get used to how God faithfully gives me manna every morning.

> Everything that was written in the past was written to teach us, so that through *endurance* and the *encouragement of the scriptures,* we might have *hope. May the God of hope fill you with all joy and peace as you* trust in Him *so that you may overflow with hope by the power of the Holy Spirit.* (Romans 15:4, 13)

Paul's letter to the Romans is a timeless manual on how to live on earth while we wait for heaven!

Revelation 2:17 says that Jesus gives *hidden manna* to those who obey and overcome!

I am completely overwhelmed by His generosity.

April 29. Day 95.

> Consider it pure joy, whenever you face trials of many kinds, because you know that the testing of your faith develops perseverance. Perseverance must finish its work so that you may be mature and complete, not lacking anything. If any of you lack wisdom, he should ask God who gives generously to all without finding fault, and it will be given to him. (James 1:1–6)

James wrote this letter to the early church, which was subjected to horrific suffering. Imprisonment, flogging, torture, and homelessness were the norm. To consider these trials *pure joy* seems to be plain crazy until you remember that the cost of following Jesus was never hidden from them. Letters like this were passed around to remind them that their suffering was temporary and that heaven was forever.

James's words about asking God for wisdom seemed strange to me, because if I was being sawed in two, I'd be asking for *courage,* not wisdom, but then it dawned on me! It is wisdom that gives me insight into what it means to *fear the Lord,* which compels me to bow down in absolute *surrender to His sovereignty,* convinced that whatever happens is for my eternal good.

Sovereign God, I need wisdom.

April 30. Day 96.

From every window I can see the old airport we flew into back in 1989. Only the best pilots in the world were allowed to land there, because the descent to the airstrip was unbelievably close to the tops of the buildings. We could stand on our street corner and count the bolts on the underbelly of the aircraft as it soared just a couple hundred feet over our heads. I can also see Munsang and the corner of our rooftop.

I miss my friend and want him to see what I see. I loved being with him. I loved it when he woke me up with kisses. I loved how safe I felt when I laid my head on his chest. My nostalgic view is a constant reminder to me that when the four of us walked off the plane carrying our suitcases into the total unknown, *God went before us*—and He's never stopped.

Take me to my manna.

> *Susan,* be patient until the Lord's coming. See how the farmer waits for the land to yield its valuable crop and how patient he is for the autumn and spring rains? *You too must be patient and stand firm, because the Lord's coming is near.* For an example of patience in the face of suffering, look at the prophets. Those who have persevered are blessed. Think about *Job's* perseverance and consider what the Lord finally brought about. *The Lord is full of compassion and mercy.* (James 5:7–11, paraphrased)

Wow, the prophets are quite the example. Jeremiah's faithfulness to the Lord landed him in the bottom of a muddy cistern. Ezekiel's wife died as an object lesson. Job lost *everything* and still *chose* to say, "Though He slay me, yet will I trust. Blessed be Your name."

Sovereign God, thank You for Your compassion and mercy that spurs me on to patiently persevere.

Thank You for the view out my window that reminds me of Your faithfulness. Blessed be Your name.

May 1. Day 97.

First Peter 1 says we are strangers in this world who have been chosen by a Sovereign God to obey Jesus. We are assured that in the midst of grief, we have a *firmly anchored hope that is secured by the very power of God.* Peter writes that we should rejoice even when we're hurting, because suffering proves our faith genuine and showcases Jesus! This temporary pain is achieving for me an eternal glory that will far outweigh this agony.

My reaction to suffering affects my healing.

My reaction to suffering affects my eternity.

God, in His perfect love, allows us to hurt so that in our sorrow we will come to realize that we are nothing and He is everything. It's easier to throw in the towel of despair than it is to persevere, so Peter writes that we must prepare our minds for action by setting our hope fully on the grace to be given us when Jesus is revealed! I can look at my contender and surrender without ever throwing a punch, or I can step into that ring with God's strength backing me up and watch my opponent fall to the mat.

Sovereign God, help me fight.

May 2. Day 98.

Like newborn babies, *crave* spiritual milk, so that *you may grow up* in your salvation. (1 Peter 2:2)

I've always tried to be disciplined in spending time in God's Word, but since Jim went to heaven, *I cannot live without my manna.* I'm ashamed that it took Jim's death to trigger this intense craving in my soul.

Widowhood bent my knee, broke my heart, and made me desperate for more of Jesus.

For the past few mornings a huge eagle has been flying outside my bedroom window. It's been magnificent to watch it swoop in and out of the clouds. My thoughts went to Isaiah 40:31, where it says that those who crave His nearness will exchange their weakness for God's strength, and instead of growing weary on the path, they will soar.

I love soaring.

May 3. Day 99.

I was soaring until I had a run-in with the cable company. I settled the final bill for our old address and gave them my new address when I moved, but a few weeks later I got an invoice stating my account was overdue. When I called customer service they assured me that it was a misunderstanding, but I've continued to get constant reminders, so I called again, and that's when it happened.

The customer service rep's attitude was condescending. She kept repeating that my payment was late, which irritated me so much that I yelled at her, refused to pay the bill, and then slammed down the receiver! I tossed and turned the whole night. I felt even worse when I read my manna: "When they hurled insults at Him, He did not retaliate. When He suffered, He made no threats. Instead, He entrusted Himself to Him who judges justly" (1 Peter 2:23). I did the *exact* opposite of Jesus. That poor cable lady was the recipient of all my bottled-up frustration that is part and parcel with widowhood.

The Holy Spirit cut me no slack.

Every verse I read was a gentle reprimand that Christlikeness is still expected no matter what we're faced with. Feeling overwhelmed is *not* an excuse for arrogance and anger. 1 Peter 3 tells me to be sympathetic and compassionate and humble. *Ouch.* It tells me not to repay evil with evil or insult with insult, but to repay evil and insult with blessing, *because to this I was called,* so that I may inherit a blessing. *Double ouch.* It tells me to keep my tongue from evil. *Triple ouch.* It tells me to seek peace and *pursue it.* Is there such a thing as a quadruple ouch?

I knew what needed to be done.

I called the cable company. The odds of getting the same customer service representative were a big fat zero *unless God is in charge.* I told her that I had represented Jesus horribly. I asked for her forgiveness, and she awkwardly said it was okay and that she would be sending me another bill next week sometime.

As I hung up the phone, the heaviness lifted and I found myself soaring again.

May 4. Day 100.

One hundred days of God's grace, comfort, and strength.

1 Peter 3:15 says, "But in your hearts set apart Christ as Lord. Always be prepared to give an answer to everyone who asks you, to give reason for the hope that you have."

The hope that keeps me going is *that this is not all there is.* My time on earth is brief compared to the eternity I'll spend in heaven with Jesus.

> Dear friends, do not be surprised at the painful trial you are suffering, as though something strange were happening to you. But rather, *rejoice that you participate in the suffering of Christ, so that you may be overjoyed when His glory is revealed!* (1 Peter 4:12–13)

I am learning to rejoice in my suffering because this God-carved path is changing me.

It has tightened my grip, firmed up my stance, strengthened my resolve, and focused my eyes on the prize.

I'm thankful for this path.

May 5. Day 101.

I have a friend who was taken to a fancy restaurant where everything that comes out of the kitchen looks like a piece of art. Dessert was a masterfully sculpted swing carved out of delicious dark chocolate on a bed of velvety melted white chocolate with a raspberry swirl. It was so intricate that you could gently push the swing backward and forward. My friend was impressed, but her boyfriend told her to look closer. She made a few more oohs and ahhs, but he still wasn't smiling. He insisted that she look *even closer,* and when she did, she gasped. There on the little swing sat a diamond ring.

It's often like that when we read God's Word. We see the obvious and miss the treasure. If we lean in closer, we see the real reason for the story and the incredible application for our lives.

1 Peter 5:5–6 says that God opposes the proud but gives grace to the humble, and in light of that we should humble ourselves *under God's mighty hand,* that He may lift us up in due time. At first glance it sounds like if we're humble, then eventually God will reward us by putting us in an honorable position. But when we lean in closer and read Peter's entire letter, we see the glistening truth and realize how we nearly missed it.

To humble ourselves means to believe and declare that God is sovereign, and then to willingly put ourselves under God's mighty hand without complaining or squirming to get out.

If we do this, God will lift us above our questions into that place of acceptance and submission. That's why the very next thing Peter writes is about casting all our anxiety on the Lord.

Instead of wasting our energy on wondering why me, we are told *to rest* under God's hand.

One of the worst things someone can do is allow me to have a pity party. I *must* resist the temptation to feel sorry for myself. If I do this, "the God of *all* grace, who *called me to His eternal glory in Christ, will restore me* and *make me strong, firm, and steadfast."*

I'm so glad I leaned in a little closer.

May 6. Day 102.

There is a piece of land that houses a tiny cottage I refer to as my Ebenezer. *Ebenezer* is one of those old King James biblical words; it means, "Thus far the Lord has helped me."

My Ebenezer is at a church camp that I went to every summer of my life until we left Canada. This church camp is where Jim and I surrendered our lives to Jesus. We also spent a lot of hours in my grandmother's cottage, affectionately known as Nanny's, playing endless games of Rook, eating toast and peanut butter, and drinking bottomless cups of tea. The memories we had, coupled with the eternal moments, made this place holy ground to us, so when my father gave us the deed to Nanny's, it was a happy day!

The cottage is over seventy years old. It has no foundation, hot water, or even a shower. It's basically just four walls waiting to collapse, but I love it. When CJ and Alison got married, Jim and I stayed there, much to everyone's horror. We pumped up an inflatable mattress, lit our candles (which in hindsight was probably a very dangerous thing to do in a dry old firetrap), and lay there feeling blessed out of our socks. We imagined what we could do to make the cottage livable and couldn't wait to get started on the renovations. We had a contractor take a look at it, and his recommendation was to tear it down. He said some of the old could possibly be incorporated into a new cottage, but if we wanted a structure that was safe and would last for our grandchildren, we had to start from scratch. We decided to follow his advice, and Jim knew exactly who to ask to build our haven.

Tim had been in our youth group, and even way back then, his carpentry skills were remarkable. Although time and distance separated us, Jim loved Tim like a brother. We decided that after the Christmas busyness, we would locate Tim and ask him if he would build us a new Nanny's.

After Jim died, returning to our church camp and rebuilding Nanny's was unthinkable. Eventually my sons convinced me that Jim would want me to follow through on what we'd decided to do, and so I reluctantly e-mailed Tim. I received a response from him and his wife that absolutely undid me.

He told me that he had been at the funeral in Canada and sat in the back left corner. After the service he wanted to talk to me, but the huge crowds made it impossible. He also wanted me to know Jesus had been waking him up most nights during the last decade to pray for us. Sometimes it would be just a short prayer. Other times he would pray for hours. During one of those prayer times, Jesus had told him that I would be needing a little house and that he was supposed to build it! He didn't really know what to make of that until he got my e-mail. He concluded by saying he would be ecstatic to build Nanny's. *Wow.*

I still don't know how I'll stay there without Jim, but Nanny's will forever be my Ebenezer, a powerful reminder of God's constant intervention and care over my life.

May 7. Day 103.

Second Peter 3:1–14 is all about my favorite topic. I don't believe it's a coincidence that the complex I'm living in is called Sky Tower. It's unusual in Hong Kong to look out your window and actually see an unobstructed view of the sky, yet that's what I see every morning, which is my daily reminder that Jesus could come today!

Peter talks about the scoffers who say, "Where is this coming He promised?"

Peter writes that the Lord is delaying the reunion that *He too is longing for* so that everyone will turn from their sins and come to Jesus.

God wants us to aggressively wait for His return.

I can't call myself a sky-gazer unless I let others in on what I'm waiting for.

Every time we give a reason for the hope we have and someone chooses to believe, we are one minute closer to hearing Him shout our names and flying into the clouds!

May 8. Day 104.

It's Mother's Day.

Like most moms, I often felt like a flop. I was too smothering or too lenient, but Jim always told me I was perfect. He truly honored me. A year ago we were in Philadelphia visiting my brother. When I woke up, Jim was lying beside me grinning, with a bag full of goodies.

I give You today, Jesus, and ask that You bring beauty out of ashes. Please be with every mom who is forgotten today. *Let them know You are lying beside them in their aloneness and that they are deeply valued by You.*

Thank You for my sons. They are my two soldiers who continually bless my heart. Since they were little boys, I sang that old hymn, "Stand Up, Stand Up for Jesus," in their ears. Whenever they went out to play, I would remind them that they were soldiers of the cross, and I have watched them grow up into just that. I've prayed for them as they have maneuvered through enemy lines and cried for them when they suffered a wound. I've breathed a sigh of relief when they made it through a barrage of enemy fire, and I will always and forever fight alongside them on my knees.

I love being their mom.

11:50 p.m.

It was a perfect Mother's Day. Curtis took me out for lunch to one of our favorite hamburger joints. The food was great, but the conversation was even better. Then he brought me home and spent all afternoon cooking me dinner. He made lamb steaks with rosemary with a side of mashed potatoes mixed together parsnips, carrots, sour cream, and pepper. He prepared a delicious salad with an olive oil dressing and a four-berry smoothie with Greek yogurt for dessert! The detail and love that went into this meal reflected the love of my Jesus. CJ called twice to tell me I was the best mom in the world and that he not only loved me, but was blessed by my life and thankful to be my son.

My most sovereign God, I thank You for this Mother's Day.

You made it flawless.

May 9. Day 105.

For I am *resolved* to know nothing except Jesus Christ and him cruci-fied. (1 Corinthians 2:2)

Being resolved *is a determination to stay the course, no matter how difficult that might be.* This sentence is part of a long letter Paul wrote to the church in Corinth about how God's power is seen in our human frailty.

Again, my reaction to suffering means everything.

It's only in those dark, lonely, anguishing times that a distinction can be noticed. While the rest of the world spirals into despair, it's my opportunity to let the peace of God rule so that others will look and see the power of God holding me steady. Every time I embrace whatever He brings into my life, I am working together with Him to fulfill His eternal purposes.

I never want anyone to think that I'm doing great or that I'm strong.

What I want is for everyone to know that I am weak but Jesus is strong, and that anything good seen in me is only because God loves me like crazy.

May 10. Day 106.

Jimbies, you are always in my thoughts. In God's grace I'm living and trying to glorify Jesus through every moment of this pain. The cards you gave me and the countless conversations we had spur me on to keep going. Jesus is looking after me as I live every unbelievable second of this journey, and when I remember that both of us are in His arms, I'm not so lonely.

Holy Spirit, take me to my manna.

Each one should retain the place in their life that *the Lord assigned to them* and to which God has called them. (1 Corinthians 7:17)

Although Paul is referring to marital status, the deeper issue is the accep-tance of God's will, so *again* on this new day, I embrace my widowhood.

This is the path that You have called me to, O Sovereign God, and I am resolved to glorify You with every step.

If I remember that this present world is fleeting, then I will be looking forward to what's promised instead of dwelling on what I don't have.

It matters how I walk this journey. It will be over before I know it.

May 11. Day 107.

Run in such a way as to get the prize. (1 Corinthians 9:27)

I loved long distance running when I was in school. There was one race I'll never forget. I was running around the track, when suddenly I felt a jabbing pain in my side. The longer I ran the worse it became, until I was no longer thinking about the race. *The pain overshadowed my desire for that coveted gold ribbon. It convinced me that it wasn't worth the agony, that it was a hopeless cause,* so I ran off the track and sprawled out on the grass.

My teacher stood over me and asked me why I had dropped out of the race. I explained that I was in pain. Instead of sympathy, he shook his head in disbelief and told me that I had been laps ahead of everyone and that if I had just kept going, I would have taken home the prize. I hadn't just let myself down, but the entire school. What I learned that day I've carried with me until now.

I cannot let the pain cloud the prize.

I have to force myself to keep running until the flag is lowered. Athletes going for gold *do not quit.* They make it to the finish line one way or the other. They may come in bleeding, blistered, and limping, and collapse into a heap of exhaustion, *but they finish.*

I will too.

May 12. Day 108.

I woke up and read Paul's words to Timothy about enduring hardship like a good soldier of Christ Jesus, then turned on the news and was amazed to hear the anchor tell two stories about two soldiers!

One stepped on a grenade and blew his foot off. After extensive surgery, he returned to the war! Although he had a very worthy excuse to stay home, he refused, saying, "I want to show the enemy I will never stop being a soldier!"

He is now on the front lines with an artificial foot, showing the enemy that nothing will hinder him in his mission. His bravery has encouraged all his fellow soldiers to keep going.

The second soldier was told by his commander in chief that his tour of duty was over. He returned to a parade in his honor and was awarded a Purple Heart. With tears in his eyes, he said that the unbelievable reception he received made the horrors of war worthwhile. I started to imagine what it will be like when my Commander in Chief says my work has been accomplished and it's time for me to come home. It makes me cry just thinking about how it will feel when He places a crown on my head because I've persevered.

Until that day comes, I want to be the kind of soldier who keeps fighting despite the wounds and missing parts.

May 13. Day 109.

I have been given another day to faithfully wage war as a good soldier.

> If only for this life we have hope in Christ, we are to be pitied more than all men. (1 Corinthians 15:19)

Literally millions around me lack hope. They count on their relatives to burn paper provisions after they've died so they will be well provided for in the afterlife. Others try to do enough here on earth so that when measured in heaven, the scales will tip in their favor. As a follower of Jesus, I know that *nothing* I could ever do could be enough, and so *all* my hope is in Jesus, not just for this life, but in the real life to come!

May 14. Day 110.

> Praise be to the God and father of our Lord Jesus Christ, the father of compassion and God of all comfort, who comforts us in all our troubles, so that we can comfort those in any trouble with the comfort we ourselves have received from God. (2 Corinthians 1:3–7)

I know that one day I will comfort others with the same comfort that has comforted me on this path. I will be able to look into the eyes of someone who has lost much and assure them of the promised nearness of our Lord. I will be able to share the secret of embracing the pain and the joy of having Jesus's hand in yours. I will cry with them and let them know Jesus cries too. *Something profoundly precious happens when we share in the fellowship of His sufferings and then in turn share in someone else's pain. Eternal worth is given to every lonely hour.* Paul describes the hardship and pressure he and his companions faced as far beyond their ability to endure and said that they despaired even of life.

Those emotions and sentiments are so familiar, aren't they? Whether it is the loss of your best friend, soul mate, and lover; the breach of a sacred vow; the termination of a job; or the intrusion of a cancer; *it leaves you wondering how survival is possible.*

Paul concludes, "Indeed, in our hearts we felt the sentence of death. But this happened that we might not rely on ourselves, but on God who raises the dead!"

We can always choose to throw ourselves into the arms of God, who will breathe life into our deathlike situations and fill us with eternal hope that we can then pass on to others.

Choosing to do this will save lives.

May 15. Day 111.

I have friends who have moved into the building across the street and friends who have moved right into Sky Tower, just for me. When God promises He will put the lonely in families, He isn't kidding.

If God says it, God does it!

> Jesus carries out and fulfills *all* of God's promises, *no matter how many of them there are;* and *we will tell everyone how faithful He is,* giving glory to His name! (2 Corinthians 1:20, *The Living Bible*)

Here's another promise:

> Now it is God who makes both us and you *stand firm* in Christ. He anointed us, He set His seal of ownership of us, and He put His spirit in our hearts as a deposit, *guaranteeing* what is to come! (2 Corinthians 1:21)

I can't stop smiling . . .

May 16. Day 112.

As I was walking out of church yesterday, a friend grabbed my arm and introduced me to a stranger.

"Sue is a widow as well. Sue, this lady lost her husband and her two children on the same day."

The impact of those words dropped me to my knees. I began to cry. I couldn't begin to grasp what she was feeling. It made the loss of Jim seem miniscule. The thought of losing Jim *and* my two sons at the same time made me dizzy. I wrapped my arms around her and whispered the name of Jesus in her ear. She shared with me that they had been one of the many tsunami victims in December 2004. They left for Thailand as a family of five and came home a family of two.

Somehow my pain, although so small compared to hers, connected our hearts. We talked about the promise of heaven and of the constant presence of Jesus. We comforted each other with the comfort God is comforting us with. I walked away so thankful for my boys but feeling guilty that I still had them, vowing to remember there are countless others who have lost so much more than I have.

Help my pain to never blind me from those who are suffering around me.

May 17. Day 113.

Lori and I refer to one another as "Jesus buddies" because whenever we get together, our conversation always turns to Him. On our recent road trip to see my brother, we cranked the volume and had church all the way to Philadelphia with the Brooklyn Tabernacle Choir! It was Lori who drove me to Jim's Canadian funeral. The choir accompanied us that day too, and the last words spoken to me before I got out of the car were, "Are you ready, Sue?" Lori is a worshiper who has taught me that I dare not take a step without first throwing myself at God's throne.

How can one person be so blessed? I have friends who take me back to all the places I've lived so I can remember God's faithfulness, who stand as sentries in the corners of funeral parlors, who encourage me to worship through my suffering, who call me daily to make sure I'm okay, and who today will fly across an ocean to give me a hug.

Self-pity and despair cannot hang around very long when God's love is expressed like that.

Paul writes that we are hard-pressed on every side, *but not crushed;* perplexed, *but not in despair;* struck down, *but not destroyed.* And that's all because of how much God loves us. If we choose to fix our eyes on Jesus, the epitome of God's love, then our hearts will be fortified to keep trusting (2 Corinthians 4:8 and 19, paraphrased).

Thank You, my Sovereign, for friends who represent Jesus so well.

May 18. Day 114.

Now we know that if the earthly tent we live in is destroyed, we have a building from God, *an eternal house in heaven,* not built from human hands. (2 Corinthians 5:1)

A tent is the perfect picture of our humanness. No matter how fancy the tent, *it's still a tent,* temporary and easily knocked over.

We were a motel-with-a-swimming-pool type of family, so when Jim and I were planning our honeymoon, I was totally enamored with the idea of camping. I thought it would be romantic to lie out under the stars in the middle of nowhere, all alone. Jim, on the other hand, had grown up camping and was really looking forward to having a key to let us into a room with a comfortable bed and a big bathtub. We ended up compromising. The first half of our honeymoon was in a tent in the Shenandoah Valley, and the second half was in a cozy cottage on a lake.

We were given an orange-and-beige tent, a Coleman stove, a cooler, and a double-sized sleeping bag for our camping adventure. As we drove into the mountains, I was giddy at how incredibly romantic this was going to be. I was totally pumped—until I saw a sign that said something about storing our food high up in the trees to keep it away from the bears. Jim said we'd *probably* be safe if we kept our supplies in the trunk of our car. *Probably* was not a good word to use. After sort of watching the sunset, because watching for bears suddenly seemed like more of a priority, we zipped up our very insubstantial door and crawled into our sleeping bag. For some reason I expected the ground to be softer. Still determined to make this what I had always imagined, I tried my best to ignore the fear and the pain.

That worked until a creature leaned against the side of our tent.

I woke Jim up with a terrified whisper, telling him that a bear was trying to kill us! Jim told me not to worry because he knew a guy who had killed a bear with his hands. I told him that he didn't really know David and that there was *no way* I was staying in this tent! When the creature was gone I ran to the safety of our car and locked the doors while Jim took down the tent. What a nice wife, eh? I made up for it on the way out of the park by telling him he was right. Camping was horrible. Jim chuckled all the way to the hotel. (By the way, when Jim was packing up, the bear came back, except it was a deer.)

Paul writes that our bodies are like tents. He says that while we are in these tents, we groan to be clothed in our heavenly dwelling. I can still see Jim grinning as we drove down the mountain with the tent in our trunk. He didn't mind that it was the middle of the night, because we were heading toward comfort and a delicious buffet.

I saw the same glimmer in his eyes the morning he went to heaven as his earthly tent was folded up and he was welcomed home.

May 19. Day 115.

When you read Paul's letter to the church in Corinth, a beautiful truth emerges.

It's always about making Jesus famous.

I've been convinced that we make Jesus known more by our reaction to adversity than by the most passionate sermon we could ever preach.

Paul and his band of brothers chose to trust when they found themselves naked and bound by chains in a dark prison cell. Out of their trust came a song. As a result of that song, a prison guard and his entire family wanted to know the Jesus they were worshiping. It wasn't the earthquake that convinced the jailor he needed Jesus; *it was two naked, bleeding men who refused to run even when they had an opportunity to do so, because they knew they had a chance to make Jesus known one more time.*

Sovereign God, I want to be Your faithful ambassador *especially* when I have been beaten, stripped of everything, and put in chains.

May 20. Day 116.

It's a colossal adjustment to be without him.

There are times on this new path when I actually throw my hands up into the air and say out loud, "Here You go, Jesus . . . take it!" Truthfully, that seems to help. There is something about vocalizing our desperation for Him that brings courage and peace.

Lori hand-delivered the quilt Aunt Carol made me from Jim's clothes. When I look at it, I don't just see a beautiful design, I see candlelit dinners at our favorite restaurants. I see us holding each other to keep warm on a cold night. I see us celebrating Eid with our Pakistani family. I see us walking the length of the beach in Guam. I see us standing outside of the Ed Sullivan Theater in front of the Letterman marquee. I see a love that was passionate and loyal.

God's Word is like my quilt.

It's so much more than words on a page. *It's a tapestry of His love and deep desire for us to be just like Jesus.* Paul writes that "we should try to live in such a way that no one will ever be offended or kept back from finding the Lord by the way we act . . . that in *everything we do* our aim should be to show that we are true servants of God . . . in great endurance; in troubles, hardships, and distresses; in beatings, imprisonments, and riots; in hard work, sleepless nights, and hunger; in purity, understanding, patience, and kindness; through glory and dishonor; in bad report and good report" (2 Corinthians 6:3–8, *The Living Bible*).

Sovereign God, please enable me to prove the validity of my claim to be Your true servant.

May 21. Day 117.

Some of my Muslim friends do something quite beautiful to mark special occasions. They invite all their friends over, and then together they read through the entire Quran. Everyone is given a small portion, and when they are finished, usually after several hours, there is a time of corporate prayer. The first time I was asked to join them, one of the older aunties told me to bring my Holy Book, so for years now I've had the huge privilege of sitting on the floor reading God's Word and praying that God would bless, in every way possible, the household and all of us who have gathered there.

Because of recent terrorist attacks, the Muslim community is often portrayed as evil. This is a hurtful assumption that pains both me and my Muslim family. There are also so-called Christians who have done horrific things in the name of righteousness, which is why I no longer call myself a Christian. I feel like I have to make a distinction, so I refer to myself simply as a follower of Jesus. The extremists on both fronts seem to dominate the airwaves, helping to solidify opinions, and so the chasm widens between them and us. It breaks my heart, because I want everyone to know the real Jesus.

My Muslim family fears the God of Abraham, Isaac, and Jacob and wants to please Him in all their ways. On the day Jim died, they actually wiped away my tears with their hands as they fell down my cheeks. They spoon-fed me soup. They rubbed my back. They took up a collection and paid for Jim's body to be sent back to Canada. One of the men, who is a tailor, stitched Jim a brand-new suit to be buried in.

I will never stop thanking them for being Jesus to me that day. We know that God has knit our hearts together and that we will be family forever. They also know that I am not their friend with an agenda to convert them to Christianity. I'm confident Jesus will show them who He is. Until my last breath, I will love my precious Muslim family *just like Jesus loves me.*

Sovereign God, as I go to another *Quran Khwani,* make me a conduit of Christ's love and hope as I sit with Your Holy Book in my hands.

May 22. Day 118.

Mr. and Mrs. Patrick were the cooks at the church camp where Nanny's is located. They followed our lives, often sending us notes of encouragement to remind us that we were in their daily prayers. When Mr. Patrick died, we were in Canada, so we went to his funeral. As we were walking away from the graveside, we felt a hand rest on both of our shoulders. It was Mrs. Patrick. She held our hands in hers, secretly giving us money. Jim and I were completely undone at her generosity. We didn't want to accept it, but she insisted, saying that it was what God had told her to do.

In her moment of deepest sorrow and personal need, she gave to us.

When we got inside our car, we decided we wanted to be just like Mrs. Patrick. The Macedonian churches sound just like her:

> Out of the *most severe trial,* their overflowing joy and their extreme poverty welled up in rich generosity. For I testify that they gave as much as they were able and even beyond their ability. Entirely on their own, they *urgently pleaded with us for the privilege of sharing* in this service to the saints. (2 Corinthians 8:2–3)

This is another one of those verses that marries the most unlikely words. Severe trials, yet they had overflowing joy. Extreme poverty, yet they were rich in their generosity. Paul goes on to write:

> And God is able to make *all* grace abound to you, so that in *all* things at all times, having *all* that you need, you will abound in every good work . . . *You will be made rich in every way so that you can be generous on every occasion* and through us your generosity will result in thanksgiving to God. (2 Corinthians 9:8, 11)

God's grace enables a widow who is living on a meager pension to put money in the hands of a couple at the open graveside of her best friend.

Sovereign God, please, *please* . . . help me to live in that kind of grace.

May 23. Day 119.

Paul's "thorn in the flesh" must have been brutal, because he begged God to remove it three times. God left the thorn but assured him that His grace was sufficient and that His power was made perfect in weakness (2 Corinthians 12:9). Paul's response to God's refusal is the only remedy for the suffering thorns inflict:

> Therefore I will boast all the more gladly about my weaknesses, so that Christ's power may rest on me. That is why, for Christ's sake, I delight in weaknesses, in insults, in hardships, in persecutions, in difficulties. *For when I am weak, then I am strong.* (2 Corinthians 12:10)

How come this is so hard to remember? Why do we still plead for a perfect life and spurn God's grace? Why is it so difficult to believe that God's way is always better? Why do we think God has forsaken us when life is tough?

I want to see things the way God does.
I've finished pleading for the thorn to be removed.

I am determined to prove that this crazy way of living can be reality for a follower of Jesus. A reality that says I must die in order to really live, that I must give generously out of my poverty, and that I must be weak for Him to be strong.

May 24. Day 120.

Curtis was granted his green card today, which means he'll be moving back to California. It was an unexpected gift to have Curtis here for the past two years, and when Jim died it became beautifully clear why.

Paul opens his letter to the church in Galatia by saying, "Grace and peace to you from God our Father and the Lord Jesus Christ, who gave Himself for us" (Galatians 1:3).

My heart is calm because I know that I can count on God's grace and peace when I say good-bye to Curtis. They are mine to hold on to.

May 25. Day 121.

On Sunday as I crossed Hong Kong's harbor on the Star Ferry, I passed the Convention Centre that was built especially for the handover in 1997. As I sailed by, it felt like yesterday when Jim and I attended a Christmas Eve service there together. We feasted on Turkish kebobs after the service before jumping into a taxi, instead of the usual bus, so that we could get home quickly. We lit our candles, put on our Natalie Cole CD, and danced in our living room with the backdrop of the twinkling lights of our little tree. It was a perfect evening that neither of us ever wanted to end.

On Sunday, Jim's death seemed like it couldn't have possibly happened four months ago, because it feels like *minutes* since we raced home to make love. Yet this morning it feels like forever. It's a very lonely journey God has ordained for me. I must dwell today on the truth that *I am not alone,* though I feel like I am.

Take me to my manna.

In Galatians 6:2, Paul writes, "Carry each other's burdens, and in this way you will fulfill the law of Christ."

Sovereign God, help me to take my eyes off my own pain and show me whose burden I can carry.

May 26. Day 122.

When Jim quoted the book of Ephesians, the words came alive. I could hear his voice this morning as I began to read how, before the world was made, God had already chosen to adopt me because it made Him happy!

I am the recipient of the richness of His grace, for He understands me well and knows what is best for me at all times.

Help me to remember all day long that I am God's daughter and that He has a perfect plan that will bring Him glory.

May 27. Day 123.

One of many reasons I'm looking forward to heaven is that there will be no more good-byes. I moved six times growing up, which meant I was the new kid in eight different schools. Then I exchanged being a pastor's daughter for being a pastor's wife, and the good-byes continued in three more cities before leaving the country to move to the Dominican Republic and then Hong Kong. *Each time, we knew we were saying yes to His call, but it always hurt to say the G-word.*

God has a plan for each of us that we must submit to. For me it has been to say good-bye all my life, but in my doing so, the Lord has allowed me to say hello to souls who needed to hear about Jesus. Wherever God calls us to, our mission is always the same: *to know Jesus more so we can make Him famous.*

My most excruciating good-bye was unexpected, yet in the heart-wrenching turmoil of those final seconds with Jim, I heard the voice of Jesus calling me to follow.

The same obedience and abandonment to His will was *still* being required. And when I obeyed, I came face-to-face with the strength that raised Christ from the dead.

May 28. Day 124.

Jim and I loved to watch *The Amazing Race*. We picked our favorites to win, groaned when mistakes were made, winced when the fast-forward meant eating the eyeballs of a cow, felt sorry when the stress of the game pitted couples against each other, and got all teary-eyed when the winners came running to the mat.

Last night's finale was great. In the episode before the win, the eventual victors came in last, but it was a nonelimination leg, which meant that they were allowed to keep racing. However, all their money and possessions were taken from them. They looked at each other and said, "*There's still hope because we have each other!*" When they finally reached the mat, everyone erupted into unhindered, explosive joy.

Their words reflect what Paul wrote in Ephesians 2: "We are God's people and members of God's extended family."

As members of that extended family, we cheer each other on all the way to heaven. Unlike the world's, our race isn't a competition, because everyone who finishes the race is a winner. But there *is* someone who stands at the finish line to congratulate and greet each of us when we get there.

May 29. Day 125.

This journey is teaching me that *praying according to God's will* is the *only* way to pray. The prayers found in Ephesians are powerful and effective because they were birthed out of suffering and uttered by a man who had learned to fix his eyes on the unseen and lived to do whatever God asked.

> I pray that from His glorious, unlimited resources He will empower me with inner strength through His Spirit. Then Christ will feel at home in my heart as I trust in Him. My roots will grow down into God's love and keep me strong. Please give me the power to understand how wide, how long, how high, and how deep Your love is for me. Let me experience the love of Christ, though it is too great to fully understand, so that I will be made complete, with all the fullness of life and power that comes from God. (Ephesians 3:16–19, paraphrased)

I like that a lot.

The more I trust Him, the more at home He'll feel and the more I'll come to know His love. I will never comprehend that love, but I know I couldn't exist without it, and I long for everyone else to know it too!

This is a prayer that I know He will answer.

May 30. Day 126.

Jim and I were invited to speak in many churches throughout Canada. Every time we pulled into another church parking lot, we saw the same thing. No matter what direction we looked, there was another church. The smaller the town, the more there were.

We couldn't help but wonder what conclusion those who don't believe in Jesus come to when they look out their windows and see multiple churches. At the very least, they have to be confused. *Why would anyone want to believe in something that even those who go to church are not able to agree on?* We would drive for hours, imagining what it would be like if each church did what Paul wrote about. Everyone looking on would be so drawn to Jesus, it would be, well, *like the early church!*

Paul writes that Jesus Himself gives each one of us grace and individual gifts so that His church can live in beautiful unity to represent Him well (Ephesians 4).

I am convinced that if His church would stand together at the foot of the cross, forsaking all the politics and doctrinal nitpicking, our hurting world would finally see their Savior and not us, and He would be simply irresistible.

This is another prayer that I know He'll answer.

May 31. Day 127.

Follow God's example. (Ephesians 5:1)

Jim imitated God the best of anyone I know. Our friends constantly told him he was too thankful and too nice; that it was unnecessary to thank taxi drivers or waiters because they were just doing their job; but all of their comments fell on deaf ears.

When he was in Grade 2, Jim was heartbroken to discover that one of his classmates had not received any valentines at their class party, so he carefully tore one of his many valentines in half, making sure his and the giver's name were removed. He lovingly addressed it to his classmate, signing it, "Love, Jimmy," and then secretly put it on her desk. Upon seeing the torn valentine, his classmate thought Jimmy was making fun of her friendless situation.

She burst into tears and ran to the teacher, which resulted in a public lecture directed at Jimmy on the consequences of being mean.

Every time Jim and his sister Kathy, visited their grandparents, Hobert, the weird, sometimes obnoxious neighbor, would offer them huge bowls of ice cream which they always accepted, even though he was a tad scary. Just months before Jim went to heaven, Kathy asked Jim if he remembered creepy Hobert. She was expecting him to make a derogatory comment, but instead Jim told her that he had made a conscious decision never to forget him. He said he was sure that there was a lot more to Hobert than met the eye and that every time he met someone a little strange, he would think about Hobert and his hurting heart.

That was my Jim.

From the time he was a young boy, he saw what no one else saw. He seized every opportunity to look past the obvious, asking Jesus to show him what was really there. *He was careful in the way he lived and made the most out of every opportunity. He spoke words of life; he made music in his heart to the Lord and he always gave thanks to God his father for everything.* Jim didn't just know how to recite the entire book of Ephesians, *Jim lived the book of Ephesians.*

I was so blessed to have a front-row seat to his life, and I will be smiling as I watch him receive his crown of righteousness one day.

I choose to imitate God like Jim did, looking through our Creator's eyes so I can see what He wants me to see.

June 1. Day 128.

The devil's schemes are endless and personal. It began in the garden of Eden when Satan asked Eve, "Did God really say . . . ?" That was enough to plant a seed of doubt in her heart that grew into disobedience.

The Enemy has not changed. He *still* whispers the same question into our ear. "Did God *really* say you're not allowed to feel sorry for yourself? Your situation is so bad . . . you are only human . . . it's okay . . ."

God does not force us to put on His armor, just like He does not force us to trust in His sovereignty, but if we do, He says we'll be able to stand our ground. We must dwell on the truth, pick up the shield of faith because our life depends on it, and apply God's Word when we're faced with the temptation to cave to the pressure. And we *must* pray, regardless of how we feel or whether we get the answer we want.

I have to constantly remind myself that I am one soldier in a battalion of billions who daily have a choice to fight or surrender. I stand in an endless line of soldiers who are facing the same arrows. We are in this war together, and we have a responsibility to pray for our comrades, that they will choose right and fight hard. We have an obligation to urge them to buckle up, hold tightly, and cover their heads.

What sweet relief it will be when we can take off our armor and lay down our weapons!

June 2. Day 129.

I woke up to a song about how God is here to bring hope and peace, mercy and purpose. There are so many who face each day without this knowledge. I pray with Paul this morning, "that whenever I open my mouth words will be given to me and that I will declare the gospel fearlessly" (Ephesians 6:19).

Jesus has many names. One of them is *Immanuel,* which means God with us.

What an honor it is to introduce my world to Jesus, their Savior and Immanuel.

June 3. Day 130.

I found an old note tucked inside my Bible from Leda, the organist at the last church we pastored before leaving Canada. I was so deeply touched by her love affair of over fifty years and ached for her as she was forced to figure out how to live without her husband after he died. I prayed I would never have to do that.

Yet, here I am.

I miss Jim's touch so much I ache. After expressing our love to one another, we would lay in a gentle embrace for a long time, just treasuring what we'd been given. Maybe it was because of friends like Leda and other widows who came in and out of our lives that we never took what we had for granted. We were always awestruck. I guess that is why it hurts so much now.

I hadn't read Leda's little note for years. It's remarkable that all these years later, when I'm wondering how I can keep going, it would once again fall into my hands. She quoted John 12:26: "Keep alert and watching, dear ones—His coming is at the door!"

I needed this reminder, because I woke up dwelling on the empty space beside me instead of looking to the sky.

Thanks, Leda.

June 4. Day 131.

Today is the anniversary of the Tiananmen Square massacre. When our sons were teenagers, we gave them each a poster of the one brave student standing in front of a tank, unwilling to move aside for the sake of his cause: freedom.

Matthew 3 says that Jesus was led by the Spirit into the desert where He was tempted by Satan. Jesus was *led by the Spirit* into a dry, lifeless, lonely, horribly difficult and frightening place to be tested . . . *so that we would know how to survive the desert.*

Jesus willingly stood in front of a moving tank and refused to budge even though He easily could have. He showed us the extent of God's love, and He showed us what it takes to be one of His followers.

I'm undone by His love.

I'm challenged by His sacrifice.

June 5. Day 132.

Satan hasn't changed. He still lives to deceive us. Thankfully, Jesus hasn't changed either, and I'm so glad that the weapons He wielded against the Enemy are just as effective now as they were then! If I can imitate Jesus when I come face-to-face with the Father of Lies, I too will be victorious in this wilderness.

I've noticed that Satan loves to plant seeds of discontent in my heart in an attempt to get me to question God's care over my life. Whenever this happens, I must follow Jesus's example and remind Satan, and my soul, that it's the eternal stuff that really matters. Any needs I have now are temporary. *I have to know what God says so I won't be tricked when Satan distorts it.*

Jesus did not fall prey to Satan's testing, and I don't have to either. Like Jesus, I can stand on *God's Word,* trust in *God's sovereignty,* and worship *God alone,* and then watch the devil walk away.

June 6. Day 133.

> The people living in darkness have seen a great light; to those living
> in the land of the shadow of death, a light has dawned. (Matthew 4:16)

When Jesus left the desert, He walked into God's plan for the world, one place at a time.

Everywhere Jesus went, He brought truth, revelation, light, and life.

The darkest place I've ever been was in an underwater cave in the Dominican Republic. We followed one of our Dominican friends into blackness, on our bellies, into what he kept saying was something we would never forget. The thought that our newfound "friend" could have been luring us into a trap to leave us for dead never even entered our minds. I could barely see my hand in front of my face, but I could feel the wet walls on either side of me as I wiggled through this cave, totally trusting our guide, who barely spoke English. Soon the walls disappeared, and the temperature dramatically dropped. Our Dominican amigo struck a match on the side of the wall, revealing a cavern filled with stalactites at the edge of a huge underground lake. It was spectacular and terrifying. *The light illuminated both the beauty and the danger.*

Perhaps that is how each person felt when Jesus walked into their lives. They suddenly saw what was there and realized how close they were to death and life all at the same time. Simon, Andrew, James, and John followed Jesus as He went throughout Galilee teaching in their synagogues. They followed Him into Syria and watched as He cast out demons, stopped seizures, and revived paralyzed limbs. *They watched the light dawn and illuminate the darkness, and surely they must have been awestruck like we were in that cave.*

Thank You, Jesus, for being my Light in this very dark place.

June 7. Day 134.

People ask me how I can call myself blessed. I believe that *being blessed is having a deeply rooted joy that is not linked to my circumstances, but rather to my obedience to God.* I know Jesus agrees, because when He talked about being blessed, He didn't equate it to a life without suffering. His teaching in Matthew 5 says that:

I am blessed if I realize that I am nothing without my God.

I am blessed when I mourn, because that's where I come to know the nearness and comfort of Jesus.

I am blessed if I follow the example of Jesus and serve selflessly.

I am blessed if I hunger and thirst for righteousness, because I will be filled with Jesus.

I am blessed if I show mercy on earth, because only then will it be shown to me in heaven.

I am blessed if I keep my heart pure, because I will see God even in the midst of pain.

I am blessed if I choose humility over pride.

I am blessed if I'm misunderstood for doing right.

When I see things the way Jesus does, it changes everything.

It's changing me.

June 8. Day 135.

Sovereign God, please help me to put my thoughts on what's to come, rather than what was.

Jesus says in Matthew 5:13 that we who follow Jesus are the salt of the earth. I looked up the uses of salt and was shocked to learn that there are fourteen thousand known uses for salt! Every breathing creature needs to have salt to live. Did you know that salt can melt the hardest of ice and be used to seed clouds to produce rain in desert areas?

If we are the salt of the earth, that means that our lives can melt the coldest of hearts. We can shoot mists of intercession into a desert situation and watch the rain begin to fall.

Jesus says this earth needs us.

We were created to be useful, productive, and effective, bringing life and flavor wherever our God puts us.

There's no time for being stuck in what was.

Sovereign God, hold me in Your hand and sprinkle me wherever You wish.

June 9. Day 136.

As of today, I am the new Bible teacher at Creative Primary School. I didn't go looking for this job; this job came looking for me, to remind me once again of God's intimate care. Seriously, it would be an insult to worry about any of my tomorrows.

I see bright twinkling lights out my bedroom window all night long. *When one goes out, it changes the landscape.* That's a constant reminder to me of the words of Jesus: "Let your light shine so that everyone can see your good deeds and praise my Father in heaven" (Matthew 5:14–16).

I know that each time I choose to trust Him, my light shines, and those around me see the power of God.

For their sakes alone, I dare not wallow in self-pity, even for a second.

June 10. Day 137.

After the doctor told us that Jim had died, I was taken home to change out of my pajamas, and my Australian friend Pam was there to meet me. For the next twenty-four hours she never left my side. She read me the Psalms into the wee hours of that first night without Jim. Her son came to visit me today, and when he walked through the door, I lost it. Sometimes I can feel the surge of emotion mounting, but other times it *just comes,* forcefully and relentlessly out of nowhere, and there's no way to stop it.

Without Jesus, I would surely die. I am so thankful that He came all those thousands of years ago. The world would be empty of hope if He hadn't. Just like it's impossible to stop the floodgates of my grief, it's impossible to keep God's commands. We just don't have it in us. *We are so prone to stray from what we know is right, and that's exactly why Jesus came.* Jesus came to showcase how helpless we are to do this on our own. Our righteousness is useless, and that's why we need His.

I am so thankful for my Jesus, both now and forever!

He's made this life, and the life to come, completely possible.

June 11. Day 138.

Another night is over.

Another twenty-four hours have begun.

Take me to my manna.

In Matthew 5–7, Jesus continued to teach the masses how to live this life on earth so we can attain heaven, touching on every topic from murder to adultery to loving your enemies. *The great news is that Jesus actually lived what He taught.* There were no discrepancies between what He said on the mountainside and how He Himself reacted when faced with evil, abandonment, unspeakable darkness, and intense sorrow.

I want my life to always mirror what I say.

This journey can't be just talk.

I have to walk what I talk for it to mean anything at all.

June 12. Day 139.

There are moments when I feel like I'm spiraling down into a bottomless abyss. I relive Jim's final moments. I beg him to come back. A faceless voice screams in my ear that it's over, and the war commences. Everything within me wants to fight with the truth and win, but I'm exhausted from the sorrow.

Last night I was at a wedding celebration with five hundred of my friends from Pakistan. Many of the men found me to express again how sorry they were about Jim. A look of genuine disbelief is still written on each of their faces. Coming home in the taxi, I physically ached to feel Jim beside me, and even though I know in my mind it is over, my heart just can't seem to stop hoping it isn't.

Jesus, is it possible for You to tell Jim that I think about him every second and can't wait for our reunion in the skies? Could You tell him that CJ and Ali bought their first little home? Could You tell him that Curtis is leaving Hong Kong to go back to America on July 19 to begin a new chapter? Could You tell him that I am the Bible teacher at Creative Primary School?

Take me to my manna.

In Matthew 6, verses 1–18, Jesus talks about three acts of righteousness that are to be done covertly:

• When you give to the needy, *do it in secret.*

• When you pray, go into your room, close the door, and *pray in secret.*

• When you fast, put oil on your head and wash your face so that no one knows you're fasting.

I love tales about undercover agents who go into dire situations, save everyone, and then are extracted out and put back into civilian life again. No one—not even their best friend—knows they just rescued the entire world from certain death! That is *exactly* what Jesus asks of us. He wants us to be undercover agents of His lavish generosity and endless grace!

Sovereign God, You have once again reminded me that pity parties are not becoming.

Here I am, reporting for duty!
Send me on a secret mission!

June 13. Day 140.

After our honeymoon, we stuffed all our mismatched used furniture into a U-Haul and drove to Peterborough. We had just enough money for our first month's rent and a few groceries. Within a few days, our tiny, L-shaped basement apartment became the hangout for Jim's buddies. I loved feeding the gang, and the gang loved coming. In fact, they loved it so much that we were forced to tell them that if the place was in darkness, that meant we didn't want visitors. One night as we were stumbling around in the dark trying to have some alone time, Jim went to the refrigerator to get himself a Coke. When he opened the door, the fridge light flooded the apartment, and immediately there was a knock at our door. Jim's buddies had been standing in our backyard waiting for a light to go on!

Despite those friendly intrusions, we obviously had sufficient time to ourselves, because just four months after we were married I was pregnant. The pregnancy was difficult, so I was forced to quit my job, but as we continued to feed the masses, *God miraculously continued to provide.* Those early days taught us that storing treasures in heaven must be an ongoing discipline regardless of how much is in our wallet.

Since Jim went to heaven, well-meaning people have reprimanded me for being so generous, telling me I have a long future ahead of me. Believe me, I don't need to be reminded about my future, but here's the deal. Jesus says in Matthew 6 that wherever I choose to put my treasure is where my heart will be. There are no little asterisks beside these words with a footnote that says, "excluding widows who suddenly find themselves living on one income," so I choose to trust Him with my tomorrows and keep my light on.

June 14. Day 141.

Do not give dogs what is sacred; do not throw your pearls to pigs; if you do, they may trample them under their feet, and then turn and tear you to pieces. (Matthew 7:6)

I believe Jesus was referring to judgmental people. Dogs gnaw at everything in sight, leaving behind a wet mess. Pigs snort, dig their snout and hooves into the ground, and destroy everything around them.

There have been times where I have poured out my heart desperately hoping for some encouragement, but instead have received a lecture that left me feeling stupid for being so honest. I've excitedly shared every detail of my manna, only to be met with a patronizing tolerance.

I've been left standing in a puddle of slobber, silenced by snorts.

So I'm learning to be careful. My heart is just too vulnerable these days to be trampled on. I'm also learning not to judge, because the fact is, people just don't understand until they've been there themselves.

June 15. Day 142.

The movie *Shadowlands* wiped Jim and I out. We clung to each other as C.S. Lewis held his beloved Joy in his arms as she took her final breaths. Long after the credits rolled, we were still sitting in the cinema. For the next several hours we couldn't speak without tearing up. Their love story totally overwhelmed us.

I'm sure that the crowds felt this way as they listened to Jesus. Every sentence He spoke was riveting. I wish I could have been there on the mountainside. I'm sure I would have been one of the last to leave.

Shadowlands was one of those marker moments in our marriage where we vowed to never take what we had for granted. What we'd seen and heard that day was unforgettable. *It changed us.*

Listening to Jesus talk must have had the same effect, because even now, all these centuries later, *thinking about His story makes me cry.* Thinking about how much He loves me leaves me speechless.

June 16. Day 143.

From the onset of this path called widowhood, I've been challenged by my manna. It has continuously put me at a crossroads where I've been forced to choose. *Do I believe what Jesus says or not? Am I going to obey Him or go my own way?* I understand now what Jesus meant when He said, "The road that leads to life is narrow and very few find it" (Matthew 7:14).

It's much easier to be angry than it is to trust.

It's much easier to pine for someone to love me than it is to find someone to love.

Jesus, take me to that narrow road and carry me all the way home.

June 17. Day 144.

Only those who do the will of the Father will enter the Kingdom of heaven . . . Anyone who hears these words of mine and puts them into practice is like a wise man who built his house on the rock. (Matthew 7:21, 24)

We used to sing a song about this story in church. When the torrential downpour came, the house built on the rock stayed standing, while the house that was built on the sand was washed away. Throughout this storm, I've come to understand that simply believing in Jesus is not enough. I must also follow His teachings to keep from collapsing.

I have to practice what He preached.

If I do this, my house will stand, and everyone in the neighborhood will wonder how, and I'll be able to tell them.

June 18. Day 145.

When Jesus came down from the mountainside, large crowds followed him. (Matthew 8:1)

Here's the thing about Jesus. *You just can't get enough of Him!* The longer you sit at His feet, the more you want to hear, which is why He was always surrounded by a crowd. Another great thing about Jesus is that He was everyone's Savior. Whether you were an ostracized leper or a highly respected Roman centurion, Jesus never withheld His compassion. Matthew records that the leper was made clean and that the centurion's servant was healed, but what spoke to me this morning was the conversation Jesus had with the centurion *before* he received his miracle.

Lord, my servant lies at home paralyzed and in terrible suffering. I am not worthy to have You come under my roof, *so just say the word, and I know my servant will be healed,* for You see, I too am a man with authority. I tell my soldiers what to do and they do it, and I believe it's the same for You! (Matthew 8:6–9)

When Jesus heard this, He was astonished and announced to everyone around Him that He had never found anyone with such faith in all of His travels (Matthew 8:6–10, paraphrased). This centurion believed that Jesus had *all* authority over *every* situation, and he *knew* that whatever Jesus said would be. *He completely trusted Him to do the impossible.*

I want to believe like that.

I want my faith to astonish Jesus.

June 19. Day 146.

Father's Day meant Jim got breakfast in bed: bacon and eggs with a side of Pillsbury cinnamon rolls smothered in icing. Every year I told him he was my "Psalm 112 guy" and the best father in the world.

> Praise the Lord! Blessed is the man who fears the Lord and who finds great delight in his commands. His children [Curtis James William and Christopher Jack Ryan] will be mighty in the land; the generation of the upright will be blessed. Wealth and riches are in his house and his righteousness endures forever. Even in darkness light dawns for the upright, for the gracious and compassionate and righteous man. Good comes to him who is generous and lends freely, who conducts his affairs with justice. Surely, he will never be shaken; a righteous man will be remembered forever. He will have no fear of bad news; his heart is steadfast, trusting in the Lord! His heart is secure and he will have no fear! In the end he will look in triumph on his foes. He has scattered abroad his gifts to the poor and his righteousness endures forever; his dignity will be lifted high in honor. (Psalm 112:1–9)

That was my man.

Jim, I hold you in the highest honor. You are unforgettable and irreplaceable. I can't believe that our grandchildren won't know you until they get to heaven. You can be sure that I will tell them that David wrote a Psalm about their Gramps.

Father God, please hold my boys.

June 20. Day 147.

I'm so tired of hearing that if we have enough faith, we can live a life exempt from suffering. A few people have actually had the nerve to imply that Jim died because I didn't believe hard enough for God's intervention. I can assure you that if Jim's resurrection hinged on my faith, he'd still be here.

The truth is that God does what He wants, including using suffering to make us fit for His kingdom.

> A teacher of the law came to Jesus and said, "I will follow You wherever You go!" Jesus said, "Foxes have holes and birds of the air have nests, but the Son of Man has *no place to lay His head."* (Matthew 8:19–20)

> Another disciple wanting to follow Jesus said to Him, "Lord, first let me go and bury my father." Jesus said, "Let the dead bury their own dead, but you go and proclaim the Kingdom of God." (Matthew 8:21–22)

> Still another said, "I will follow You, Lord; but first let me go back and say good-bye to my family." Jesus said, "No one who puts his hand to the plow and looks back is fit for service in the Kingdom of God." (Luke 9:61)

When I think of all Jesus endured, how could I ever demand a get-out-of-pain card?

Instead, I must *choose* to do the will of the Father, holding on to *nothing* in this world, remembering that my real home is in heaven and my inheritance is Jesus Himself. *If* I do this, *then* I will be fit for service in the kingdom of God.

June 21. Day 148.

One of my students asked me if the stories in the Bible were true. There is nothing I love more than to answer that kind of question. Not only do I believe each story to be true, but I also believe they were preserved just for us. Take me away, Holy Spirit, and deposit me in the midst of one of those true stories, and reveal to me why it's relevant to me on this new day.

Matthew 8:23–27 records the story of when Jesus and the disciples were caught in what Matthew describes as an unexpected, furious storm. Jesus was asleep, so they woke Him up and begged Him to do something.

In 1994, the capillaries around my heart seized up during a treadmill test, landing me in the hospital for a few days' worth of tests. During that hospital stay, Jim and I talked about this story and how Jesus stood up, rebuked the elements, and brought an instant calm, and then asked His friends why they were so afraid. We wondered out loud to each other what it would have been like if instead of freaking out, His disciples had simply trusted, remembering that the Maker of the wind and the waves was in their boat.

That discussion is what prompted me over a decade ago to write beside these verses, "Which is the greater miracle: to have the wind and waves instantly silenced, or to go through a storm cradled in His unexplainable peace?"

On the morning of January 25, an unexpected, furious storm threatened to capsize my boat. A second before, all had been calm as we talked about the wonder of God's strength. But in less time than it takes to blink, I was screaming at Jesus to wake up and do something. He didn't give me what I was begging for, but He did give me peace and courage to weather the storm.

Some days the wind scales down from a tornado to almost a breeze. Other days, all I can do is fiercely cling, grit my teeth, and keep trusting Jesus, despite what it looks like.

I'm living a miracle.

June 22. Day 149.

It must have been seriously wild to be one of the disciples. They saw firsthand what we are *still* talking about. When they disembarked after the storm, they were met by two crazy, naked, and very dangerous men who were inhabited by two thousand demons! After a confrontation with Jesus, the throngs of evil spirits left the men and housed themselves in a herd of pigs, which rushed down a steep bank into a lake and died. The pig farmers and the townspeople were so outraged they pleaded with Jesus to leave their region (Matthew 8:24–34). Unlike other places where others begged Him to stay, the folk in Gadarenes actually wanted *their pigs* more than Jesus! It didn't matter that the men who had been tormented for years were now clothed and in their right minds. *The temporal won over the eternal.*

Jesus climbed back into the boat, and although the two men He had set free wanted to come with Him, He told them to go and tell everyone all about how His mercy had rescued them (Mark 5:19).

I'm so glad that Jesus never gives up on us, even when we push Him away. *Send me to someone today who needs to hear about Your mercy.*

June 23. Day 150.

A paralytic was brought to Jesus by his four determined friends. The doors were jammed with people, so they ripped open the roof and lowered him into the house on his mat. Jesus looked right past the obvious physical need of this man into the eternal need and forgave him of his sin (Matthew 9:1–7).

In that moment, was the paralytic disappointed that he was still lame, or did the assurance of a clean heart outweigh his desire to walk?

Eventually Jesus did heal him, but only to make a point to the Pharisees, who were all in a tizzy because Jesus had just announced that He forgives sin.

> Which is easier to say, "your sins are forgiven" or "get up and walk"? So that you may know that the Son of Man has authority on earth to forgive sins . . . I say to you, "My son . . . get up, take your mat and go home!" (Matthew 9:6)

Instantly, the paralytic's muscles were filled with stamina, and he jumped for joy all the way home. I guess we'll never know (at least on earth) exactly what made him the happiest. I'll bet you a Coke (yes, there will be Coke in heaven) that he was more excited over the fact that his sins had been erased then he was about being able to walk.

I have to believe that whatever Jesus chooses to do for me is right.

If He bypasses my wish list and goes straight to the eternal that has to be okay with me.

June 24. Day 151.

I was fifteen when I saw Jim for the first time. His tanned face accentuated his blond hair and blue eyes. Jim told me that when he first laid eyes on me from across the room, he wrote in his diary that he'd seen the most beautiful girl in the world and that he wanted to marry her one day. We lived in different towns, so we were pen pals for the first two years of our romance, until his father got a job transfer that brought the Keddy family to my hometown and Jim to my high school. Three decades later, I'm still amazed that Jim *chose me* to grow old with. Out of all the girls who came and went, *he only had eyes for me;* in fact, the last time we danced together in our tiny living room, it was to the song, "It Had to Be You."

Jesus *chose* to be friends with liars, prostitutes, cheaters, and adulterers even though it made the religious leaders angry. When they demanded an explanation, He said, "It is not the healthy who need a doctor, but the sick. But go and learn what this means; 'I desire mercy, not sacrifice,' for I have not come to call the righteous, but sinners" (Matthew 9:12–13).

To put it in today's vernacular, *Jesus only had eyes for the lost.* Every time Jesus hung out with sinners, He was saying, "It had to be you."

My heart still pounds a little faster when I think about how Jim chose me to spend his life with, but I'm undone when I think about how *Jesus chose me* to be His forever.

June 25. Day 152.

Nine months ago some friends called to tell us that they were pregnant with baby number four. They were terrified because thirteen years had gone by since baby number three. *It takes time to adjust to change, because all the questions tend to overshadow the joy.* I think that's exactly how the disciples of John the Baptist were feeling. They had heard John talk about the one who was to come, but when Jesus came, all the changes left them rattled. They wondered why fasting wasn't a regular discipline for Jesus' disciples like it was for them. Jesus talked to them about the futility of sewing new fabric on something old and pouring new wine into old wineskins, showing them that the newness He was offering couldn't be confined within the old traditions created by the teachers of the law (Matthew 9:14–17).

Jesus changed everything.

I've promised my friend that I will come and help her when baby number four arrives. I've assured her that I'll be there to do whatever I can for her as she and her family get to know this new miracle.

Jesus does that with us.

He comes alongside with His grace, enabling us to embrace the new with total joy.

He shows us that change is good because it ushers in life.

June 26. Day 153.

According to the Oxford dictionary, the word *desperate* means "willing to do anything to change the terrible situation you're in." When CJ was thirteen months old, he had to have major surgery, which left the poor little guy writhing in pain. The doctor prescribed codeine, and within a few hours of taking him home, CJ had a seizure and stopped breathing. *That's when we knew what desperate meant.* We splashed cold water on his face, shook him, hung him upside down, but nothing worked! Jim and I cried out to Jesus, and CJ's stiff body jerked, then relaxed as he gasped for air. We called the doctor, and he reasoned that the seizure was likely due to the stress of the surgery. Jim and I took turns staring at CJ all night long just to make sure he was still breathing. It happened again the next day when we were at church. My friend Marion grabbed him from my arms and administered CPR to no avail. I will never forget the look on her face when she hollered for someone to call an ambulance.

We explained to the nurses exactly what had happened, and naturally they were skeptical. While they were telling us to calm down, CJ seized again. Much to our horror, they just stood there waiting to see what would happen. Eventually a code blue was issued, and a tube was stuck down CJ's throat so he could breathe. After some tests they concluded that a severe allergic reaction to codeine had shut down his respiratory system. The medical staff apologized for not believing us and then told us there was no way our little boy could have begun to breathe on his own without medical intervention. They conceded we were recipients of a few miracles.

Reliving those moments makes my palms sweat. We felt so helpless. *Our desperation drove us to cry out to Jesus.* It was that same desperation that caused a father to fall on his knees before Jesus, begging Him to come and raise his daughter from the dead. Desperation convinced a woman who had been hemorrhaging for twelve years to leave her home and somehow push through a crowd, knowing that if she could touch Jesus, she'd be healed (Matthew 9:18, 21).

Desperation can lead us down one of two paths.

It can take us to a pit of despair, or it can take us to Jesus.

Jairius could have joined in with the mourners, and shame could have kept that sick woman behind closed doors, but when they heard that Jesus was in their reach, nothing could keep them away.

Jesus, I am desperate for You.

June 27. Day 154.

It feels so strange not to be able to tell Jim that I finished my TESL course! He was the first one I called when I got my driver's license, the first one to know when I got my letter of acceptance into college, and the first to find out we were pregnant. Both times the doctor confirmed we were expecting, we tried to keep it a secret until I started to show, but we found out that was impossible because exciting news is too hard to contain!

I have so much to celebrate! I completed my TESL course with honors! I get to teach hundreds of Chinese students about Jesus! I have friends I get to cook for every day! I have two sons who love me!

I have Jesus!

Bring out the balloons and put on the music!

It's party time!

June 28. Day 155.

When I was sixteen I surrendered my life to Jesus, promising Him I'd do anything and go anywhere. Would I have reneged on that promise if I had known widowhood was in His plan?

Honestly, I wouldn't change a thing.

Is that because I'm strong and have it all together? No, it's because I'm so weak and such a mess that Jesus has become more precious to me than life. Jesus told His disciples what to expect, and miracles and suffering were both on the list. They'd feel the joy of watching the impossible happen and the agony of a whip ripping up their back. Sometimes they'd be welcomed, other times they'd be hated.

Jesus never once promised a pain-free existence or a happy life. Jesus has not guaranteed rescue operations every time we find ourselves in danger. He didn't say that God keeps sparrows from falling. What He said was *that He sees each sparrow that falls, and that if He cares about birds, then just imagine how He cares for us.*

The conditions to following Jesus have not changed.

Surrender is surrender.

"Whoever finds their life will lose it, and *whoever loses their life for My sake will find it*" (Matthew 10:39).

Jesus, I'm completely Yours.

June 29. Day 156.

When I opened the door, she started to cry. I held my friend and told her my comfort was found in knowing God was sovereign and that I would see Jim again in heaven. She had a lot of questions about Jim's death, and although it's agony to relive those moments, I live for them. Talking about the wonder of Jesus strengthens my spirit. The days that are empty of conversations about my faith are the days when it's hardest to make sense out of everything. Maybe that's why John the Baptist felt uncertain. It's almost unbelievable that John was wondering if Jesus was really the Messiah, unless you've been in a dark place and experienced how that darkness can convince your heart that God has abandoned you.

Jesus says, "From the days of John the Baptist until now, the kingdom of heaven has been forcefully advancing, and forceful men lay hold of it!" (Matthew 11:12).

John the Baptist joined a long list of those who died believing, yet never seeing. I need that same grit to be infused in my spirit. I wish it was a onetime miraculous injection, but it's not. *The journey is not easy, but it leads to a place where there are no nights, no prisons, and no questions.*

June 30. Day 157.

The permanence of this life without Jim has put my life on pause.

I remember a shadow of this feeling the hour before we got married. I was sequestered in the church nursery just off to the side of the vestibule for what seemed like hours. My bridesmaids were talking and laughing, but for me life was on pause until I finally heard the organ strike its first note. As I walked down the aisle, we never took our eyes off of each other, not even for a second. It feels like such a long time since I've seen his smile and felt his touch. I just want the waiting to be over. I want the door to open. I want the organ to play. I want to walk into his embrace.

Holy Spirit, take me to my manna.

> Come to Me, all you who are weary and burdened, and I will give you rest. (Matthew 11: 28)

I come.

July 1. Day 158.

Last night I met a man crushed by grief. He and his wife were in a car accident that killed their twelve-year-old son. With teary eyes, he asked me how I sleep and cope with the loneliness. With tears in my eyes, I told him how Jesus continually bids me to come to Him, and how when I do, *His peace stills the struggle.* I explained that Jesus's invite is also for him, but he said he was still too angry to come to a God who allowed his son to die. I wish I could drag him into the arms of Jesus, but sadly it doesn't work that way.

On one of our trips to London, England, Jim and I visited the Churchill Museum and Cabinet War Rooms. We were so challenged as we read his writings that we were ready to enlist!

> We shall not fail or falter, we shall not weaken or tire. Neither the sudden shock of battle nor the long-drawn trials of vigilance and exertion will wear us down. Give us the tools and we will finish the job.
>
> You ask, what is our aim? I can answer in one word. It is victory, victory at all costs, victory in spite of all terror; victory, however long and hard the road may be; for without victory, there is no survival. (Winston Churchill)

Sovereign God, I pray for every heart that has been hardened by pain. Please prove to them that You love them despite their anger. *May the hope of heaven unclench their fists and silence their accusations. Give them grace to trust, courage to fight, and strength to endure so that they too will know that victory is certain!*

July 2. Day 159.

A bruised reed He will not break, and a smoldering wick He will not snuff out. (Isaiah 42:3)

Jesus came for the wounded.
Jesus blows on ashes and rekindles life.
Jesus kisses our hurts and puts us back on our feet.
I am living proof.

July 3. Day 160.

When people ask me how I'm doing, I often say, "Heaven's coming!" Yesterday someone asked me what that meant. I told her what Jesus said:

> Do not let your hearts be troubled. Trust in God and trust also in Me. In My Father's house are many rooms; if it were not so, I would have told you. I am going there to prepare a place for you, and if I go and prepare a place for you, I will come back and take you to be with Me so that you can be where I am. (John 14:1–3)

It's true! *Jesus is coming, and everything will be just fine.* He'll escort me to my room, and who knows, maybe Jim's room will be right next door! All I know for sure is that *heaven's coming,* and when I get there, *it will be forever.*

July 4. Day 161.

Whenever Jim and our two sons talked, it was as though the rest of the world ceased to exist. As they quoted authors and screenplays, everyone listening was amused but totally lost. No one knew our sons like Jim. He was the first to hold them, and as they grew up, he was very present and in the most natural of ways taught them eternal truths. Jim cared about everyone, but his sons were in a league of their own. *They were his mission.*

Jesus was like this with His disciples. He explained exclusively to them what others couldn't understand. He had no secrets from the disciples. *He wanted them to know everything, because He knew that one day they would change the world.*

The disciples had to learn to live without Jesus, just like my sons have been forced to live without their dad. I have to believe that the same Holy Spirit who gave comfort to the disciples will do the same for our two boys. They have been placed on a lonely path, but all Jim instilled in them will not be lost. The Holy Spirit will lead them exactly to where they were destined to be and use them to make Jesus famous.

July 5. Day 162.

I woke up thinking about an old cemetery I stumbled upon when I was fifteen. The headstones were broken and the inscriptions barely readable. I still get goose bumps when I remember the strong sense of the presence of the Lord in that forsaken place. In fact, I trace my realization of there being an actual heaven back to those moments as it dawned on me that a cemetery is merely a holding place until Jesus comes back to take His followers home.

I needed to be reminded of this, and *I must be faithful in sharing this hope.*

July 6. Day 163.

Sovereign God, *may Your Kingdom come and Your will be done as it is written in heaven.*

Help me to walk away from the lure of despair.

Please give me my daily manna . . .

His kingdom uses the smallest and the weakest to showcase God's magnificent glory, and to prove His point He uses a mustard seed—the tiniest of all seeds—as an example of how greatness grows out of nothing (Matthew 13:31–32).

His kingdom is like an expensive pearl or a priceless treasure. Nothing compares to its beauty or worth, so letting go of it becomes unthinkable (Matthew 13:44–46).

Use my weakness to turn eyes to Your strength.

I ask that my choice to trust You will inspire others to follow suit, so that my world will see You are worth believing in.

July 7. Day 164.

Our sudden good-bye makes me deeply thankful for the love we shared. I was the only one he ever gave himself to. One of my dearest friends has just been cast aside by her husband for someone else. The public betrayal and blatant rejection has left her heart in pieces. We are walking side by side through our individual sorrows, realizing that the more we care for one another, the more our own pain is lessened.

I have found that it's not finding someone to love me, but finding someone to love that has transformed this lonely path into something beautiful. The secret is to find someone who needs a hug rather than to dwell on how much I long to be hugged. Instead of moping over how there's no one to make me a cup of tea, I must look for someone I can make a cup of tea for.

Jesus did this. When He heard that John the Baptist had been beheaded, He climbed into a boat, rowed out into the deep waters, and poured His heart out to His Father. Jesus could have stayed away wallowing in His loss, but He chose to come back to the crowds and do what He was sent to earth to do. *Jesus put aside His own needs and looked after the needs of others.* He fed thousands of people with five loaves of bread and two small fish, and the power of God was displayed for all to see.

Jesus says, "Bring me what you have," and just like He did with the little boy's lunch, He takes our meager resources, lifts them up with thanksgiving to His Father, and then does the impossible.

Use me to distribute baskets full of the miraculous to the hungry!

July 8. Day 165.

I just woke up from a wonderful dream where Jim and I were expressing our love to one another. It felt so real. Opening my eyes was like a knife being twisted in my chest as I lay there alone trying to breathe. What am I to do without him?

Jesus, hold me in Your arms and sustain me once again.

> Jesus made the disciples get into the boat and go on ahead of Him to the other side, while He dismissed the crowd. After He dismissed them, He went up on a mountainside by Himself to pray. (Matthew 14:22–23)

This is such a perfect story. There's a storm! Jesus walks on the water! *Peter walks on the water!* The storm instantly stops! There are a dozen sermons in there, but what *really* speaks to me is what happened between Peter and Jesus. Peter's response to being swallowed up by the waves left me a perfect example to follow.

"Lord, save me!"

Peter *knows and declares* that his only help is Jesus! I love how Jesus immediately scoops him out of the water, and how together they walk back to the boat on top of the water! I woke up this morning needing rescuing, and Jesus has come through once again, assuring me that when I call, He comes. Like

Peter, I have felt the waves underneath my feet and climbed back into the boat with Jesus, and I am going on to the next destination where I will see with my own eyes even more miracles.

July 9. Day 166.

On Friday nights a few of us unwind by going to our favorite Reflexology Spa. I can tell you from experience that Lily gives the best foot massage on the planet. Last night as her fingers did their magic, she asked me an unusual question that I am still thinking about this morning.

"Susan, do you have to pay to go to church?"

Before I could answer, she told me how she and her friends went to church but were told they couldn't stay unless they gave at least 10 percent of their income in the offering plate. I told Lily that Jesus wants our lives, not our money. Her eyes lit up when she heard how we could never buy His mercy or forgiveness because it was all a gift. I explained that when I give money to the church, it is just one of the ways I have to express my love and thanks to Jesus for all He's done for me.

Jesus talked about people who followed traditions set out by men in Matthew 15. *He said that these people honored Him with their lips, but their hearts were far from Him, and that they worshiped Him in vain because their teachings were but rules taught by men.* A Pharisee mentality has seeped into the church, and as a result there are Lilys being turned away because they don't have enough money.

It's not money that gains you entrance into heaven.

It's all about our brokenness and His mercy.

July 10. Day 167.

I went to a farewell dinner last night for my son. We were in a beautiful home with a panoramic view of the harbor. There were three couples, plus me.

It hurts to be number seven.

As everyone stood by the window watching fireworks explode over the South China Sea, I stood off to the side imagining Jim pressed against me with his arms wrapped around my waist. I thought back to when he slipped my engagement ring on my finger during the Canada Day celebrations and how just as I said "Yes!", the first fireworks of the night erupted in the sky over our heads. From that moment on, we loved fireworks.

I am telling my soul that this is a temporary separation, but this morning my flesh is arguing against that truth.

Jesus, help me!

How many broken hearts have uttered those words? In Matthew 15, a Canaanite woman came to Jesus, crying out, "Lord, Son of David, have mercy on me!" She personified the definition of broken. Her daughter was suffering from demon possession, and she knew Jesus was her only hope.

Jesus answered her with silence.

This is one of those really hard-to-understand stories. Jesus eventually responded to her by telling her that He was sent only to the lost sheep of Israel. Refusing to be discouraged by His answer, *she asked again.* Jesus told her it was not right to take the children's bread and toss it to the dogs. Unfazed, she cried out, *"Yes, Lord, but even the dogs eat the crumbs that fall from their master's table!"* (Matthew 15:27). Jesus told her she had great faith, and He granted her request.

I'm crying out for mercy today. I'm asking for just a crumb from Your table. Please don't be silent.

July 11. Day 168.

Our last forty-five minutes together were so normal. I was flipping through a cookbook full of healthy recipes and writing a menu plan for the week when Jim walked into the living room. After a hug and kiss, he hopped into the shower. Without him knowing, I stood behind the curtain to make sure he was okay. When he turned off the water, I slipped out of the bathroom and prepared two bowls of shredded wheat with fresh blueberries that we ate while we watched the news. We read God's Word together, and just as I went to take his hand to pray, he went to heaven.

Today I realized what a gift those forty-five minutes were. He could have died in our bed or in the shower, but our sovereign God mercifully let him begin his new life *after* I'd been in his arms one last time.

Take me to my manna.

> The people were amazed when they saw the mute speaking; the crippled made well, the lame walking and the blind seeing. (Matthew 15:31)

Jesus is famous for doing the impossible and creating oxymorons.

Mute speaking, lame walking, blind seeing, *Sue living, Sue smiling.*

Last night I had a few friends who don't know Jesus yet over for dinner. Just before they left, they asked me to pray for them so that God would bless them as He has blessed me. I am thrilled that everyone in my little world has front-row seats to watch God's strength surpass my weakness.

They are seeing things that don't make sense and are standing amazed!

July 12. Day 169.

The Pharisees and Sadducees had Jesus right in front of them, but they refused to believe unless they witnessed a miracle. Jesus—knowing we are capable of being just like they were—says to us, "Be careful. Be on your guard against the yeast of the Pharisees and Sadducees" (Matthew 16:6).

A storm can threaten to capsize the boat, but if Jesus is in the boat there is peace, even if the winds keep howling. A person can be blind, but if Jesus is with him he can see, even in the darkness. A person can be deaf, but if Jesus is with her she can hear God speak.

The Pharisees and Sadducees saw but were blind. Their ears heard, but they were deaf. Instead of falling to their knees and acknowledging that Jesus was enough, they demanded a sign, and they missed out on being handed the keys to the kingdom of heaven!

I shout it from the rooftops this morning that *I don't need a sign. I don't need a miracle.*

I don't need anything but You, Jesus!

July 13. Day 170.

After my father preached, he would often invite everyone to come forward to pray. I know that the hours I spent on my knees were where God fortified my soul for the days I am living through now. I woke up this morning singing a chorus that was sung during those prayer vigils:

Jesus, Jesus, Jesus, never have I heard a name that thrills my soul like thine.

Jesus, Jesus, Jesus, O the wondrous grace that links that lovely name with mine.

When I think about all Jesus did *to* link His name with mine, it makes me cry. Jesus told His disciples that if anyone was to follow Him, they *must* first deny themselves and pick up their cross (Matthew 16:21, 24). The usage of the word *must* speaks of a definitive, nonnegotiable choice.

My flesh *must* be put to death if I want Jesus to be seen in me.

It *must* . . . for the sake of His sweet name and for those who have yet to hear it.

July 14. Day 171.

What a magnificent moment for Peter, James, and John to witness the transfiguration of Jesus and be privy to a visit from Moses and Elijah! Whatever was spoken on the mountaintop gave Jesus the courage to come down and finish what He came to accomplish.

God is the same today as He was then. *God is in our corner, sending us the encouragement we need to keep obeying until eternity begins.*

I feel like Peter, James, and John.

I don't know what to do except to fall facedown trembling in the presence of my God.

July 15. Day 172.

When they came together, Jesus said to them, "The Son of Man is going to be betrayed into the hands of men. They will kill Him, and on the third day He will be raised to life!" And the disciples were filled with grief. (Matthew 17:22–23)

The disciples could have been anticipating the third day, but instead they stopped listening after the "they will kill me" part. *The now was so unbelievably sad and horrific, they found it impossible to look ahead to the hope!*

It is so easy to live like that!

Jesus says, "I tell you the truth, if you have faith as small as a mustard seed, you can say to this mountain, 'Move from here to there' and it will move. *Nothing is impossible for you!"* (Matthew 17:20).

I choose to look past the grief and live in anticipation of what's sure to come!

I choose to exercise my faith and say to the mountain of despair that stands before me, "Move over there!"

July 16. Day 173.

Our twenty-fifth wedding anniversary was August 4, 2004, but because CJ and Ali were getting married that month, we decided to postpone our anniversary extravaganza to the following summer, which is now.

We did, however, mark our day in true Keddy style. We enjoyed a leisurely, five-star dining experience overlooking the harbor at Morton's Steakhouse, which is housed in the Sheraton Hotel. After dinner we rode the elevator up to our incredibly lavish room and made love. In the morning we talked about how remarkable and rare it was that even after twenty-five years, we still desired each other.

Today we would have been busy preparing for our trip to Italy. The closest we got to our dream of someday visiting that country was New York's Little Italy, which was so enchanting that my mild-mannered, no-fuss-please husband held me in his arms and danced with me on the cobblestone street. We made our own music, and it was magical.

Take me to my manna.

Jesus says, "I tell you the truth . . . unless you change and become like little children, you will never enter the kingdom of heaven" (Matthew 18:3). When I thought about this, I was reminded of Gracie and her unbridled response after hearing Jim was in heaven. She jumped up and down yelling, *"Hokey toot! Uncle Jim's in heaven!"* Her eyes shone with a quiet strength, an unflappable trust and a complete understanding that when someone stops living here on earth, they begin a new life in heaven. For Gracie, *trusting is effortless, and every day is an adventure.*

I must become like Gracie if I want to truly live and not just exist.

July 17. Day 174.

I just woke up from a vivid dream and want to return to where it took me.

We were driving, and there was that comfortable feeling of oneness between us. The car stopped. Jim got out, telling me he'd be right back, but as quickly as the car had stopped, it began to move and I found myself alone in the backseat with a new driver. I looked out the rear window and frantically yelled out Jim's name as he tried to push through the throngs of people to get back to the car.

Our eyes locked.

As the car drove away, his image faded until he was gone. I grabbed my mobile phone and began to push in his number while pleading with the driver to stop because my husband was going to get back into the car! The driver apologized and told me his instructions were to keep driving.

My mobile phone beeped, indicating that I had a message: *"I'm so sorry, Subies. I love you so very much. I fully expected to get back into the car, but I had to get out, to let others in."* This message looped on my screen a few times and then went black.

The next thing I saw was me walking off a platform. I had the sense that I had just spoken to a large group of people. As I was leaving, I was handed an ornately carved wooden box. Suddenly, Jim was right there. He took my hands in his and told me that he *had* to come, that I was doing really good, and that there was a gift for me inside the box. I carefully opened the lid. The gift was shrouded in soft satin. I removed the satin and found a scroll. I carefully rolled it open and discovered it was covered with names. When my eyes reached the bottom of the page, more names appeared. *It was a living parchment!*

Still holding my hands, Jim smiled and said, "Keep going, Subies! Don't stop! We're all cheering for you! It won't be long . . ." And then he was gone and I was awake, still feeling the warmth of his hands.

Thank you, Jesus! You sent Jim to remind me that the sky is full of saints who are cheering me on!

When faced with his own death, Jesus said: "Now My heart is troubled so what should I say, 'Father, save Me from this hour?' No! It was for *this very reason I came* to this hour! Father! Glorify Your name" (John 12:27–28).

I believe on the morning of January 25, 2005, Jim echoed the words of Jesus and embraced God's plan for his life. Jim got out to let others in . . . so there is *no way* I am going to keep them out by my actions.

I choose to run this race well.

I hear cheering . . .

July 18. Day 175.

I went to Curtis's church yesterday for his final service. He led the congregation in a beautiful song that I later found out he'd written:

> We will run the race. We will reach that line.
> We will not give up. We will receive the prize.
> Which is to see Your face and to know Your Name,
> And to bow at the feet of the King of Kings.

How does God do it? There are billions of us, yet He makes me feel like I am the only one He cares for! It blows my mind that Curtis would write and sing a song that was a postscript to my dream!

Jesus says, "And everyone who has left houses or brothers or sisters or father or mother or children or fields for My sake will receive a hundred times as much and will inherit eternal life" (Matthew 19:29).

I am not the first to say good-bye.

It is for *Your sake,* Jesus, that I am an ocean apart from both our sons and a heaven apart from my true companion . . . *and remembering that makes me want to run faster toward You, my precious prize.*

July 19. Day 176.

Curtis leaves today.

I opened my eyes just as the sun was rising over the mountains. It was a perfectly rounded, blazing orange sphere that cast a pale pink shadow on the horizon. The Lord spoke to me: "From the rising of the sun, to the going down of the same; the Name of The Lord is to be praised!" (Psalm 113:3)

From this moment to the moment I hug Curtis good-bye, I will *choose* to praise the name of the Lord.

July 20. Day 177.

My good-bye with Curtis was short and sweet.

Over the years, we've learned that the best way to leave is quickly. I will always be thankful that Jim was taken to heaven in the blink of an eye. My brother's exit from earth is far different. Multiple myeloma has forced our family into a painfully slow good-bye. If I didn't know Jesus was going to come back and remove us from this pain, my face would be buried in a bottle.

Matthew writes about two blind men who found out Jesus was passing by. Knowing He was the promised Messiah, they yelled, "Lord! Son of David! Have mercy on us!" (Matthew 20:30). Even though the crowd told them to be quiet, these blind men knew that their only source of mercy was walking by . . . so they yelled even louder!

I love how Jesus responds.

He hears. He stops, and He asks them what they want.

"We want to see."

He touches them, and *immediately they receive their sight and begin to follow Him.*

Jesus hasn't changed.

When we call out for mercy, *He still hears, He still stops, He still listens, and He still opens eyes* so we can follow Him to that place where blindness and pain are erased forever.

July 21. Day 178.

Matthew writes that when Jesus rode into Jerusalem on the back of a colt, the whole city was stirred and asked, "Who is this man?"

Surrounding Jesus were paralytics who were now walking and the blind who could now see. There were those who had been delivered from demons, healed of diseases, and raised from the dead. *This* was the crowd that proclaimed with conviction, "*This is Jesus!*"

I wasn't there when He made His entrance into Jerusalem, but I'll be there when He comes on the clouds! The whole world will be stirred that day, and this time, I'll be the one shouting!

July 22. Day 179.

In 1940, a young pastor was martyred for his faith in Africa. After he died, the statement below was found scribbled on a piece of paper with his belongings. It makes me want to stand up and declare my allegiance to Jesus even though I am on a plane heading to England.

I'm part of the fellowship of the unashamed. I have Holy Spirit power. The die has been cast. I have stepped over the line. The decision has been made. I am a disciple of HIS. I won't look back, let up, slow down, back away or be still. My past is redeemed, my present makes sense, and my future is secure! I'm finished and done with low living, sight walking, small planning, smooth knees, colorless dreams, tamed visions, mundane talking, cheap giving and dwarfed goals. I no longer need pre-eminence, prosperity, position, promotions, plaudits or popularity. I don't have to be right, first, tops, recognized, praised, regarded or rewarded. I now live by faith, lean on His presence, walk by patience, lift by prayer and labor by power! My face is set, my gait is fast, my goal is heaven, my road is narrow, my way is rough, my companions are few, my guide is reliable and my mission is clear! I cannot be bought, compromised, detoured, lured away, turned back, deluded or delayed. I will not flinch in the face of sacrifice, hesitate in the presence of adversity, negotiate at the table of the enemy, ponder at the pool of popularity, or meander in the maze of mediocrity! I won't give up, shut up or let up until I have stayed up, stored up, prayed up, paid up, preached up for the cause of Christ. I am a disciple of Jesus. I must go until He comes, give until I drop, preach until all know and work until He stops me! And when He comes for His own, He will have no problem recognizing me . . . My banner of identification with Jesus will be clear!

If anything should be made into a wall hanging, it's this.
Jesus, my Captain, I salute You.

July 23. Day 180.

A year ago, Jim and I were here speaking at a missions conference. Before it began, we managed to squeeze in a whirlwind tour of London. We were awed at the magnificence of Westminster Abbey, impressed by the grandeur of Buckingham Palace, and deeply moved as we imagined the array of flowers on the mammoth grounds at Kensington Palace the day Diana died. We enjoyed fish and chips in a pub and devoured scones topped with clotted cream and strawberry jam in the famous Harrods Tea Room. *And we did all of this is in the span of twelve hours.* That was our life, full and never boring.

I'm sure the disciples felt the same way about their time with Jesus. Can you imagine all the stories they told their families? I'm sure one of them would have been about the time Jesus cursed a fig tree because it didn't have figs. He was hungry and could do the impossible, so why did Jesus make the tree wither and die if He wanted figs?

I wish they'd asked, "Why did you do that?" instead of "How did you do that?" (Matthew 21). His explanation was strange: "You can ask for whatever you need, and if you believe you'll receive it." So again, if He wanted something to eat, why didn't He make figs suddenly appear? Could it be that Jesus wanted to leave His disciples with an unforgettable illustration of the importance of bearing fruit?

I'm guessing that as Jesus talked to them just hours before He was betrayed about *remaining in Him and bearing fruit* (John 15:1–8), their minds went back to that morning walk, and suddenly the *how* became insignificant as the *why* came into focus.

Jesus, it's encouraging to know that even when I don't ask the right questions, You will continue teaching me until I get it.

July 24. Day 181.

Matthew talks about the Sadducees, who disputed the resurrection of Christ. There's an exchange that I've never liked between the Sadducees and Jesus. Our first conversation about it was shortly after we began dating. We were literally counting the seconds until we could get married. There was nothing on earth I wanted more than to be Jim's wife, *forever.* So you can imagine how upsetting it was to read that there was no marriage at the resurrection! After we were married it continued to bother me, and I secretly harbored a hope that when I got to heaven, I'd be pleasantly surprised. Until today.

The story the Sadducees told Jesus was about a woman who was a widow seven times! She had been passed from brother-in-law to brother-in-law until mercifully, she finally died. In an attempt to trip Jesus up, they asked Him whose wife she would be at the resurrection. Jesus told them they were in error because they *didn't know the Scriptures or the power of God* (Matthew 22:23–30).

The Scriptures tell me that when we die our physical bodies cease to function, but because of His resurrection power, our spirits soar into eternal life with God in heaven, where we will become the Bride of Christ.

As great as it was to be Jim's bride, *it pales in comparison to being part of the Bride of Christ!*

I finally get it.

July 25. Day 182.

Six months ago today Jim went to heaven.

I choose to look at the sky and cling to the hope of the resurrection. I choose to imitate His endurance and set my eyes on His face . . . one more time.

Matthew 23 describes a brokenhearted Jesus. His words condemned the Pharisees, yet His tears showed how much He longed for them to understand.

> Everything you do is done for men to see . . . you shut the Kingdom of heaven in men's faces . . . you travel over land and sea to win a single convert, and when he becomes one, you make him twice as much a son of hell as you are . . . you give one-tenth of your spices *but you have neglected justice, mercy and faithfulness* . . . you clean the outside but the inside is full of greed and self-indulgence . . . you look beautiful on the outside but on the inside you're full of dead bones and everything unclean . . . *I have longed to gather you as a hen gathers her chicks under her wings . . . but you were not willing.*

Jesus! I am willing. I run to You. Cover me with Your mercy.

Help me to forever hold in my heart the picture of Your tearstained face so that I never make You cry.

July 26. Day 183.

After a long bus ride, I arrived in Wales and fell into the arms of my dearest friends. They lived beside us in our very first apartment complex in Hong Kong, and although they are Muslims and I am a follower of Jesus, our hearts beat as one. We don't have a conversation these days without talking about Jim, which always leads to heaven and the hope I have in Jesus. We cry. We laugh. We remember. It's healing.

As we sat together last night, they expressed to me that there is not another man on earth like Jim. They said Jim was kind, quick to forgive, patient, selfless, obedient to his God, loving, gentle yet strong, faithful, and confident that nothing was impossible for his God to do. They told me that from everything I have told them about Jesus—Jim must have been just like Him.

There is no greater legacy than that.

July 27. Day 184.

I have another day to make Jesus famous! It's always an honor to give reason for the Hope that keeps me alive!

Jesus says that no one knows the day or the hour of His return except for His Father in heaven (Matthew 24:36). So that means that *even Jesus is waiting for that day* that has been set aside when He will bring us to a place free of sorrow and sin.

I wonder if He's as excited as I am?

I bet He is.

July 28. Day 185.

When I was a teenager, there was nothing that could keep me away from coming under one roof with a thousand other teenagers to worship Jesus! I heard about a girl who was so excited the night before Youth Convention that she couldn't sleep, so when morning came she decided to stay home because she was too tired. Seriously, it's been thirty-seven years since I heard that story, and it's still annoying!

The eve before we got married, I watched the clock all night long. My mind was on overdrive as I rehearsed my vows, which we'd decided to recite from memory. When my dad came into my room to wake me up for breakfast, I was already dressed and wondering how I was going to get through the next eight hours before our wedding ceremony actually began. It would have been crazy not to go to my wedding because I was too tired!

Jesus tells a story about ten bridesmaids who fell asleep while waiting for the bridegroom. Five of the bridesmaids came with enough oil to keep their lamps lit throughout the vigil, so at midnight when it was announced the bridegroom was coming, the five who didn't have enough oil begged to borrow some from the others. *But there wasn't enough.* While they were gone searching for oil, the bridegroom arrived. The bridesmaids who were ready accompanied him to the wedding banquet and watched as the door was shut.

When the others returned, they pounded on the door to be let in, but they were turned away. Jesus finished His story with this: "Therefore, keep watch, because you do not know the day or the hour when I will return" (Matthew 25:1–13).

The prepared bridesmaids could not share their oil. *As someone who loves Jesus and is longing and watching for His return, I cannot give part of my faith away, even though I wish I could.* It is the responsibility of each and every person to *choose to believe or not.*

I want everyone to be ready for the return of Jesus!

I don't want anyone to roll over and go back to sleep and miss out on the event of a lifetime!

I am resolved not to lose heart on this journey so that others who are still deciding will choose to believe, because they will not be able to deny His existence as they watch me.

July 29. Day 186.

The day I am longing for is a day that will mean the end of my sorrow, but for some, that day will be horrible.

Jesus tells a story in Matthew 25:14–30 about a man who goes on a journey and entrusts his property to his servants. He gives each of them money and instructs them to put the money to work until he returns. Two of the men invest their money, doubling its value. The third hides his money under the ground. When the Master of the household comes home, he rewards the two obedient servants, calling them good and faithful. The one who buried his money is called wicked and worthless.

We can be called faithful or worthless.

We can share in the Master's happiness or we can be thrown into the darkness.

The choice is ours.

Until that day comes, we who follow Jesus have been clearly told how to live. We are to feed the hungry, give water to the thirsty, invite strangers in, clothe the naked, look after the sick, and visit those in prison. *Our choice to believe in Jesus comes with a responsibility to be like Jesus.* It is not about how big our church is or how holy we've been.

It's about how much we have loved.

It's about seeing Jesus in the face of a starving child, a homeless drunk, a hardened prisoner, or a lonely old lady. It's about choosing to love our enemies, realizing that God loves them as much as He loves us.

I want to be called faithful. *Jesus, help me to see You today, in every face.*

And Jesus . . . may every face that looks at me see You and be persuaded to believe.

July 30. Day 187.

I'm having a tough morning. Tears won't stop, and the ache in my gut won't go away. I am longing for what used to be. I have lost my best friend, my only true confidant, and my protector. He made me laugh. He held my hand, wrapped me in hugs, and kissed my neck. He lit candles and lowered the music and beckoned me to come. We were comfortable with one another. When we were with other people, we counted the minutes until we would be alone again.

Sovereign God, I have a world that is watching, and I so want Your strength to be made perfect in my weakness. Take me away to the feast You have prepared and strengthen my resolve . . .

Just hours before Jesus dies for the sins of the world, He gathers his disciples together to have one last meal. Jesus breaks the bread and tells them, "This is my body which is broken for you." Jesus pours the wine and says, "This is my blood which is poured out for many." Maybe in an attempt to bolster their resolve, but for sure to strengthen His, He has them sing a hymn from David's psalms (Matthew 26:26–30):

> The cords of death entangled me, the anguish of the grave came upon me; I was overcome by trouble and sorrow but then I called on the name of the Lord: "O LORD, SAVE ME!" The Lord is with me so I will not be afraid! He is my helper! I will look in triumph on my enemies! Despair and deep sorrow surrounded me, but in the name of the Lord I cut them off! This is the day that the Lord has made so I will rejoice in it!

I'm such a wimp.

My resolve is back.

July 31. Day 188.

Yesterday was full of moments that took on eternal value, and I think I know why. When Jesus went into the garden of Gethsemane, *He relinquished His desires* and prayed to His Father, "May Your will be done, not Mine." Whenever we pray this prayer, we can be assured that our day will have eternal significance, because God's will is always perfect.

After Jesus cried out this prayer, He was betrayed, arrested, deserted, and unfairly tried in a rigged trial. He was beaten beyond recognition, nailed to a cross, and mocked. As He endured *His Father's will,* He reminded His soul of what was true: "In the future you will see the Son of Man sitting at the right hand of the Mighty One and coming on the clouds of heaven!" (Matthew 26:64). As He hung suffocating on the middle cross between two criminals, He turned His head toward the one who had asked to be remembered and declared to him, "I tell you the truth! Today, you will be with me in paradise!" (Luke 23:43). *He was telling the world and Himself that this was not the end!*

Jesus suffered unspeakable pain, was tortured until He was unrecognizable, and with His final breath uttered the words, "It is finished." He died knowing that His day had eternal worth.

Sovereign God, may Your will be done, not mine.

So be it. Let it be so.

August 1. Day 189.

My heart is broken, *yet filled with joy.*

I have constant pain, an unrelenting ache, and overwhelming loneliness, *yet I've never felt so empowered.*

My thoughts are scattered and even the simplest of decisions are impossible, *yet when I speak about Jesus, it is with absolute clarity and authority.*

I will grow old without Jim, never again feel his arms hold me in the night or his kisses wake me up, *yet my heart pumps with a hope that is sure.*

Jim's death has pushed me into the arms of my Savior, where every morning has become a feast, every day has become a miracle, and every night brings anticipation of what God will show me at sunrise.

I have absolutely nothing to complain about.

August 2. Day 190.

I woke up to the sun blazing through my window today. What a lovely change from the dreary dullness that's hung over the Cardiff sky since I arrived! I wish all days could be sunny, but I have learned that Jesus is the only absolute.

He is the Anointed One. He is the Savior. He is God with us. He is my King. He is my Shepherd. He is my Lord. He is my Judge. He is my example to follow. He is my Teacher. He is my Healer. He is my Deliverer. He is my financial adviser. He is my Rock. He is my Peace. He is my Friend. He is merciful. He is compassionate. He is my rest. He is the mender of my broken heart. He is my hope. He is my family.

He is more than enough.

He is the Servant of all. He is the Master. He is my Bridegroom.

He is the One who will be faithful to the end!

Whether the sun is blazing in the sky or not, that is all I need to know!

August 3. Day 191.

I'm a sky-gazer. I have chosen daily to raise my eyes to the heavens, even though it's much easier to look at the sidewalk. My sadness seems to be attached to my neck because there is a constant pull to lower my gaze, but I've learned that if I choose resist that pull, God's own hand lifts my head.

Right from the start, Adam and Eve were faced with a choice to believe what God said or not. They didn't and were banished from the garden. Abraham was presented with a choice to obey or not. He did, and God provided a ram.

Everyone in God's Word had to choose, and so do I.

The sky is beautiful.

August 4. Day 192.

Twenty-six years ago today, I said "I do." Just like I have at the 191 sunrises before this one, *I choose trust.*

Just before Joshua died, he brought everyone together to remind them how God had brought them out of slavery, through the Red Sea, and then *into the desert so that they would learn to trust and obey Him.* He reminded them how God fought their battles and brought them into the land of promise and then presented them with a choice: "Choose for yourselves this day who you will serve" (Joshua 24:15).

The people responded with shouts of surrender to serve only God the rest of their days. Joshua cautioned them that God is jealous and accepts all or nothing. *We fear and serve the Lord* not *for what He does for us, but simply because of who He is!*

Joshua took a large stone and declared it a witness to their choice. "See! This stone will be a witness against us. It has heard all the words the Lord has said to us. It will be a witness against you if you are untrue to your God!" (Joshua 24:27).

I don't have a stone, so this journal will be a witness to my vow: that for the rest of my life, I will daily present myself before the Lord and proclaim, "As for me . . . I choose to serve only You, no matter what."

August 5. Day 193.

Jesus held my face in His hands yesterday and lifted it to the sky.

On all twenty-five of our anniversaries, we stopped whatever we were doing at precisely 2:00 p.m. to wish each other a happy anniversary. There was only one anniversary where that didn't happen. I was on a plane heading back to Canada for my aunt's funeral, and Jim was in Hong Kong. At 1:58 p.m., using the phone attached to the back of the seat in front of me, I punched in my Visa number and then carefully dialed our phone number. I was so excited that the poor guy next to me heard all about it: "It's connecting . . . one ring . . . three rings . . . five rings . . . *Oh no! I got the answering machine!*"

I ended up leaving a message telling Jim how much I loved him. I thought of calling him back a few minutes later, but it was very expensive and 2:00 had come and gone. Jim called me when I landed and told me that at the same time I was calling him, he was sending me a romantic e-card. In those days we only had one line that served both the computer and the phone, which is why the answering machine had picked up. As soon as he logged off, the phone beeped, telling him he had a message. When I arrived at my hotel, there were two dozen roses waiting for me. Some of the petals are pressed inside my Bible.

Yesterday at exactly 2:00 p.m., I looked up into the sky in Cardiff's quaint downtown and bid Jim "Happy anniversary." I came home wishing for roses but thankful for the hope that holds my heart.

August 6. Day 194.

I'm trying to stop crying, but my heart won't be comforted. The intensity of grief comes unannounced, and my only hope is for Jesus to break through and quiet my heart.

When Jim went to Bible college, his class chose John 15:16 for their theme verse. "You did not choose me, but I chose you and appointed you to go and bear fruit—fruit that will last. Then, the Father will give you whatever you ask in my name." On days like today, it's hard to believe that I am capable of bearing fruit.

I know what I must do.

Thirty-seven years ago today, one of my most precious friends was born in Karachi, Pakistan. In God's plan, she and her husband immigrated to Hong Kong and became our neighbors. They are now my family. Today I will focus on giving her a birthday to remember! I will slow cook a big chunk of prime rib that we purchased at the halal market yesterday, whip up a mountain of creamy mashed potatoes, prepare at least three kinds of vegetables, toss a salad, make some rich gravy, prepare a yummy Black Forest cake smothered with dark chocolate icing, cover it with candles, and celebrate her life! We will celebrate our friendship and thank God that He brought us together.

I think heaven just applauded.

August 7. Day 195.

Since I was a little girl, it has made me sad that I knew Jesus and others did not. I will be forever thankful that Jesus chose to reveal Himself to me, but with that revelation comes a responsibility. *Just as Jesus revealed Himself to me, I must share Him with everyone He puts in my path.*

There's an old hymn penned by Major D.W. Whittle that I've dubbed my funeral song because it says all there is to say:

> I know not why God's wondrous grace to me He hath made known,
> Nor why unworthy, Christ in love, redeemed me for his own;
> I know not how this saving faith to me He did impart,
> Nor how believing in His word wrought peace within my heart;
> I know not how the Spirit moves, convincing men of sin,

Revealing Jesus thro' the Word, creating a faith in Him;
I know not what of good or ill may be reserved for me,
Of weary ways or golden days, before His face I see;
I know not when my Lord may come, at night or noon-day fair,
Nor if I'll walk the vale with Him, or meet Him in the air.
But I know *whom I have believed, and have been* persuaded *that He is able;*
To keep that which I've committed, unto Him against that day!
("I Know Whom I Have Believed"—Daniel W. Whittle, James McGranahan, 1883)

It's time to represent You well.

August 8. Day 196.

But God chose the foolish things of the world to shame the wise; God chose the weak things of the world to shame the strong . . . so that *no one* may boast before Him. . . . . . Therefore as it is written, *"Let him who boasts—boast in the Lord!"* (1 Corinthians 1:27, 31)

These were among the last verses we read together the morning Jim died. There could not have been a clearer or more needed message for my heart to hear.

Way back in 1860, Anna B. Warner wrote a song that is still being sung today, at least by me:

Jesus loves me this I know, for the Bible tells me so.
Little ones to him belong, they are weak, but He is strong.
Yes, Jesus loves me! Yes, Jesus loves me!
Yes, Jesus loves me! The Bible tells me so.

In those few simple lines is everything the world needs to know.

August 9. Day 197.

We watched the DVD of the Canadian memorial service last night. All our cheeks were wet as our hearts tried to comprehend what our minds have been forced to believe. As they watched and listened to the congregation sing, *"Turn your eyes upon Jesus; look full in his wonderful face; and the things of earth will grow strangely dim, in the light of his glory and grace*" ("Turn Your Eyes Upon Jesus"—Helen H. Lemmel, 1922), the question was asked how everyone could remain so strong.

The answer to that question is actually found in the song.

We smile because we have hope. We have hope because we have Jesus. We have Jesus because God sent part of Himself here to earth to become the final sacrifice for our sins so that we could know the extent of His love, and be forgiven and live forever though we die.

Unbelievable, but nothing could be truer.

August 10. Day 198.

All of Paul's writings in the New Testament were hand-delivered letters that he wrote to various churches. They were life-giving, full of encouragement, instruction, and revelation. It is simply amazing that the same words that spurred on the early church spur us on today! The church in Thessalonica was going through a rough time. Although they were suffering, they kept going, inspired by the hope they had in Jesus, and Paul was blessed by their attitude. He boasted to other churches about their perseverance, and he thanked God for them. *Their tenacious faith bolstered his.*

Paul encourages them, and now us, to stand firm and hold on to the teachings found in his letters. If we do this, just like Paul boasted about the persevering saints in Thessalonica, *Jesus will boast about us to the Father* and present us to Him on that day of all days as His very own bride. Paul goes on to write that on that day, Jesus will destroy the Enemy with a mere breath!

Until that breath ushers us into an eternity where all things will be made new, I pray that we will live in such a way that Jesus has something to boast about.

August 11. Day 199.

It's been so good to be with my dear friend. We have cooked together, feasted on the finest of foods, and laughed ourselves silly. We have talked about the truth of the gospel and the choice we have to accept it or reject it. We have thought a lot about eternity and how, in a split second, life can drastically change.

Jesus has been with us, and whenever Jesus comes close, it's simply unforgettable.

Mary and Martha were superwomen! Martha invited thirteen men over for dinner, and Mary walked into the room where they were waiting for the feast and plopped herself down in front of Jesus. Luke writes that Martha was distracted by all the meal preparations and that Mary, according to Jesus, "had found the better way." Honestly, the disciples must have wondered who on earth these two women were. One was sitting on the floor staring at up Jesus, and the other one was having a complete hissy fit demanding her sister get up and help her.

I love what Jesus said to Martha. I can hear Him saying it to me too.

> You are worried and upset about many things, but only one thing is needed and *Mary has chosen what is better* and it will not be taken away from her. (Luke 10:41)

Mary chose to put aside her culture and what was expected of her and make Jesus the most important thing. She chose not to be distracted because she knew that the promised Redeemer was sitting right in her living room! Martha's zeal to treat the men to a feast wasn't bad—it just wasn't *needed,* and sitting at His feet was.

Jesus will never send anyone away who comes and sits at His feet.

To get there requires courage, but once you're there, you realize there is no place you'd rather be.

Jesus, help me never to forget that you are in the room.

August 12. Day 200.

British Airways is on strike, and I'm scheduled to fly to Canada on this airline in two days. The world has come face-to-face with the reality of how nothing on this earth is certain. Life has been paused because of a union that is demanding fair treatment for baggage carriers.

I am choosing to sit at the feet of Jesus.

I am choosing not to be distracted.

There is a very real chance that this strike might prohibit me from getting to Canada, but somehow, from where I am sitting it doesn't matter.

His face is all I can see, and it's oh so beautiful.

August 13. Day 201.

I love that God wants us *to remember*. Jim and I had a list of "firsts" we celebrated. January 31 was the first time he told me he loved me. February 8 was the day I finally told him I loved him too. November 28 was our first real date and our first kiss. June 30 was the day he put a ring on my finger. August 4 was our wedding anniversary. October 22 was the day God challenged us to start to obey Him in every little thing. Our calendar was full of days that made us pause to remember.

During the Feast of Tabernacles, God's people were told to remember how He took them out of their bondage in Egypt and brought them to the Promised Land. Halfway through this seven-day celebration, Jesus went to the temple courts and began to teach that it was God's will to do that again, only *this* time He would be freeing them from their sins and bringing them to a place of eternal rest and fellowship with Him! The first time they had to choose to believe Moses. *This time they would have to choose to believe Jesus!* (John 7:16–19.)

God is holding out the same challenge for all of us right now, and the choice is still ours to make.

I long for all my friends to embrace God's will.

This is a date I want circled on everyone's calendar so that we can stop and remember everything Jesus has made possible!

August 14. Day 202.

I'm sitting outside of Gate 6. I've been transferred to another airline and told I won't be getting any meals, but that's okay! I'm just thankful to be going to Canada! It was hard to say good-bye. The hugs were long and it felt terribly lonely to walk away alone; yet I know that Jesus is with me and has gone before me. He is an awesome mystery.

The book of Hebrews shines a light on Jesus that both deepens the mystery and brings clarity to who Jesus is. Jesus is God's spokesperson and the exact representation of God, who sustains all things.

It's *this* Jesus who is sitting with me outside of Gate 6. *The exact representation of God will fly with me to Canada. The Sustainer of all things will sustain me as I go to the cemetery and supervise the laying of Jim's marker. The joy of Jesus will anchor me through the waves of sorrow that are sure to come.*

And it will be *this* Jesus who will one day show those who find it inconceivable that God would become flesh and die for their sins the scars in His hands.

This Jesus will tell them not to be afraid, but to just believe.

August 15. Day 203.

I had my first Popsicle and my first kiss at Braeside Camp. Whenever we came back to Canada, Jim and I lived at Braeside in the "Keddy Kottage," which is a stone's throw away from Nanny's. I insisted that I would never come back to these grounds without Jim, but the moment we drove through the gate I felt like I'd come home. I felt safe. I felt hugged by Jesus.

The writer of Hebrews writes,

> It makes good sense that the God who got everything started and keeps everything going now completes the work by making the Salvation Pioneer perfect through suffering, as He leads all of us to glory. Since the One who saves and those who are being saved have a common origin, Jesus doesn't hesitate to treat them as family. (Hebrews 2:10–11, *The Message*)

Jesus considers me family!
No wonder I feel hugged.

August 16. Day 204.

My father-in-law has a saying that he never speaks without a playful punch on the arm: *"I'm proud to know ya!"*

That's something Jesus would say, because Jesus is our biggest cheerleader!

> Because He himself suffered when He was tempted, He is able to help those who are being tempted . . . *and we are* His house *if we hold on to our courage and the hope of which we boast!* (Hebrews 2:18, 3:6)

Jesus became one of us, so He knows the struggle and what we need on this journey from earth to glory.

When you cling to the courage and hope He has provided, you can be sure that: *"Jesus is proud to know ya!"*

August 17. Day 205.

The best compliment I can be given is to have friends show up for dinner. I love that *they love* to sit around my table. I'm sure that's how God feels every morning when I come to Him for my manna. I can't wait to see what He dishes up, and I know He loves to fill up my plate!

> Let us *hold firmly to the faith* we profess, for we do not have a high priest who is unable to sympathize with our weaknesses, but we have one who has been tempted in every way just as we are—yet was without sin. Let us *approach the throne of grace with confidence* so that we may receive mercy and find grace to help us in our time of need. (Hebrews 4:14–16)

Whenever we come to God, we will always leave satisfied and wanting more. His manna encourages, strengthens, guides, and offers hope! Just as my friends know they're always welcome at my table, God wants us at His table anytime! I always have enough, but *God has an endless supply.* He too never heats up leftovers or microwaves frozen dinners—*His meals are freshly prepared, and they always hit the spot.*

August 18. Day 206.

Once we know who Jesus truly is and all He endured so that we could have eternal salvation, we dare not spurn His lavish grace. We cannot become lazy and trust God only when we feel like it. Instead, we must "imitate those who through faith and patience inherited what was promised" (Hebrews 6:12).

Abraham did it without a Bible in his hand, *so surely we have no excuse!*

We must hold tightly to His promise, never forgetting what it cost for us to feel His hand gripping ours.

August 19. Day 207.

Hebrews 7 tells us that Jesus is forever indestructible; the only guarantee of our salvation; and that He intercedes for us continuously!

I love words like *indestructible, guarantee, forever,* and *continuously!*

Jesus, Your mercy, Your grace, Your presence, and Your power are indeed *indestructible, guaranteed, and continuous . . .* even on this day when I will go to the cemetery to see Jim's gravestone for the first time.

Later.

The day is over, and Jesus did not let me down.

The skilled engravers did a great job, and the beautiful marker that lies in the ground just beyond the entrance near a cluster of trees is one-of-a-kind. As I stood there, a huge flock of birds perched themselves in one of the big trees and began to chirp a contagious anthem to their Creator. I found myself humming along as I placed some lilies and sunflowers at the spot where Jim's body is buried. The sunflowers instinctively turned their faces to the heavens, reminding me where my eyes should be.

The words that sank deep into my spirit this morning rang in my heart: *indestructible . . . guaranteed . . . forever.*

I got back in my car and turned the key. A song began to play that talked about how Jesus is the best friend we'll ever have. I don't even know who the artist was, *but I know who arranged to have that song playing as I drove out of the cemetery.*

I have no words to thank You, Jesus, except to promise that I will serve You the rest of my days.

August 20. Day 208.

I met with Tim and Karen last night to talk about Nanny's. My heart is conflicted. I'm thankful they are going to build our haven, but I'm not sure how I will live there without Jim. What I do know is that I want Nanny's to be that place where everyone loves to come. I want people to leave well fed and more in love with Jesus.

In just a few hours, I am bringing the Keddy family to Jim's grave. It will be their first time to see the marker and stand on the piece of earth that holds Jim's body. I pray that the living hope we have will trump the sorrow. I can't take a step toward that place without my manna. Hebrews 8:10 assures us that He is our God and we are His people. Hebrews 9:12–14 tells us that because of Jesus, our sins are completely forgiven. When Jesus gave His life for us, we were saved from death *so that we could serve the living God, first on earth and then in heaven!*

Today could be the day when He comes to take us home!

As I stand at the graveside with all the family, I choose one more time to look at the sky.

Sovereign God, fill our hearts today with thankfulness for all Jesus has done. Place an expectation in our spirits for that day of all days. Remind our souls that death has no victory over those who belong to You and that we live to do Your bidding.

August 21. Day 209.

God was there. We lifted our eyes to the sky and sang the required song and left Jim's grave convinced that a day is coming when heartache and good-byes will be banished forever!

But I can't survive on yesterday's grace, so take me to my manna.

Hebrews 10:7 quotes Jesus: *"Here I am. It is written about Me in the scroll. I have come to do Your will, O God."* Wow. That really spoke to me, for if Jesus said these words knowing what was ahead, then how can I not say these words too? Jesus set aside perfect heaven, so how can I ever question the path God created for me?

On this new day—I choose to draw near to my God with a sincere heart, in full assurance of faith. I choose to hold unswervingly to the hope I profess, for He who promised is faithful. I choose to spur those around me toward love and good deeds so that others will come to know Jesus. And I choose to encourage everyone to continuously look at the sky as we see that day of all days approaching! (Hebrews 10:22, 24–25.)

August 22. Day 210.

I love that God calls me His friend and is my constant companion. Like David wrote in the Psalms, "He makes me glad."

My friend, do not throw away your confidence; it will be richly rewarded! You need to persevere so that when you have done the will of God you will receive what He has promised! For in just a little while . . . He who is coming will come and won't delay . . . but until then . . . my righteous ones . . . *my friends* . . . you must *live by faith*. If you shrink back, I will not be pleased with you . . .

So says GOD! (Hebrews 10:35–38.)

On Day 210 of this unexpected journey, *I will persevere* . . . I will not throw away my confidence. I will not shrink back. I will remember that the living God is my friend, and by doing this I will please Him.

And so begins another day.

August 23. Day 211.

A year ago today, Jim and I blew up an air mattress and slept on it in the middle of Nanny's cottage. He was alive and happy and looking forward to coming back every autumn so we could drink in the color of the leaves. Your Word tells me to persevere, but I'm losing my footing. Rescue me . . .

> Now faith is being *sure* of what we hope for and *certain* of what we do not see . . . and without faith it is impossible to please God, because anyone who comes to Him must believe that He exists and that He rewards those who earnestly seek Him . . . Abel, Enoch, Noah and Abraham were still living by faith when they died. *They did not receive the things they were promised; they only saw them and welcomed them from a distance.* They admitted that they were aliens and strangers on earth who were longing for a better country—a heavenly one! Therefore . . . God is not ashamed to be called their God for He has prepared a city for them! (Hebrews 11:1–16)

I too admit that I am an alien and a stranger on this earth, longing for that place where my faith will become sight! I am resolved not to squander even a second of this pilgrimage! I want to please my God! I see You, Jesus, through eyes of faith, riding on the clouds, and I welcome You from a distance!

I'm standing again.

August 24. Day 212.

I know God wants me to return to Hong Kong, but part of me wishes I could stay. It would be nice to be like other families who live near their kids, but in a few hours I will somehow say those goodbyes one more time, and with a courage that comes from heaven I will board that plane that will take me back to what God has called me to do. *I live for Him and not myself.*

> Moses regarded disgrace *for the sake of Christ* as of greater value than the treasures of Egypt, because he was *looking ahead to his reward. He persevered because he saw Him who was invisible.* Therefore, since we are surrounded by such a great cloud of witnesses, let us throw off everything that hinders and the sin that so easily entangles, and *let us run with perseverance* the race marked out for us! Let us *fix our eyes on Jesus,* the author and finisher of our faith, who for the joy set before Him endured the cross . . . *Consider Him* so that you will not grow weary and lose heart. (Hebrews 11:24–27, 12:1–3)

Hong Kong . . . here I come!

August 26. Day 214.

Twenty-four hours later, I'm home. I miss seeing my kids' faces and having a cottage full of friends, but I am back in Hong Kong and have a job to do, so I will try my best to keep my eyes fixed on my prize and keep running! Take me to my manna.

> Endure hardship as discipline. God is treating you as sons and daughters. (Hebrews 12:7)

I've noticed that *God never gives me permission to wallow in my pain.* Words like *endure* keep popping up.

Every lonely second, each agonizing good-bye, gives me the opportunity to endure like Jesus did, thus making me fit to rule with Him in eternity. Although I don't understand what ruling with Him will look like, I do want to please Him, so I will follow His teachings here on earth so I can be ready for heaven.

> Take a new grip with your tired hands and stand firm on your shaky legs. Those who follow you, though they are weak and lame, will not stumble and fall but will become strong! (Hebrews 12:12–13)

Others who are hurting will take their cue from me, so I *must* endure, *hold on tight, firmly plant my feet, and remain focused on what's coming* so that they will put their trust in Jesus and come to know His strength!

It's not necessary for me to fully understand, but it *is* necessary for me to fully obey.

August 27. Day 215.

I only slept four hours thanks to jet lag and an upsetting phone call. A representative from the insurance company that is handling Jim's life insurance policy called to let me know they are investigating a visit Jim made to the doctor a year before he went to heaven. They have to rule out that he had any preexisting conditions before they give me any insurance money.

That short conversation made me nauseous. Do they think I care about insurance money?

All I want is Jim.

Just thinking about that doctor's appointment makes me confused and angry. He left the doctor's office with a clean bill of health. I still have the reports, and the word *normal* is everywhere. Stress test—*normal.* Blood work—*normal.* Cholesterol—*normal.* Upper and lower GI series—*normal.* Blood pressure—*normal.* It's like a neon light flashing all over the page—*normal, normal, normal.*

I hung up the phone and collapsed in a fit of tears. *How is it possible that I am a widow having a conversation about life insurance? How could Jim's heart be normal just twelve short months before it stopped?* I picked the phone up again and called a dear friend. All she heard were sobs, so she began to pray, and when she did, Jesus reached down and pulled me close.

I am so thankful that even when I have no strength to fall into His arms, I end up there anyway.

I let His peace whoosh over me, and as I lay in the embrace of Jesus, my thoughts went to Mary and how she chose the better way. I heard the Holy Spirit whisper in my ear, "Sit at His feet, Susan . . .

"Choose not to be distracted by all the questions . . .

"Choose not to look away from His face . . .

"Keep yourself right there."

Jesus, You have once again convinced me that Your strong arms that have held me throughout this journey thus far will never, ever let me go.

August 28. Day 216.

Today is the anniversary of when Jim and I first met. I was in London, Ontario, where my dad was preaching from a flatbed truck stationed in a plaza parking lot. All the cars were parked in rows with their windows down. A few of us kids were standing outside toward the back, and this is where the introduction was made. Jim went home and wrote on a piece of paper that he had met the most beautiful girl in the world with the most gorgeous blue eyes he'd ever seen and that he hoped to marry her one day. I too was smitten. I had never seen anyone more handsome. He wrote me a letter that same week, and that was the beginning of what I thought would be forever. *But on this earth there is no forever.* I have the urge to tell every wife I see, whether I know her or not, to appreciate each moment. I want husbands to bring their wives flowers every day. I want couples to hold hands and dance in their living rooms, realizing that it could all end in a heartbeat.

I feel drawn to the book of Revelation. Sovereign God, open my eyes to whatever You want me to see.

> The Master Jesus declares, "I'm A to Z. I'm The God who is, The God who was and The God about to arrive. I'm the Sovereign-Strong." (Revelation 1:8, *The Message*)

My romance with Jim didn't last forever, but the love Jesus and I share will. *Master Jesus, I can't wait to see Your face.*

August 29. Day 217.

Sovereign-Strong, take me to my manna.

John writes to the churches that he is their "brother and companion in the suffering *and* in the kingdom *and* in the patient endurance that is theirs in Jesus" (Revelation 1:9).

We followers of Jesus are a band of brothers and sisters who are indeed companions on a journey to forever. In the kingdom of God we walk together, reminding each other that the best is yet to come!

Further down in chapter 1, John attempts to describe Jesus. Wow. If a police artist took a crack at what John described, it would be a pretty strange portrait. Commentaries have all sorts of things to say about what it all means, but what spoke to me was John's reaction when he saw Jesus. *He fell at His feet as though he was dead. Jesus literally took his breath away!*

I think Jesus is just too beautiful for words.

You know what else is just too beautiful for words?

The Body of Christ standing beside me.

Both are indescribable.

August 30. Day 218.

I sat in staff meetings yesterday that left me terrified. All my lesson plans have to be submitted into a computer program that I know nothing about. What have I said yes to? *Jesus, You have to help me! Together we can do this, right?! I need my manna!*

In Revelation 2, Jesus tells the church in Ephesus that He knows their good deeds, their hard work, and their perseverance. He knows they hate wickedness and have endured hardship, but *they have forgotten how in love with Jesus they once were.* He wants them to remember and go back to how it was. He wants the church in Ephesus *to look only at Him and love Him the most.*

He wants me to do that too.

I can't be distracted by the demands of my new job. I must love Jesus completely, and everything else will fall into place.

Jesus, as I begin this new adventure, I must guard my heart from letting the busyness of my duties rob me of my intimacy with You.

I can breathe now.

August 31. Day 219.

Jesus tells the church in Smyrna that He is aware of their pain.

> I know your afflictions and your poverty, yet you are rich . . . I know the slander against you . . . Do not be afraid of what you are about to suf-fer . . . Be faithful, *even to the point of death, and I will give you the crown of Life!* (Revelation 2:9–10)

Did they wonder why instead of removing their pain, He was allowing more? Did they understand that although they were poor on earth, their suffering made them rich in heaven?

The original meaning for "crown" is a garland that is placed on the head of someone who wins a race, so the church in Smyrna was being reminded to keep running toward the finish line no matter what was thrown in their path! Jesus assured them that their suffering had a purpose and that if they were faithful to the end, they would be rewarded.

My pain is a test.

I cannot stop running.

September 1. Day 220.

Sovereign God, my need for You is great. Take me to Your table one more time.

The words of Jesus to the church in Pergamum remind us that sin is never overlooked. He is pleased that they have remained true even in the midst of horrific evil, but He points out that there are some who have become involved with idolatry and immorality. Jesus tells them to repent and says that "those who overcome will be given hidden manna" (Revelation 2:17).

I want that hidden manna!

In fact, I can't live without it!

I never *ever* want to jeopardize those feasts, so I will guard my heart against sin until I'm finally around God's throne with those who obeyed Jesus from the church in Pergamum.

September 2. Day 221.

During Jim's first year of Bible college, a farmer from our church employed him to work in his cornfields. Most days I would pack a lunch and then wander through the stalks until I heard Jim's radio. We always had the sense that our farmer friend could have looked after the weeds himself, but this was his way of being a part of what God was doing in Jim's life. Today that very kind farmer joined Jim in heaven, and his wife has joined me on this well-worn path of loneliness. She is about to come to know Jesus in a brand-new way. If I were across the table from her right now I would tell her *that God has put*

her on this path, that His hand will always be in hers, and that if she yields to His
sovereignty, she will live in the miraculous. Holy Spirit, please whisper comfort
into her heart on this, her Day 1.

Jesus tells the church in Thyatira that He has seen their deeds, love, faith,
and perseverance but cautions them to stop believing that sexual immorality
and idol worship are permissible. He tells them there is hope for them if they
"only hold on to what they have until He comes" (Revelation 2:18–25).

Jesus, You see what no one else can see. Keep me pure. I will hold fast to
Your teachings and firmly to my faith. *Jesus, You are our prize when all of this
is over.* Seal that in my heart today and in the heart of the farmer's wife who
has just begun this journey.

As You hold on to us, help us to hold on to what we have until You come.

September 3. Day 222.

Take me to my hidden manna.

The church in Sardis had a reputation of being alive, but Jesus said they
were dead. He says to them:

> Wake up! *Strengthen what remains* and is about to die, *for I have* not
> *found your deeds complete* in the sight of My God. Remember what you
> have received and heard and then repent and obey! (Revelation 3:1–3)

I love that He doesn't just leave them sleeping. He shakes them from their
slumber because He longs for His church to be wide awake and effective. *He
wants His church to view everything in the light of eternity, walk in obedience, and
represent Him well, being famous for its love, mercy, and generosity.*

Jesus, wake me up when I fall asleep.

I aim to be dressed in white so You will acknowledge me before Your Father.

September 4. Day 223.

My back has seized up. I need a miracle, because it's a forty-five-minute
bus ride to where I'm speaking this morning. Take me to my manna.

The church in Philadelphia has really blessed Jesus. His message to them
is total encouragement:

> I know your deeds. See, I have placed before you an open door that no one can shut. I know that you have little strength, yet you have kept My word and have not denied My name. (Revelation 3:7–8)

He assures them that He will fight on their behalf and that they will be rewarded because they have kept His command to endure patiently. He tells them He is coming soon, so they should hold on to what they have so that no one will take their crown (Revelation 3:10–11).

There it is again! *Endure. Hold on to what you have.*

How can I not keep holding on?

There is just too much at stake to ever let go.

September 5. Day 224.

Yesterday was a miracle. My stubborn muscles refused to relax, but God's power enabled me to preach both services and convinced hearts to never let go of Jesus. When I got home, my precious friend Mohsina was there with an ice pack for my back, a delicious dinner, and a hot cup of milky tea. I am so thankful for our sisterhood! I woke up more limber this morning. Take me to my manna.

Laodicea was famous for its financial institutions, extensive textile industry, and the eye salve they manufactured; yet Jesus called them wretched, pitiful, poor, blind, and naked! He said to them, "Because you are lukewarm—neither hot nor cold—I am about to spit you out of My mouth" (Revelation 3:16).

Did they hear those four little words of hope?

"I am about to . . ."

He was *still* giving them time to repent! He wanted them to be clothed in white garments reserved for those who overcome and to apply His salve to their eyes so they could see. He was rebuking them because He loved them.

> Here I am! I stand at the door and knock. If anyone hears My voice and opens the door, I will come in and eat with them and them with Me! (Revelation 3:20)

Jesus is extending the same longsuffering to us as He did to the church in Laodicea. He stands at the door of our lukewarm hearts and knocks, *giving us a chance to do the right thing. He compels us to believe that He is all we will ever need.* I don't know what the church in Laodicea did, but I am running to the door of my heart.

I open it wide to You, Jesus.
Come in and eat with me.
Rub my eyes with Your salve so I can see what is real and eternal.

September 6. Day 225.

Part of Jim's last message was taken from Revelation 4. He told the congregation that he couldn't wait to see what was waiting for him beyond the door that opened to eternity. *Jim has now seen what he looked forward to his whole life.* For the last 224 days he has been where, according to John, there is a continuous chorus of worship around God's throne (Revelation 4:8, 11).

Until that door opens for me, my prayer is that I will represent Jesus well on this pilgrimage to heaven. While here on earth, my little voice joins in with those who sing around God's throne, because without Him . . . I couldn't bear the wait.

September 7. Day 226.

I asked my Grade 6 students to describe God. A few used words like *friendly* and *good*. Others said they didn't know. *I can't wait to tell them all about Him!*

> Worthy is the Lamb, who was slain to receive power and wealth and wisdom and strength and honor and glory and praise! To Him who sits on The Throne and to the Lamb be praise and honor and glory and power for ever and ever! (Revelation 5:12–13)

Last night the doorbell rang, and when I opened the door, there stood a man who was clearly disturbed and mumbling something incoherent. He had a scowl on his face, thick glasses, and a bright yellow T-shirt tucked in his jeans that were pulled up above his waist. He forced his way into my apartment, and I pushed him right back out! I slammed the door shut, locked it, and called the management office. They quickly came and took him away. Evidently he had wandered out of a psychiatric ward and somehow ended up in my building, on my floor, at my door!

I am truly never alone! *The One who sits on the throne watches over me!* Jesus, the Lamb of God—the One who was slain for me *and for every student I will stand before this year*—is my companion and protector!

It's unbelievable, but exactly how it is.

September 8. Day 227.

I looked and there before me was a great multitude that no one could count, from every nation, tribe, people and language! They were standing before the throne and in front of The Lamb! They were wearing white robes and crying in a loud voice: *Salvation belongs to our God, Who sits on the Throne and to the Lamb!* (Revelation 7: 9–10)

Never again will we hunger. Never again will we thirst. The sun will not beat upon us or any scorching heat because the Lamb at the center of the Throne will be our Shepherd. He will lead us to springs of living water . . . and *God will wipe away every tear from our eyes!* (Revelation 7:16)

Somewhere around that throne one day will be Jim, my boys, and their families. As far as the eye can see will be the great cloud of witnesses that have cheered me on as I've walked this unexpected path. With *one voice* we will worship our King and the lover of our souls, *forever.* Never again will we feel loss, sorrow, pain, separation, loneliness, hunger, thirst, or longing. *It will finally be over.*

Help me to live here on earth with *that day* in my sights.

September 9. Day 228.

Twenty-five years ago today at 3:31 p.m. we had our first son. Jim took him in his arms, leaned in close, and whispered a prayer in my ear, giving Curtis James William back to the Lord. *Jesus, please be with Curtis today. Bring hope and healing into Curtis's wounded heart as he learns to celebrate without his dad.*

John writes that one day "the kingdom of this world will become the kingdom of our Lord and of His Christ, who will reign forever"! On that day "the one who accused us day and night will be hurled down by the blood of the Lamb and by the word of our testimony"! (Revelation 11:15 and Revelation 12:10–11.)

What a moment it will be when our accuser is destroyed! The fight will be over! An eternal celebration around God's throne will begin, and not one of us will be missing!

Bring it on! I can't wait!

September 10. Day 229.

Before the celebration in heaven begins, there will be days of persecution. Some of us will be imprisoned. Some of us will be killed (Revelation 13:10). This is already happening in the nation I am living in right now.

John writes that the Beast will be given power and great authority. Men will proclaim, "Who is like the Beast?! Who can make war against him?" (Revelation 13:4). This Beast will be handed power to conquer and rule every tribe, people, language, and nation (Revelation 13:7).

These verses aren't pleasant to read, but without this horribleness, we wouldn't have reason for the celebration. *You have to know pain to know relief.* Revelation makes it clear that those of us who belong to Jesus will not be exempt from suffering, which is why John wrote, "This calls for patient endurance and faithfulness on the part of the saints" (Revelation 13:10).

I choose to endure. I choose to be faithful to what I know is true.

Most of us have never known real persecution, but I suspect there is coming a day when we will.

This journey of sorrow is good practice.

September 11. Day 230.

Hundreds of widows woke up this morning reliving the day when the Twin Towers fell. *Bless each of my sisters with an abundance of Your grace. Bless every son and daughter who was left without a dad. Bless the parents who had their child die before them. I pray that everyone who is reeling with the aftereffects of those tragic moments will come to know how much You care.*

In the Old Testament, the word *endure* is set in conjunction with God's love, mercy, and faithfulness; however, in the New Testament it is *always* connected with pain, suffering, and hope. I'm learning that to endure means *to patiently trust, believing that something better is coming.*

Looking ahead, John wrote:

> I saw the victorious ones holding harps given to them by God and they were singing the song of Moses and the Song of the Lamb . . . "Great and marvelous are Your deeds, Lord God Almighty . . . Just and true are Your ways, King of the ages . . . Who will not fear You O Lord and bring glory to Your Name? For You alone are holy. All nations will come and worship You, for Your righteous acts have been revealed!" (Revelation 15:3–4)

Moses knew and bowed to God's ways. There were more hard times than celebrations in his days. Jesus was mocked, beaten, and crucified so that the world could be rescued from eternal separation from God. He wondered if there could be another way but ultimately surrendered, saying, "Not My will, but Yours be done." *Through all their suffering, Moses and Jesus bowed to God's sovereignty, declaring that His deeds were great and marvelous and that His ways were just and true.*

Their song *must* be my song.

September 12. Day 231.

John writes that he heard what sounded like the roar of a great multitude in heaven shouting, "Hallelujah! Salvation and glory and power belong to our God, for true and just are His judgments. Hallelujah! Our God almighty reigns. Let us rejoice and be glad and give Him glory! For the wedding of The Lamb has come, and *His bride has made herself ready!*" (Revelation 19:1–7).

Yahoozie! My heart is pounding out of my chest! This journey from earth to glory is where all the preparations are made! *I must love Him more than life. I must endure. I must fix my eyes on Him and trust Him no matter what it looks like. I must continuously remember that heaven is coming and that this path of sorrow is making me ready to be His Bride.*

When Jim and I got married, we had endless lists. Each detail was written down, then checked off when it was done *because we wanted our day to be perfect.* By the time I walked up the aisle, *there was nothing left undone.* We drove away from our reception smiling, *with no regrets, so looking forward to the next chapter!*

Today is another day for me, *His called, His chosen, and His faithful follower,* to check off that list!

September 13. Day 232.

Every Christ-follower has an invitation to the wedding supper of the Lamb. It's different from every other invitation because there is no set date. Instead, we have to be ready to go at the drop of a hat—or should I say the sound of a trumpet?

It's sort of like when I was pregnant with our boys. We had a bag packed and sitting at the foot of our bed. We knew that I had to be right ready to waddle to the car as soon as that first contraction hit. *We knew the boys would be born, but we weren't exactly sure when.* As it turned out, we were surprised both times because they both came early!

We know Jesus is coming back. He says that nation will rise against nation and kingdom against kingdom. He says that there will be famines and earthquakes and that all these are the beginning of birth pains. He goes on to say that no one knows the day or the hour except for His Father in heaven, so we have to keep watch.

We have to live ready to go.

September 14. Day 233.

There will be no more night. They will not need the light of a lamp or the light of the sun, for the Lord God will give them light. And they will reign forever and ever. *These words are trustworthy and true.* (Revelation 22:5)

I love that there will be no more night, because I find the night hours the hardest. Both the darkness and the pain of separation will be erased on that day, because Jim and I will be on the same side of the door.

"Yes! I am coming soon," says Jesus.

"Amen! Come, Lord Jesus," says me.

(Revelation 2:20.)

September 15. Day 234.

I went to sleep last night singing my cemetery song. It has become my anthem ever since the sun broke through the dark clouds as I stood ankle-deep in the snow at Jim's grave. This morning I woke up singing another ancient church song:

> Oh! Won't it be wonderful there, having no burdens to bear?
> Joyously singing with heart bells a ringing,
> Oh won't it be wonderful there?
> ("Won't It Be Wonderful There?"—James Rowe, 1865)

I am so grateful for the hope of heaven. Take me to my manna.

The Gospel of Mark is a compilation of Peter's teachings preserved for us by Mark. He begins by talking about how John the Baptist announced that he would be followed by someone whose sandals he was not worthy to untie. Untying sandals was a task reserved only for slaves. John was exalting Jesus to His rightful place and basically saying that he was less than a slave in His presence.

As I read these words, I thought ahead to when Jesus knelt at the feet of His disciples and washed their feet. No wonder Peter initially refused! It was unthinkable, but Jesus said that He did it *to set an example for us.* I'm flabbergasted that Jesus left the perfection of heaven and came to earth to be the servant of all, which included washing dirty feet, then making the sins of the entire world His own, so that we could be part of His kingdom.

It really will *be wonderful in heaven!* Not only will our burdens be gone, but we will be able to thank Jesus throughout eternity for all He did to get us there.

September 16. Day 235.

I've been using Steven Curtis Chapman's song, "For the Sake of the Call" with my Grade 6 students. The lyrics of this song were taken straight from Mark's writings where Jesus stops in front of two fishing boats and calls out to a few fishermen to come and follow. Mark records that *at once,* Simon and Andrew left their nets, and that James and John actually *left their father behind* in the boat with the hired help!

No questions were asked.

They didn't make a list of pros and cons.

They simply dropped their nets, got out of the boat, and were forever changed by their obedience.

They left everything, because *nothing holds a candle to having Jesus, the One who spoke the world into existence, call you by name and ask you to come.* The last thing I tell my Grade 6 students every day is that *nothing compares to getting to know Jesus.* My prayer is that by the end of the year they will understand why millions have given their lives for the sake of the call, and that they too will follow.

Jesus, give me Your strength to always forsake who I am, and what I want, for who You are and what You want for my life.

September 17. Day 236.

The first place Jesus takes His four new companions is into a synagogue. As Jesus is teaching, a man possessed by an evil spirit screams, "What do You want with us, Jesus of Nazareth? Have You come to destroy us? I know You are—the Holy One of God!" (Mark 1:24). Jesus tells the spirit to be quiet and to come out of the man, and it does.

I can just imagine the two sets of brothers looking at each other, feeling exhilarated and terrified all at the same time! I have a feeling that after that visit to the synagogue, catching fish was a distant memory. There would be no turning back for Simon, Andrew, James, and John.

There's no turning back for me either.

I've seen too much to ever go back to how it was.

September 18. Day 237.

Another sunrise! Another day to follow!

Jesus left the synagogue and went to Simon and Andrew's home. When they arrived, Simon told Jesus his mother-in-law was sick. When Jesus heard this, *He went to her.* I love the compassion of Jesus, *and I love that He's the same today as He was then.* Jesus walked over to her bedside, took her by the hand, and helped her up. I can't count how many times Jesus has taken me by the hand and helped me up. The fever instantly left her, and she began to serve them.

I'm convinced that Jesus lifts us up to serve. He doesn't lift us up to feel better, although we do; *He lifts us up so that we can serve one another in love.*

A few days ago I heard that one of my friends from Pakistan was in the same hospital where Jim was pronounced dead. My first impulse was to run in the opposite direction, but instead I asked Jesus for help. He took me by the hand and walked through the hospital doors with me, down the hall right into my friend's room.

You have given me so much, Jesus. I am here on this earth to pay it forward.

September 19. Day 238.

Last night I took a houseguest to the Mid-Autumn Festival. It's a fun night for families to fill the parks with lanterns and laughter. Jim loved this time of year, and I missed him much, but as always Jesus gave me *something else to focus on rather than my pain.* The guest I have in my home is a friend of a friend who is on a journey to discover who to believe in. Her search has taken her to Asia, and I pray that she will come to see that the answer to her question is Jesus.

The morning after Jesus healed Simon's mother-in-law, He got up while it was still dark and went off on His own. When Simon and his friends realized He was missing, they went searching for Him to let Him know everyone was looking for Him. Although it's nice to be wanted, it can be exhausting . . . which is why I completely understand why Jesus might want some time to Himself!

But as I read these verses, I realized that this was *not* the reason He left. *That would be* my *reason.* But no—*Jesus left to spend time with His Father.* He wasn't under a tree reading a book; He was praying. When Simon found Him, Jesus's response was not a deep sigh of regret that He'd been discovered, but rather it was *one of compassion.*

> Let us go somewhere else to the nearby villages, so I can preach there also! *That is why I have come.* (Mark 1:38)

Jesus received direction and compassion when He spent time with His Father. He never tired of touching the untouchable or loving the unlovable *because that's why He came!*

Father God, I need to pray more. Please direct my heart into Your love and Christ's perseverance. Fill me with the knowledge of Your will. I want my labor to be prompted by love. I want my endurance to be inspired by hope. Clothe me with compassion, kindness, humility, gentleness, and patience.

That's why I'm here.

September 20. Day 239.

It must have been pretty amazing to host Jesus. Simon's wife would have had the honor of cooking for Jesus and doing His laundry. She also would have been there when four men ripped open her roof and lowered the paralytic at the feet of Jesus, who was standing in her living room! Her house would forever be part of that man's story, just as much his healing would be part of hers (Mark 2:1–12).

Jesus, You are amazing. Just like You made Yourself at home in Simon's house, You delight in making Yourself at home in my house! *You are here to do what no one else can do, so give me boldness to tell my friends You are here!*

I want everyone to go home with a story.

September 21. Day 240.

Back when Jesus walked this earth, tax collectors were despised. So when Jesus invited Matthew, *a tax collector,* to follow Him, it was scandalous. Clearly Matthew felt no judgmental vibes coming from Jesus, because he left his table and invited Jesus over for dinner so He could meet all of his friends. Eating together in the Jewish culture was and still is a sign of friendship, so the statement Jesus made that day was enormous. The religious crowd was outraged, but Jesus didn't budge.

> It is not the healthy who need a doctor, but the sick. I have not come to call the righteous, but sinners. (Mark 2:17)

In other words, "I've come to hang out with them to make them whole."

For those He has already rescued, we live to imitate Him and be the best friend a sinner could ever have.

I have a feeling it's going to be a great day!

September 22. Day 241.

Does Jesus care when my heart is pained too deeply for mirth or song,
As the burdens press, and the cares distress, and the way grows
weary and long?

Does Jesus care when my way is dark with a nameless dread and fear?
As the daylight fades into deep night shades, does He care enough to
be near?

Does Jesus care when I've tried and failed to resist some temptation
strong;
When for my deep grief there is no relief, though my tears flow all
the night long?

Does Jesus care when I've said goodbye to the dearest on earth to me,
And my sad heart aches till it nearly breaks—is it aught to Him?
Does He see?

Oh, yes, He cares, I know He cares, His heart is touched with my grief;
When the days are weary, the long nights dreary, I know my Savior cares.
("Does Jesus Care?"—Frank E. Graeff/J. Lincoln Hall, 1901)

Today, *this is all I know.*

September 23. Day 242.

It's been an uphill challenge this week. I've been feeling that "wet blanket"
Curtis talked about back in February. *I still believe God is sovereign,* and I will
endeavor to embrace the path He's chosen for me to walk. *I still believe He
cares.* My faith is not weakening, and my resolve is strengthened every time I
choose to look at the sky.

I am just really lonely.

This is the first time I've been alone in my entire life. I went from living with my parents to boarding with a family in my college years to getting

married. I don't think I'm made to live alone. I see advertisements for holiday destinations and cry. We were planning on taking vacations more often. *We had a plan.* I look at all my tomorrows, and it's just desperately sad to envision them without Jim.

It's with clenched teeth and pure grit I'm continuing to trust in what I do not see. *Jesus, please give me a double portion of Your perseverance and power.*

Jesus tells a story about a farmer who went out to sow his seed. Some fell along the path and was eaten up by birds. Some fell on rocky places where there wasn't much soil, so when the sun came up, the plants withered because there was no root. Other seed fell among thorns which grew up and choked the plants. But others fell on good soil, so it grew and produced a crop that multiplied (Mark 4:1–20).

Jesus used this story to illustrate the condition of our hearts. If we are *not* rooted in Him, our Enemy can snatch away the truth, and the worries of this life and the deceitfulness of wealth can prevent us from being fruitful. But if we *are* rooted in Him, *then there will be fruit that multiplies!*

Thank You, Sovereign God, for good soil. Thank You for being my gardener, for breaking up the soil in my heart, for adding nutrients and supplements along the way so that now my roots are deeply planted in You. Thank You for every hour I had around an altar growing up when You came near and enveloped me in Your presence.

I have heard Your voice, and I know exactly what I need to do!

I'm ready for Day 242.

September 24. Day 243.

The story of Jesus sleeping in the boat during a storm made it into three out of the four Gospels. Repeating something is a pretty good indicator that there is a lesson within this story that God wants us to learn.

When the storm hits, all the disciples can think about is how they want it to stop. They had seen Jesus heal the sick and muzzle evil spirits. They were recipients of His lavish love and compassion. He had called them family.

But in those moments of sheer terror, they forgot what they had seen, and heard, and come to know.

Today I am reminded that I need to trust Jesus always, *especially* in the midst of a storm. No matter how strong the wind or how much water is filling the boat, Jesus said, "'We *are* going to the other side!"

On the Sea of Galilee, Jesus stood up, and with a simple *hush,* stopped the storm. It was only when the disciples watched the wind stop and the waves turn to ripples that they realized who was in their boat.

They fell on their knees and feared Him instead of the elements.

I'm learning that it's in that holy fear where you learn to trust.

Everything is fine. I'm going to the other side.

September 25. Day 244.

When they reached the other side of the lake, a man screaming and full of thousands of evil spirits rushed up to meet Jesus. I can only imagine the hellish torment this poor man felt until, into his hopeless existence, *Jesus entered.* Jesus, who did in a few seconds what no one else could.

Jesus commanded the legion of spirits to come out of him, and instantly this man was set free and made completely sane. He begged Jesus to let him go with Him back to Capernaum (who wouldn't?), but Jesus said no, because *Jesus had another plan.*

> Go home to your family and tell them how much the Lord has done for you, and how He has had mercy on you! (Mark 5:19)

This nameless man from the Gerasenes obeyed and became the first missionary to the Decapolis! He told everyone what had happened, and Mark records that all the people were utterly amazed. I wish I could have seen the faces of his family when he walked back into their lives with clear eyes and a huge smile, fully clothed and in his right mind! When I'm in heaven, I'm going to find this man and ask him to tell me all the details.

Jesus, amaze me today as You do what no one else can do.

September 26. Day 245.

I am learning that it's only in the midst of uncertainty that the definition of faith is fully realized. Believing in what you do not see and being certain of what you hope for comes out of a desperate situation.

Jairus exercised his faith when he told Jesus that he believed Jesus could raise his daughter from the dead. The woman with the issue of blood showed complete trust in Jesus when she declared that all she needed to do was touch

His coat to be made whole. *Both Jairus and the woman believed before they received, and both were rewarded for their faith.*

I want to believe like they did, because *faith is always rewarded by the miraculous.* Although, to be honest, it actually feels like *more* of a miracle to me to keep trusting when the bleeding continues or death doesn't let go.

When we live a life of trust, His presence is constant, and this to me is the biggest miracle of all.

September 27. Day 246.

Jesus goes home to Nazareth and is amazed at their lack of faith (Mark 6:6). *I never want to be indifferent to Jesus.* I never want to amaze Him by my lack of faith! When He looks into my heart, I want Him to see awe and wonder! *I want Him to see that I believe He can do absolutely anything!*

I trust You today, Jesus! I reach through the sadness and the pain determined to touch You one more time, *knowing* that when I do, Your power will flow into me so that on this Day 246, I *will* glorify You! The same words You spoke to the woman who reached out to You in desperation, You speak to me:

> Daughter, your faith has healed you. Go in peace and be freed from your suffering. Don't be afraid. Just believe. (Mark 5:34, 36)

September 28. Day 247.

I was part of a conversation yesterday with some friends who don't follow Jesus. They were talking about world religions and debating what gets us entrance into heaven. I was thrilled when they asked for my opinion.

I told them the story about a jade master and his new apprentice. The master placed a piece of jade into the hand of his young apprentice and told him he was not allowed to let go of it for an entire year. When the year was over, the master removed the jade and replaced it with a fake piece of jade. Immediately, his apprentice felt the difference because he had been holding on to the real thing for a year.

I told them that I knew *without a doubt* that Jesus was the real deal and the only way to God because *I have been hanging on to Him for a very long time.* I live for moments like this when I get to boast about my Jesus. The conversation shifted to what it looks like to be a Christian. It was fascinating to hear their perception, and it made me glad I was in their lives to show them what Jesus is really like.

A real Christian is a "little Christ" who loves and talks like Jesus. We are His hands, feet, and heart extended to the world. Mark 6:7–13 tells us about when Jesus sent His twelve disciples out, in teams of two, to be little Christs. They had the time of their lives making Him famous.

I have to say that I am too.

September 29. Day 248.

The little Christs did a great job! I love that the apostles didn't become well known through that trip, but *the name of Jesus became famous!* (Mark 6:14.) That's what I want! *When I leave a place after speaking, a classroom after teaching, or a home after eating, I want them to talk about JESUS!*

Mark 6:31 says that while the disciples were excitedly telling Jesus about their adventures, people were constantly interrupting them, so Jesus said to them, "Come with Me by yourselves to a quiet place and get some rest." Jesus understands our needs. *He knows that it is only in that quiet place with Him where we find true rest.*

Jesus, before I face the crowds outside my door today, I come to You.

> Sweep over my soul, sweep over my soul
> Sweet Spirit, sweep over my soul
> My rest is complete, as I sit at Your feet
> Sweet Spirit, sweep over my soul.
> ("Sweep Over My Soul"—Author Unknown)

September 30. Day 249.

I told my Grade 6 students about Mother Teresa yesterday. It took twenty-three years for God's calling to be fulfilled in her life. She was called to be a missionary when she was twelve, but she had to wait six years to enter the convent where she spent the next seventeen years. After teaching for a few more years, she *finally* found herself amongst the poorest of the poor.

Standing in front of my class, I had an epiphany that *what is still ahead for me could be what I was born for.*

It was overwhelming to consider that all of my yesterdays were preparation for something I have yet to see.

Nothing is ever wasted.

I really do believe that the best is yet to come!

October 1. Day 250.

Mark writes that Jesus tells His disciples to go on ahead of Him to Bethsaida. After they set sail, Jesus climbs up the side of mountain to pray. During the night a strong wind whips up that leaves the disciples straining at the oars. Here's the kicker: *Jesus sees them straining but doesn't come to their aid.* Just before dawn, Jesus walks out on the water and is about to pass them by. *That's right, He was planning on going right on by even though He knew they were in trouble!* (Mark 6:48.)

Trust is a big deal to our God.

Could it be that Jesus was hoping that He would see trust in their eyes as He walked by their boat?

He must have been disappointed, because instead of trust He saw fear.

They were so afraid that they didn't even know who He was.

I need to guard my heart against fear so my faith remains strong.

I want Him to see trust in my face while I strain at the oars.

October 2. Day 251.

> Whatever is true, whatever is noble, whatever is right, whatever is pure, whatever is lovely, whatever is admirable—if anything is excellent or praiseworthy—think about such things. (Philippians 4:8)

That is easier said than done these days, but that's what God commands. God tells us through Paul's pen to dwell on things *that are the opposite of what we see in our world,* and because Paul learned to do this, he was able to be *content in every situation,* whether he was in dire need or satisfied. *He knew that Jesus was all he needed.*

Paul's life inspires me to be a better Christ-follower, and his teachings have taught me ten things:

1. I must sing when I am in prison!
2. I must surrender everything to God and let Him do what only He can do!
3. I am hard-pressed, but not crushed!
4. I am perplexed, but not in despair!
5. When I am persecuted, God stands with me!
6. I am Christ's ambassador!
7. I must patiently endure suffering so that others can see God's power at work in me!
8. I should be marked by my love, mercy, and generosity!
9. I must remain true to Jesus whether I'm honored or despised!
10. I must always remember that when my heart aches, nothing can take away my joy!

I want to live the way You command me to live.

I don't want to just talk about trusting; I want to truly trust.

October 3. Day 252.

Jesus and the disciples are in a remote place with four thousand hungry people, and He wants to feed them. Even though the disciples have seen Him feed multiple thousands with a little boy's lunch, they have the audacity to wonder where in the middle of nowhere anyone would get enough bread to feed everyone! *Seriously, how could they ask that question?*

The same way we do.

How many times do we wonder when there's no need to wonder? How often do we let the magnitude of the situation push out the memory of God's faithfulness?

Despite their forgetfulness, Jesus holds up seven loaves of bread to His Father in heaven, and the twelve disciples plus the four thousand eat and digest the miraculous. As they climb into their boat at the end of the day, the disciples start bickering with each other because they realize the leftovers have been left on shore. Jesus tells them to watch out for the yeast of the Pharisees. They assume He's talking about the bread, until He looks at them and says,

> Why are you talking about not having any bread? Do you *still* not see or understand? Are you hearts *still* hardened? Do you have eyes that fail to see

and ears that fail to hear? *And don't you remember?* When I broke the loaves for the five thousand, how many basketfuls of pieces did you pick up? And when I broke the seven loaves for the four thousand, how many basketfuls did you pick up? Do you *still* not understand? (Mark 8:17–21, paraphrased)

His questions pierce my heart!

Sovereign God, I vow to remember how You have provided, intervened, and carried me in all my yesterdays. I will never forget how You have given me Your courage, strength, and grace to face each morning.

Give me eyes that see.

Give me ears that ear.

Soften my heart so that I will never doubt that You can do anything.

October 4. Day 253.

Sovereign God, I thank You for another day *to remember* Your faithfulness. I'm going out for lunch with a lady who needs You but can't wrap her mind around Your love. She can't believe that You know her and long for her to know You. Only You can help her understand. Help me to represent You well to my doubting friend.

Take me to my manna.

Jesus asks questions that force us to make a choice to believe or not to believe.

"Who do you *say that I am?"*

Our response to His commands determines our eternity.

For whoever wants to save his life will lose it, but whoever loses his life for Me and the gospel will save it. (Mark 8:29, 35)

Sovereign God, I offer myself to You as a living sacrifice.

Jesus, please be seen in me today.

My doubting friend's eternity depends on it.

October 5. Day 254.

I grieve every day for my sons. I wish more than anything that I could take away their pain and bring their dad back, but it's impossible for me to fix their broken hearts, and *that* pain is greater than my own.

Sovereign God, take me to my manna.

A distraught father brings his hurting son to Jesus. His boy is possessed by an evil spirit that has rendered him mute and thrown him into convulsions.

"How long has he been like this?" Jesus asks (Mark 9:21).

"He's been like this since childhood. It has often thrown him into fire or water to kill him. *If You can do anything . . . please take pity on us and help us*" (Mark 9:21–22).

"If you can?" says Jesus. *"Everything is possible for him who believes!"* (Mark 9:23).

The boy's father exclaims, "I do believe! Help me overcome my unbelief!" (Mark 9:24).

Immediately *Jesus does what* only *Jesus can do.* He commands the evil spirit to leave and sets the son free.

Jesus never disappoints. *It can look hopeless, but it's never hopeless. It can seem insurmountable, but it's never insurmountable.* Nothing is impossible. *Everything is possible for those who believe.* So like that dad, I come to You today, Jesus, and bring You my sons whose hearts have been crushed.

And I say to You, "I do believe. Help me to overcome my unbelief."

October 6. Day 255.

People were bringing their children to Jesus to have Him bless them. I am moved as I imagine moms making their way through the crowds, hoping to have a chance of putting their priceless treasure into the arms of this amazing Jesus. They somehow knew that *the blessing of Jesus was necessary.*

The disciples had a different opinion. They actually told these people to stop! Somehow they had forgotten that just a few days ago in Capernaum, Jesus had called a child out of the crowd and said that whoever welcomes a child in His name welcomes Him, and whoever welcomes Him, welcomes the One who sent Him (Mark 9:36–37). I'm thinking their memories were jogged when they saw the look on Jesus's face and heard the anger in His voice. Mark writes that Jesus was indignant. Yup, He was ticked, and everyone knew it.

> Let the little children come to Me and do not hinder them, for the Kingdom of God belongs to such as these! I tell you the truth; anyone who will not receive the Kingdom of God like a little child will never enter it! (Mark 10:14–15)

As the disciples sheepishly stepped out of the way, one child after another was placed in the arms of Jesus, and He blessed them. It's comforting to know that I can bring my sons to Jesus and place them in those same strong arms and know that He will hold them and bless them.

The wonderful truth is that *Jesus loves to bless all of us.*

He loves to clear a path and draw us into an embrace that is like no other. *Jesus, I run to You today for a blessing.*

October 7. Day 256.

At this the man's face fell. He went away sad, because he had great wealth. (Mark 10:22)

This man's story begins with so much promise. The rich young ruler runs to Jesus and falls on his knees in front of Him and asks, "What must I do to inherit eternal life?" (Mark 10:17). The man tells Jesus that he has kept all the commandments since he was a boy. Mark writes that *Jesus looked at him and loved him.* No judgment. Just love. Then He spoke the words that would assure him eternity in heaven, "There's just one thing you lack. Go and sell everything you have and give to the poor and you will have treasure in heaven. Then, come and follow Me!" (Mark 10:21).

The young man refused Jesus's invite and walked away sad because he knew that he had just chosen money over eternity with God. Jesus lets him go and then tells His disciples that it's easier for a camel to go through the eye of a needle than for a rich man to enter the Kingdom of God. The disciples wonder if it's possible for anyone to be saved, and Jesus concedes that with men, it is indeed *impossible,* but with God, *all things are possible!* (Mark 10:25–27).

No one ever needs to turn down an invite from Jesus. He extends it with a look of love that assures us that if we choose to follow Him, *we will lack nothing.*

I see that look of love today, Jesus.

I am not going to walk away sad.

I am going to follow You all the way to heaven.

October 8. Day 257.

Jesus says:

> Mark My words, no one who sacrifices house, brothers, sisters, mother, father, children, land—whatever—because of Me and the Message, will lose out! They'll get it all back, but multiplied many times over, along with troubles and the bonus of eternal life! (Mark 10:29-30, *The Message*)

I have to remember this all day long.

There is nothing too precious to give up for Jesus. Nothing, especially when you look at what awaits those who have said yes to His call. I am living proof of how He provides not only material blessings, but family, no matter where you are in the world. He surrounds His followers with all they need. He's totally trustworthy even when the troubles come.

If *Jesus* says, "Mark My words," how can I not believe Him?

October 9. Day 258.

My brother asked me if I could please fly my boys to Philadelphia for a visit while he could still eat and throw a good party. He has a bone marrow transplant scheduled for October 18, which will be followed by three weeks of complete isolation. He's lost a massive amount of weight and is terribly weak, but this weekend my brother is happy. He has his only two nephews around his table.

I called a few moments ago and could hear my boys laughing in the background. Dwight thanked me for making this possible and told me he wished I could have come as well. He is celebrating life and hope! Today, on the other side of the ocean, I celebrate with him and toast to the joy that is deep in our souls no matter what is looming ahead.

Take me to my manna.

Bartimaeus was a blind beggar who screamed for mercy until Jesus heard him. When Jesus told him to come, he threw off his coat and ran toward the sound of His voice, and within seconds he could see (Mark 10:46–52).

The way Bartimaeus responded to Jesus reminds me of what Paul wrote in Hebrews 12:1–2:

Since we are surrounded by such a great cloud of witnesses let us throw off everything that hinders and the sin that so easily entangles and let us run with perseverance the race marked out for us! Let us fix our eyes on Jesus, the author and finisher of our faith!

Bartimaeus's response to the call of Jesus was as immediate as his healing! Bartimaeus threw his coat aside so he could get there as fast as possible, and when he could see, *he never let Jesus out of his sight!*

I want my faith to be determined and my response to be immediate.

I want my gaze to be fixed on the One who gave me sight to see what is invisible.

October 10. Day 259.

I wish I could call heaven. The transition from talking about everything to not being able to talk about anything is awful. Take me to my manna.

Mark writes that as Jesus rode into Jerusalem on a donkey, the crowds covered the road with their coats and branches. I bet you Bartimaeus was the first one to rip his coat off and laid it on the road. I'm also sure he was there when Jesus flipped over tables, reclaiming the temple as a house of prayer. He also would have seen the consequences of the fig tree that bore no fruit. In just three short days, Bartimaeus saw with his new eyes *the majesty, authority, and power of Jesus!*

Following Jesus is never boring.

I need to focus on Jesus more than my grief.

I know that as I do, I will be wowed by what I see!

October 11. Day 260.

Today is the Chung Yeung Festival. Families sweep the graves of their loved ones, then lay out food offerings for the dead to consume. So today is a public holiday, but the thoughts of relaxing scare me. Our definition of a perfect day off was going out for a feast of Thai food, coming home to watch a few episodes of our favorite television shows, and then having a date. If willing something into existence made things happen, I'd be in Jim's arms right now.

Holy Spirit, I need You. Please take me to that place of abundance so I remember how blessed I am.

Love the Lord your God will all your heart, mind, soul and strength
and love your neighbor as you love yourself. (Mark 12:30)

If I'm loving God and my neighbor the way He commands, then I will
be thinking more about how to showcase the love of Jesus to everyone around
me—who think that their dead relatives are actually going to benefit from the
roasted pig they will leave at their graves today—than about making love to
my husband.

Cleanse me, Jesus.

*Forgive me for being so full of myself when so many in my world need to
know You.*

October 12. Day 261.

Dwight has spiked a fever and is in the hospital. Both boys called to tell
me they were sure last weekend was the last time they'd ever see Dwight on
this earth. The doctors are saying that he's too weak to survive a bone marrow
transplant. My heart is just so sad. I don't know how I'll comfort my parents
if Dwight goes to heaven.

Before I finished that last sentence, Jesus had already given me the answer:
you comfort with the comfort you've been comforted with.

As long as I have arms, I can hug, and as long as I have breath, I can pray.
Everything here, good and bad, is all temporary, and remembering that helps
put death into perspective. To die is gain when you know Jesus. To live here
on earth without the people you love is agony, *but it's doable* when you know
there is a glorious end to the story.

Jesus says:

When you hear of wars and rumors of war, do not be alarmed. Such
things *must* happen, but the end is still to come. Nation will rise against nation.
Kingdom will rise against kingdom. There will be earthquakes and famines in
various places. These are the beginning of birth pains. (Mark 13:7–8)

Our world is in labor, which means the coming of Jesus is certain, and
when He comes there will be no more fevers, or lurking death, or having to be
comforted anymore.

October 13. Day 262.

I don't know when Jesus is coming, but I know that whenever the angel finally blows that trumpet, I will be ready! Whether I rise up from a grave that holds my ashes or I'm alive and looking at the sky, I *will* see Jesus, and He *will* take me home.

Jesus tells the disciples that while they wait for His return, they should expect to be flogged in the synagogues, but persecution will bring them before governors and kings so they can proclaim the gospel; to expect to be arrested and brought to trial, *but the Holy Spirit will fill their mouths;* to expect to face betrayal from those closest to them and be hated by many, *but if they stand firm to the end, they will be saved.*

Comparing these coming trials to birth pains was a perfect analogy because anyone who has given birth knows three things: it hurts like nothing else; you want it to be over *now;* and when it is, *the reward you hold in your hand makes all the pain worthwhile.*

I know how tempting it is, when faced with suffering, to crawl into the pit of despair and believe the lie that we've been forsaken instead of remembering that God uses suffering to advance the gospel. Our *only* defense is for the soon return of Jesus to be at the forefront of our minds.

There will be times when we think we can't endure for another second—and there will always be an Enemy who tells us to curse God and be done with it—but that shouldn't be a surprise if we've read the words of Jesus. *Suffering is a sure thing, but so is the crown we will receive because we've endured.* And even more precious than that is that Jesus will acknowledge us before His Father and call us faithful.

I don't know about you, but that gives me the courage I need to keep looking at the sky!

October 14. Day 263.

Dwight's cancer has spread to his lungs. *Sovereign God, I give my brother to You. Make his heart brave. Give him a glimpse of what awaits. Hold everyone close, and steady them with Your grace.*

I need courage to face what's coming. I assumed Jim would be with me when we buried Dwight. Together we would try to comfort my parents. Down the road he would stand with me when we buried our parents, and then, in my perfect world, we would die at the same time so that neither of us would ever have to exist alone.

But here I am.

Take me to my manna.

Jesus says we need to be *alert and on guard* for His return.

> You do not know when that time will come . . . *therefore keep watch* . . . If He comes suddenly, do not let Him find you sleeping. (Mark 13:35–36, paraphrased)

Again I'm reminded that this is no time for self-pity or questions.

It is a time for obedience and alertness.

Sovereign God, when my eyes get heavy, nudge me back to alertness.

Jesus, I stand on guard for You.

October 15. Day 264.

Three out of the four gospels write about how Mary broke open the alabaster jar full of nard and poured it on Jesus's head and feet, but Mark includes one sentence that the other two do not: "She did what she could" (Mark 14:8).

Mary had likely been saving that expensive perfume for her wedding night, but God had a purpose for Mary's treasure, and it wasn't for her; *it was for Jesus.* Throwing culture and reputation to the wind, she interrupted dinner and did the unforgettable. She poured her nard over Jesus, and although others judged her, Jesus was impressed and said she'd done a beautiful thing. Mary is the perfect picture of what it looks like to be completely devoted to Jesus.

We need to be willing to do what no one else understands, knowing that when we do, He thinks it's beautiful.

October 16. Day 265.

> My soul is overwhelmed with sorrow to the point of death . . . Abba, Father, everything is possible for You. *Take this cup from Me.* Yet, not what I will, but what You will, be done. (Mark 14:34–36)

Jesus understands the conflict of choosing to embrace pain for the greater good.

After Jesus is arrested, the disciples go into hiding and Jesus finds Himself alone in front of the high priest.

"Are you the Christ, the Son of the Blessed One?"

"I am. And you will see the Son of Man sitting at the right hand of the Mighty One and coming on the clouds of heaven!" says Jesus (Mark 14:61–62).

Wow! I don't think Jesus is speaking to the high priest only here. He is reminding His soul that death will not be permanent; that part of God's plan is to resurrect Him and place Him at God's right hand where He will stay forever! He showed us exactly what to do when faced with hardship. We too are to remind our souls the end of the story!

Sovereign God, I want only what You want.

October 17. Day 266.

I couldn't deny God's nearness yesterday even if I tried; it was tangible. But a new day has come, and I need You again. Take me to my manna.

I held God's Word in my hands but didn't open it.

He enveloped me in His presence.

Waves of mercy swept over my soul.

I lifted my voice and cried, "Worthy is the Lamb!"

I declared it was well with my soul, and I realized that *He is my manna and all I will ever need.*

October 18. Day 267.

Proverbs 17:22 says, "A merry heart is good medicine, but a crushed spirit dries up the bones." If I think about how Jesus will one day crack the sky, call me by name, and take me to heaven, *how can I not have a merry heart?* Once again, the seemingly impossible becomes possible!

Take me to my manna.

The depth of physical and emotional agony Jesus felt in His final hours is unspeakable. *He was mocked, punched, spit on, insulted, stripped naked, and crucified.* The crowds that had cheered His arrival into Jerusalem were long gone. Only a few of His followers dared to be near the cross.

Jesus knows what alone feels like.

He cried out from the cross, "My God, My God, why have You forsaken Me?" (Mark 15:34).

We truly have a sympathetic Savior.

After all Jesus has done for me, I would be an ignoramus to walk around with a frown, so with a merry heart and a smile on my face, I walk into another day.

October 19. Day 268.

I invited a few friends over last night to watch a powerful story about Jim Elliot and his four companions, who were martyred for their faith in Ecuador in the 1950s. They felt a strong call to introduce Jesus to the Waodani Indians, but before they had a chance, they were speared to death. Jim's widow made a comment at the end of the movie that I'm still thinking about this morning: "The men were successful. They were obedient."

What happens as a result of our obedience is not as important as our obedience.

Before John the Baptist was born, God sent an angel to his father to tell him that John would grow up and prepare the way for Jesus. John did exactly what he was created to do. He preached repentance and introduced Jesus to the world, *but he was beheaded without hearing Jesus speak or seeing Him do one miracle.*

John the Baptist obeyed. John was successful.

God has a sovereign plan for everyone, but not all of His plans make sense, at least to us. When I was born, God knew exactly what I would be doing today. It was His idea to create me, not my parents'. My mother's womb housed me, but God Himself knit me together for His purposes.

I was made to obey Him.

I was made to be Jesus to a messed-up world.

Sovereign God, help me to remember this truth when my grief makes me question what use I could ever be.

October 20. Day 269.

I love You, Jesus. When I think about You, all worries vanish. Take me to my manna.

When the angel told an aging Zechariah that he and his barren wife were going to be parents, he asked how he could be sure this was actually going to happen. *He wanted proof.* The angel declared him mute until John was born.

When the angel appeared to a young teenager called Mary, and told her that she had been chosen to house Jesus, the promised Messiah in her womb, she asked, "How will this happen, since I'm a virgin?" *She wanted details.* The angel told her the plan.

> "I am the Lord's servant," Mary answered, "May it be unto me as you have said!" (Luke 1:38)

And there it is *again . . . obedience.*
God wants us to believe what He says.
I want to be like Mary. When I'm presented with the impossible, I want to say with anticipation, *"How will this be? Give me the details! I am the Lord's servant. May it be unto me as you have said!"*

October 21. Day 270.

> Blessed is she *who has believed* that what the Lord has said to her *will be accomplished!* (Luke 1:45)

Elizabeth spoke these words to her cousin Mary, but I receive them into my own heart today. The Lord has said that *He has a plan for my aloneness and a purpose for my sorrow.* The Lord has said that because of Jim's death, many will come to know Him.
The Lord has said this, and therefore it will be accomplished!
I believe it! I believe that You will surround me again on this new day of this predetermined path. I believe that You are my companion on this journey that was chosen for me before time began.
I am blessed.

October 22. Day 271.

Mary is a pregnant, unmarried teenager who could be fretting over the ramifications of God's plan, but instead she is full of thanksgiving that God picked her to house His Son. She is so happy that she writes a song!

> My soul glorifies the Lord and my spirit rejoices in God my Savior, for He has been mindful of the humble state of His servant. From now on all generations will call me blessed, for the Mighty One has done great things for me—Holy is His name! His mercy extends to those who fear Him, from generation to generation. (Luke 1:46–50)

My soul glorifies the Lord, and my spirit rejoices in God my Savior, for He has been mindful of the humble state of His servant.

My grandchildren will know that their Nanny is friends with God, who still does the impossible!

October 23. Day 272.

Today is our secret anniversary of when Jesus gloriously intruded into our lives. He spoke the same words to each of our hearts, even though Jim was out of town at a conference and I was at home with our boys.

You need to start obeying Me in every little thing, or you'll be on your own.

When Jim came home, we stayed up all night talking and repenting. When the sun rose, we were different.

Our marriage changed. Our home changed. Our church changed. Our lives were turned inside out. Homeless strangers started showing up at our door, and we let them in. We became a family to women who were recovering from drug addiction. October 23, 1987, is the day our adventure with Jesus truly began. So when this day came around every year, we celebrated God's grace in our lives.

I knew today would be tough, so I invited the ministry team from my church—all twenty-five of them—over for dinner tonight. I'm roasting a humongous turkey and a ham with all the trimmings, and in my heart I will be commemorating this special day, thanking my Sovereign God for His mercy, His power, and His willingness to transform us into something He could use.

Thank you, Jimbies, for obeying Jesus in every little thing.

I am celebrating God's grace today, but in a brand-new way. Eight long months ago on January 25, Jesus intruded into our lives one more time. He took you home and placed me on a path that was always meant to be. The second you left, God's grace overwhelmed my soul and filled me with the perseverance of Jesus so that in His strength I could make Him famous on this journey.

Happy secret anniversary.

I stand at the throne of grace this morning, saying thank you to Jesus, and I know you're there too.

October 24. Day 273.

We had ourselves a party! As everyone feasted, my heart was privately celebrating God's glorious intrusion, but this morning the party in my heart is a distant memory. I've lost my joy.

Take me to my manna.

The angel Gabriel has a great job. First he's dispatched to Zechariah to announce the supernatural birth of John; then he is sent to Mary to tell her that Jesus will be housed in her womb; and after Mary gives birth, he is commissioned to go to a hillside to a group of unsuspecting shepherds to tell them their long-awaited Messiah has finally arrived, *in a manger!* (Luke 2:11–12).

I love how the shepherds respond: "Let's go to Bethlehem and see this thing that has happened" (Luke 2:15).

They *don't* say, "Let's go and see *if* it's true"; they say, "Let's go and see," and then they hurry off, find Jesus, and run out to tell *everyone they meet!*

Oh! I want my heart to be just like theirs! *I want to tell people what I've seen and heard! I want to tell them who He is and how they can find Him!*

The joy's back!

On this new day, I say . . . "Let's go!"

October 25. Day 274.

As I read Simeon's story in Luke's Gospel, three things impress me:

1. *He was waiting expectantly* for the comfort the promised Messiah would bring. (Luke 2:25)
2. *He was friends with the Holy Spirit.* The Holy Spirit revealed to him that he wouldn't die until he had seen the Anointed One. (Luke 2:25b–26)
3. *He was led by the Holy Spirit.* The Holy Spirit moved him to go to the temple courts. (Luke 2:27)

It was in those temple courts that Simeon saw Jesus nestled in Mary's arms and immediately knew He was the Christ. Simeon held the promised Messiah and praised God for keeping His word.

I want to live like Simeon. Completely devoted to God, waiting expectantly to lay eyes on Jesus, and guided by the Holy Spirit until that moment comes. Just like Simeon, the longing in my heart will be met, but instead of me holding Jesus, *He'll hold me.*

October 26. Day 275.

> Oh say but I'm glad, I'm glad!
> Oh say but I'm glad, I'm glad!
> Jesus has come and my cup's overrun!
> Oh say but I'm glad!
> (James P. Sullivan, 1930)

What was once a whimsical tune from my childhood is now my life. This journey has taught me that because of Jesus, a broken heart can still be glad. *He has turned my mourning into dancing, not by giving me back what I had, but by giving me more of Himself.*

Take me to my manna.

Simeon wasn't the only one waiting for Jesus in the temple. Anna, a prophetess and a widow, had lived in the temple for sixty years fasting and praying her way through decades of aloneness. When she saw Simeon holding Jesus, she too instantly knew that his arms held her Redeemer. She walked over to where they were standing and thanked God that her eyes had beheld the Messiah.

Anna was a young widow *who grew old worshiping God instead of questioning His ways.* She refused despair and waited expectantly for her Savior. Luke doesn't describe Anna's appearance, but I'm guessing she was always smiling and maybe even singing.

I choose to be like Anna.

October 27. Day 276.

An unexpected visitor showed up at my door yesterday wanting to talk. She's nineteen and struggles to walk because her one leg is much shorter than the other. This week she was traded in by her boyfriend for someone else, which left her feeling that life wasn't worth living. With a numbness in her voice, she told me how she can no longer stand the loneliness.

I was so honored to be the one to tell her all about my Jesus! My pain has become a gift, for it has pushed me into His arms. *It is there that I have found comfort, purpose, and peace, which I can now share with new friends who show up at my door desperate for an answer.*

Take me to my manna . . .

John, the miracle son of Zechariah and Elizabeth, grows up and moves to the desert where God tells him to go and preach repentance and forgiveness throughout the country (Luke 3:3–6). John's message is as relevant today as it was then. *Repentance always prepares the way for Jesus to come, and we are all sinners needing to repent.*

Jesus is God's mercy in the flesh.

Mercy puts us on level ground.

I pray that my new friend will have courage to believe, though she does not see. I pray that she will revel in the mercy of Jesus because she is the reason He came.

October 28. Day 277.

There's a home prepared where the saints abide, just over in the glory land!

And I long to be by my Savior's side, just over in the glory land! (James W. Acuff, 1906)

By and by when the morning comes
When all the saints of God are gathered home,
We'll tell the story of how we've overcome,
For we'll understand it better by and by!
(Charles Albert Tinley, 1906)

Those "lookin' at the sky" words that were penned more than a century ago have turned this girl's eyes to the sky and her thoughts toward that celebration of all celebrations! There can't be anything better to wake up to than these reminders of what's promised. Thank you, Brooklyn Tabernacle Choir!

Sixteen years ago today, our little family of four stepped off a plane with eight suitcases and Jim's guitar. We had no idea where we were going to live or exactly what we would be doing. We were picked up by a representative of the organization that had invited us to come and driven to a small apartment occupied by another family. We were given one bedroom and instructions not to eat anything in the fridge.

It wasn't quite the welcome we expected, but it was okay because it threw us into a place where we had to trust God completely. Within forty-eight hours, He had led us to a fully furnished apartment. We unpacked our suitcases, put up our pictures, and the rest is history. *The same God who has ordered our steps here on earth has promised us an eternity in heaven.* How can I not shout and sing?

> When we all get to heaven what a day of rejoicing that will be . . .
> When we all see Jesus, we'll sing and shout the victory!
> (Eliza E Hewitt, 1898)

But until I'm there, I must "produce fruit in keeping with repentance!" (Luke 3:8). The crowd asks John the Baptist how to do that, so he tells them that those with two tunics should share with those who have none, and those with food should do the same. He turns to the tax collectors and tells them that they should only collect what's owed, and he admonishes the soldiers to be honest and content with the salary they're receiving.

Sovereign God, You woke me up with songs about heaven, but You have reminded me that the way I live here on earth needs to honor the mercy and grace You've extended to me.

October 29. Day 278.

A year before Jim went to heaven, we took out a small life insurance policy as a favor to a friend. The insurance company called me yesterday to tell me that the investigation into Jim's sudden death has been completed and that my cheque is ready to pick up. I stood in front of Jim's photo and told him I'd rather have him than the money. *How can this all be real?*

Lifting my widowhood and loneliness to God is a willful, determined choice every moment. It's a good thing that His strength is constant, or else I'd still be on my hands and knees in the ER. Take me to my manna.

The Holy Spirit led Jesus into the desert where He withstood relentless temptation from Satan. His defense was God's Word (Luke 4:1–13).

I find myself in a wilderness these days, and the same Enemy who tempted Jesus tempts me. He taunts me by trying to get me to believe I am alone. He whispers in my ear that I should curse the God who took my husband from me.

Jesus has shown me how to fight against these lies, so the ball is in my court. I can follow His example or let the Enemy destroy me.

I choose to fight.

October 30. Day 279.

I've had another houseguest for a few days. She's been teaching in China, and like the backpacker who bunked in with me a few weeks back, she too is on a journey of faith. As she's travelled Asia she's come to know a lot of wonderful people, and she wonders how God could condemn her new friends to eternal damnation when their faith is just misguided. How do we know that Jesus was the final sacrifice for our sins? Is it not arrogant to think that we have the only answer? There are other religions that demand devotion and have martyrs to prove it. *What makes us different?* Those are the questions we've been talking about all weekend, and my answers always go back to Jesus and the personal relationship I have with Him.

Jesus understands my weaknesses and temptations because although He is God, *He became one of us!* He became flesh and blood, lived here on earth, and *learned obedience,* which took Him to a cross where He became sin for us so that we could be forgiven. His dead body was resurrected, and He now sits at the right hand of God, praying for us as we journey to heaven.

I don't have a religion, I have a best friend.

Take me to my manna.

Jesus walked into the synagogue, unrolled the scroll, and began to read words written by Isaiah:

> "The Spirit of the Lord is on me because he has anointed me to preach good news to the poor. He has sent me to proclaim freedom for the prisoners and recovery of sight to the blind, to release the oppressed and to proclaim the year of the Lord!" As Jesus rolled up the scroll He announced, *"Today, this scripture is fulfilled, in your hearing."*

On the day Jesus read those words, His listeners mistook His divine authority for eloquence, because to them, He was just the son of a carpenter.

Jesus called them on their attitude so they went from being amazed to being irate and driving Him out of town! (Luke 4:18–30).

Jesus, I know who You are.

I long for everyone in my tiny world to know You like I do.

I want them to know that You're not a religion; You are their Savior and very best friend.

October 31. Day 280.

One year ago tonight, we lit our candles, enjoyed a nice dinner, danced in our living room, and then made love. We fell asleep holding each other until we were awakened by the doorbell. It wasn't until we opened the door that we remembered it was Halloween. We chose to have a pretty amazing love life. We couldn't imagine anything better than what we had. That's why it hurts so badly now.

Jesus, I run to You.

What Jesus couldn't do in Galilee, He did in Capernaum. While He was speaking in the synagogue, a man possessed by an evil spirit called Jesus by name and demanded to know what He wanted. Jesus silenced the spirit and cast it out of the man, and within no time, *the whole region was talking about it.*

When Jesus speaks, things change.

The tormented are set free and hope is restored.

Speak to me, Jesus.

And speak *through me* as I spend time with a friend who doesn't know You.

Silence the Enemy.

Give this city something to talk about.

November 1. Day 281.

I lift my aloneness to You. I send self-pity to hell and purpose in my heart to submit to Your will. Take me to my manna.

When Jesus told Peter and his gang to cast their nets out into the water, Peter told Him they'd been fishing all night and hadn't caught one single fish. With resignation in his voice he said, "But *because You say so* I will let down the nets" (Luke 5:5).

Jesus asked Peter to do something he'd already tried and failed to do. In the natural it seemed not only impossible, but a waste of time. However, Peter was beginning to understand that if *Jesus said something, it would be,* so he did *exactly* what Jesus asked him to do. There were so many fish they had to ask their friends in a nearby boat to help them. Soon both boats were sinking and caught up in the miraculous!

It's so important to do whatever Jesus says, because our obedience has a domino effect on everyone around us.

I don't know how I am going to grow old without Jim.

I have no idea how You are going to bring beauty of these ashes, *but because You say so,* I will keep looking at the sky so that others will look there too.

November 2. Day 282.

I got an advert in the mail from the Burlington Memorial Cemetery with an order form to buy a Christmas wreath for Jim's grave. *I just want it all to stop.* I still sit watching the door, listening for his familiar whistle and expecting him to come walking in.

Soul, *this temporary separation will feel like seconds in the light of eternity!*

Holy Spirit, take me to my manna.

"I am willing. Be clean," says Jesus, and *immediately* the leprosy left (Luke 5:13).

"Friend, your sins are forgiven," says Jesus, and *immediately* the man who had been lame stood up and walked home (Luke 5:20, 25).

I like the word *immediately.*

Jesus, I give You my loneliness and pain, one more time.

My sorrow has been exchanged for a remarkable joy that does not depend on how I feel.

I pray that the joy of Your salvation will be evident on my face as I walk through Day 282 in Your strength.

November 3. Day 283.

My favorite choir is singing, I'm sipping a cup of milky cinnamon tea, and I am taking in the sunrise. A beam of light just pushed through the darkness, transforming the expanse into a palette of blues, reds, and oranges with scattered puffs of white. *I'm stunned at the beauty one shaft of light can bring.* Take me to my manna.

I really don't like the Pharisees. They were always looking for a reason to accuse Jesus, so they watched Him like a hawk, but their anger and arrogance kept them blind to His true identity (Luke 5:29–33). Jesus was unfazed and kept doing whatever His Father told Him to do, becoming increasingly famous for His compassion and mercy.

I want to be like You, Jesus.

I want Your compassion and mercy to be what I'm known for.

I want my love to be like Yours—lavish and unforgettable.

Thank You for the object lesson in the sky this morning, illustrating how You take great delight in breaking through the darkness. You are the light of the world, and You reside in me! Shine through me today and bring jaw-dropping beauty to the darkness around me.

November 4. Day 284.

It's Eid today in the Muslim world. This is the day when Ramadan is over and God's provision of a ram for Abraham is remembered. So today I will celebrate Eid and feast with my friends. I will be thanking my God for the example of obedience that Abraham left us and for His provisions, *especially my Jesus.*

I just got a call from my parents. Dwight is in the intensive care unit. He is bleeding from his nose and ears. His voice is barely audible. I want him to be released from his pain. *Holy Spirit, please hover over that room and infuse both Dwight and Sheri with comfort and courage. Bolster my parents' hearts as they face the inevitable. I am counting on Your provisions as we face this oncoming sorrow.* Take me to my manna . . .

Jesus says in Luke 6:21, "Blessed are you who weep now, for you will laugh."

Thank You, my Sovereign, for this morsel of manna. *That's all I needed.*

November 5. Day 285.

Before my Eid celebrations, I taught four classes. In between those classes, two separate teachers took me aside and poured out their heartbreak. What an honor to be able to tell them about Jesus and the promise of laughter that is ahead for those who believe! Take me to my manna.

There was a story in the news about a group in the United States that is trying to make it illegal to talk about Jesus on radio or television. Christian organizations are asking believers across the world to sign petitions to fight for their rights. *Jesus says to expect persecution. Jesus says to bless those who curse us and pray for those who mistreat us. Jesus says that we are to be merciful just as our Father God is merciful* (Luke 6:22–42). Jesus says nothing about protests and petitions; in fact, the only time Jesus got angry was when He was dealing with the religious, judgmental crowd.

I think the best sermon ever preached was the way Jesus lived His life.

I so want my life to be like that.

I don't want to waste my energies on fighting against what Jesus said was sure to come. *All I want to do is make Him famous to the hopeless.*

November 6. Day 286.

Jesus says:

> Why are you so polite with Me, always saying "Yes, sir," but never doing a thing I tell you? These words I speak to you are not mere additions to your life. They are *foundation words,* words to build a life on. *If you work the words into your life,* you are like a smart carpenter who dug deep and laid the foundation of his house on bedrock. When the river burst its banks and crushed against the house, nothing could shake it; it was built to last. But if you just use My words in Bible studies and don't work them into your life, you are like a dumb carpenter who built a house but skipped the foundation. When the swollen river came crashing in, it collapsed like a house of cards. It was a total loss. (Luke 6:46–49, *The Message*)

Jesus, I never want to be guilty of knowing what You want me to do and not doing it. I am so thankful for the principles You have shown me on this journey. For 285 days, the floods have risen and the torrents have slammed against me, threatening to reduce my faith to a pile of rubble.

You are the firm foundation that has kept me standing.

I will keep working Your words into my life!

November 7. Day 287.

On my fortieth birthday, Jim and I climbed an escarpment that juts out of the landscape in the New Territories in Hong Kong. When we reached the summit, we sat on a big boulder looking out over our beloved city and talked about the plans we thought God was unfolding. Oh, how different those plans turned out to be.

Yesterday I was there again with some friends and felt deep sorrow that my future will only have memories of our past. My loneliness got the better of me, so I came home, put my pajamas on, and tried to push away the pain by watching some television. Sitting there alone just made it worse because all I could think about was how we used to watch our favorite shows while eating dark chocolate and drinking Coke. I should have stayed with my friends and chosen to work His words into my life.

Forgive me, Jesus. I'm thankful for a new day.

Take me to my manna.

There is a story in Luke's writings about a Roman centurion who sent for Jesus because his servant was dying. As Jesus was approaching the house, the centurion sent friends out to Jesus to tell Him He didn't need to come to his house. He knew that all that was necessary was for Him to just say the word, and his servant would be healed. The friends explained that the centurion too was a man of authority who knew that when he told his men to do something, they would do it. When Jesus heard this, *He was amazed* and said that He had never seen such faith (Luke 7:1–10).

I had the centurion's kind of faith the morning Jim died. I remember saying that exact phrase: "Just say the word . . . and I know Jim will be healed!" There wasn't an ounce of doubt in my heart, but unlike the centurion, I *didn't* get what I asked for. He went home and found his servant healed. I went home to an empty house and chose not to be offended by God's ways.

Luke also writes about a widow from Nain who was burying her only son. When Jesus saw her tears He was deeply moved, so He stopped the procession, touched the coffin, and raised the boy from the dead and presented him to his mom (Luke 7:11–17).

I know that Jesus saw my tears on the morning Jim died. I'm certain He could have stopped the horror and given me back my husband, but instead, *He gave me courage to embrace His sovereignty.* With that acceptance came an unexplainable peace and an undeniable strength to walk this road trusting Him with all the uncertainties ahead.

I believe that my sorrow will not be wasted, so I choose to look at the sky rather than shake my fist at it.

I want to amaze Jesus.

November 8. Day 288.

Luke tells a beautiful story about a prostitute who walks into Simon's house and anoints Jesus with her perfume. Perhaps Simon had hired for her services in the past, which would explain why he was so indignant that Jesus was not sending her away as she knelt weeping at His feet. She removed her scarf, allowing her long hair to tumble out, and then, using her hair as a towel, she wiped the feet of Jesus dry. She kissed His feet and then, as one final act of lavish love, she drenched them with perfume (Luke 7:36–38).

Jesus explained that "he, who has been forgiven little, loves little, but he who has been forgiven much, loves much" (Luke 7:47). This woman entered Simon's home broken, wounded, and trapped in her sin, but she left whole, healed, and completely forgiven, *all because of Jesus.*

Jesus, I love Your mercy.

I love You.

November 9. Day 289.

The doctors let Dwight go home on the condition that someone brings him daily to the hospital for blood and platelet transfusions. He's disoriented and needs constant care, but I've been calling every day, and he still knows who I am. Our conversations are short. He continues to fight to live, and as long as he believes for God to intervene, so will I.

Take me to my manna.

> No one lights a lamp and hides it in a jar or puts it under a bed. Instead, he puts it on a stand so that those who come in can see the light. (Luke 8:16)

Jesus, I love to put You on display. When people ask me how I can be happy when so much is going wrong, I love telling them that it's all because of You. Shine brightly in me as You enable me to live out another day for Your glory!

10:30 p.m.

Dwight has been taken by ambulance back to the hospital. He's having difficulty breathing, his lower limbs have swelled, and he's bleeding again from his nose and mouth. A healthy platelet count ranges from 150,000–450,000. Dwight's platelet count is 5. I asked to speak to him, but Sheri said he was too weak to talk.

Exactly one year ago, I was in this same place. I was sure Dwight was going to die. Jim held me for a very long time. Within a few days, Dwight had once again defied death. My heart is so lonely for Jim's arms tonight. I've had to learn how to do many things by myself these past 289 days, but comforting my parents when Dwight goes to heaven will be the hardest thing yet.

Jesus, help me.

November 10. Day 290.

This morning's song tells how God is here to heal the hopeless heart and bless the broken. There couldn't be anything more true or more needed for my heart to be reminded of:

> He is here to bear my burdens.
> He knows what I'm going through and what is still ahead.
> He promises me joy even in sorrow and assures me that the best is
> yet to come!

Martha Munizzi had no idea when she recorded this CD that it would become a soundtrack for my path of aloneness. I'll likely never have the opportunity to thank her for her songs here on earth, but I will for sure find her in heaven!

Jesus, You are speaking loudly to me today!

You are here, so there is absolutely nothing to be afraid of, not even another good-bye.

November 11. Day 291.

My Brooklyn Tabernacle Choir started the day right by belting out another song about heaven, reminding me that on that day, we will rise and turn our eyes to the Lord Jesus Christ!

Holy Spirit, put this hope in Dwight's heart this morning! The doctors have said the cancer has invaded his body and that there is nothing more they can do. They have him sedated to make him comfortable. *Fortify Sheri's heart, and prepare her for the path she is about to embark upon. Hold my parents in your arms, and fill their minds with thoughts of heaven. Be their glory and the lifter of their heads.*

Take me to my manna.

While we are waiting for heaven, Jesus equips us to do His work here on earth. In Luke 9, Jesus calls the twelve together and gives them power and authority to go out and preach about the kingdom of God, to cast out evil spirits and heal diseases.

Use me, Jesus.

Equip me to do Your work.

Send me to those who have yet to hear so that everyone can come to know The Hope who anchors my soul.

November 12. Day 292.

As I read about how Jesus fed five thousand men, their wives, and all their children (Luke 9:10-17), the Holy Spirit impressed three things on my heart:

1. Jesus is always available. No matter how He felt, He welcomed the crowds, spoke to them about the kingdom of God, and healed all those who needed healing. He never forgot why He was here. *Jesus lived for interruptions.*

2. Jesus loves to provide. He could have sent the crowds away to the surrounding villages to find food, but He insisted on feeding them. *Jesus loves to look after us.*

3. Jesus makes much out of our little. When that mother packed her little guy's lunch that day, she had no idea what Jesus would do with it! When we place whatever we have in His hands, *He does the miraculous.*

I'm so thankful that Jesus is always available, that He loves to provide, and that he is willing to take my nothing and make it His something.

November 13. Day 293.

Jesus says those who follow Him *must* deny themselves; they *must* daily take up their cross; and they *must* lose their life to save it. He also says that if we're ashamed of Him and His words, He'll be ashamed of us when He comes (Luke 9:21–27).

I can't bear the thought of Jesus being ashamed of me! When I imagine seeing Jesus for the first time, He hugs me, tells me that He's seen my perseverance, then smiles and says, *"Susan, your faith has amazed Me!"*

On this new day, I am more determined than ever to die so that He can live. I *must,* or this journey will all be for nothing.

November 14. Day 294.

My dad just called, and Dwight is at the end of his journey. He's unresponsive. I want to be there so badly. I need to say good-bye. We spoke about hope in our last conversation. I want to talk to my brother one more time. There are things I need to say. *Holy Spirit, fill Dwight's hospital room with courage and comfort. Plant Your hope in everyone's hearts.*

Hold Sheri. Hold my parents. Hold me.

I feel so alone on this side of the ocean.

Give our family the grace to endure another loss . . .

November 15. Day 295.

My trust is in You because You have never failed me yet.

I am leaning on Your throne because it is unmoveable.

You are my hiding place because my soul is restless anywhere else.

Dwight is still with us, but Dad says his breathing is becoming shallower. The doctor predicts one or two more days. He says the end is near, but really, he couldn't be more wrong. *For those of us who follow Jesus, death is just the beginning of eternity with Him.*

I asked my dad to tell Dwight I love him and that what awaits him is going to be incredible. I asked him to find Jim and tell him I am okay because of Jesus. Dad promised he would whisper my message in Dwight's ear. Sheri told me to book a flight as soon as possible, so I'm flying to Philadelphia tomorrow. It would be a gift to arrive before he goes to heaven. I pray that Dwight's heart will be infused with an expectation and perfect peace.

I desperately need my manna.

In Luke 9:51, Jesus is teaching His disciples about dying.

> As the time approached for Him to be taken up to heaven . . . Jesus
> *resolutely* set out . . . for Jerusalem.

Jesus knew His time was near, so He fixed His eyes on the joy set before
Him and never looked back.

He expects the same from His followers.

I cannot ask for Jim to still be here or for my brother to remain.

I must purposely resolve to embrace God's perfect will.

I have to resolutely set my sights on eternity.

No matter what happens today, Jesus will hold me steady.

November 16. Day 296.

Dwight is in heaven.

Yesterday, just as I got to school, my dad called me to tell me he was gone.
I was in the back of a taxicab. The driver saw my tears, offered me a tissue, and
told me to stay as long as I needed. After a few moments I walked into my staff
room, sat down at my desk, covered my face, and wept. One of the teachers came
over and gently rubbed my back. The bell rang, indicating it was time to teach
my first class. A few moments into my lesson, my principal walked into the room
and gave me a long hug. She told the class my brother had just died and then told
me that I could go home. I looked at her and said that if it was okay with her, I'd
rather stay and talk about Jesus and the hope we have because of Him.

Making my Jesus famous eased my pain.

Dad said they were all standing around his bed. Jesus spoke to my mom's
heart and said, "I'm going to take him now." Dwight opened his eyes and breathed
his last breath here on earth. I wonder what it's like. I know he's seen Jesus, but
has he seen Jim? Has he met Peter or Daniel? Was Nanny there to meet him?

I leave today at noon, and Debbie is coming with me! Unbeknownst to me,
she purchased a ticket so I wouldn't have to make this trip alone. She's flying
seventeen hours, then returning the very next day! Ruth and Alf are meeting
me in Philadelphia to stand in for Jim and Mohsina, and the girls are coming
over in a few minutes to make sure I eat breakfast. I am completely surrounded.

Take me to my manna.

Yet be sure of this; the Kingdom of God is near! (Luke 10:11)

Rejoice that your names are written in heaven! (Luke 10:20)

You have given me two thoughts to cling to as I walk through the next few days. *I am sure* that one day the sky will open and Jesus will come and take us home, and *I rejoice* that because our names are written in heaven, we will all be together soon.

November 17. Day 297.

When I landed in New York, my connecting flight to Philadelphia was grounded due to torrential rains, so I took the train. A friend of Dwight's picked me up and took me to my hotel. I asked reception for my parents' room number. The walk down that hall was one of the longest of my life. I felt so inadequate. I knocked on their door, and Dad answered. Mom jumped off the bed and threw herself into my arms and began to sob. Dad rubbed her back and encouraged her to sit down. Worry was written all over his face. Mom has an aneurysm in her brain and a bad heart, which make her a walking time bomb, and stress is the trigger. I stayed until she was settled down and then found my room.

Jesus, I need You to speak into this pain. I am leaning on Your throne. If it wasn't there, I'd be on the floor.

Midnight.

When I saw Sheri, no words were necessary. We hugged and quietly cried. She talked about the difference between our journeys. I am still recovering from the shock of Jim's sudden departure. Sheri has been saying a good-bye that lasted four years and nine months. Although she misses what used to be before cancer consumed their lives, she is so thankful and relieved that he is finally free of his pain, and she feels a sense of closure.

Ruth and Alf had arrived when I returned to the hotel, and seeing their faces let me know everything was going to be okay. We picked up supper for my parents and then made our way to the funeral home.

Sheri and I stood behind my parents as they knelt on a bench in front of the casket. My mom held my brother while my dad held my mom. When they stood up, Dad was crying as he said, "There's something very wrong with this picture. This is not the way it's supposed to be." Sheri hugged Mom, and I held my dad. I couldn't help but wonder how long it would be until I would be standing at their caskets.

I stood beside Sheri as friends began to come and express their sympathy. Nurses who had cared for Dwight talked about how courageous he was through his war with cancer. Everyone mentioned that whenever Dwight posted on his blog, he always ended by reminding everyone that when they prayed for him, they should also pray for those without a voice. It was quite a sight. Two young widows, one a little further along on the path than the other. Two broken hearts trying to grapple with the reality that our lives haven't turned out like we dreamed. Both of us leaning on the throne and dwelling on heaven.

When the room was empty, I went up to the casket and stood there alone. I looked at his face, remembering him as a little kid when he used to call me "Mama Sue." I could see him sliding across the floor on his stomach with cardboard tubes stuck in the back of his shirt, pretending he was scuba diving. I could hear his grown-up voice that commanded a room and his persuasive arguments that could make anyone change his mind. I smiled at our mutual love for good food and adventure.

I miss you, Dwight.

I felt very alone as I walked into my hotel room tonight.

I wasn't meant to be alone.

Jesus, please help me sleep.

November 18. Day 298.

I managed to get four hours of sleep. To get through this day, I need to be like Mary and stick close to Jesus. I choose not to be distracted by death, but instead to look to the sky focusing on our very sure hope. Sovereign God, take me to my manna.

> If you then, though you are evil, know how to give good gifts to your children, now much more will your Father in heaven give the Holy Spirit to those who ask Him. (Luke 11:13)

Sovereign God, we need the Holy Spirit, the ultimate Comforter, to come alongside us. He is our source of stamina, and today I know He will do what only He can do.

Fortify the hearts of everyone who comes to Dwight's funeral. I pray they will leave looking to the sky.

November 19. Day 299.

Dwight's funeral was beautiful. One of his old professors gave a very intel-
lectual and wordy homily that Dwight would have applauded. His close friend
talked about God's grace, and Dad reminisced about Dwight's life. Another
friend read the poem "Death, be not proud," written in 1901 by John Donne.
I read from 2 Corinthians 4:13–5:1:

> We're not keeping this quiet, not on your life. Just like the psalm-
> ist who wrote, "I believed it, so I said it," we say what we believe. And
> what we believe is that the One who raised up the Master Jesus will
> just as certainly raise us up with you, alive. Every detail works to your
> advantage and to God's glory: more and more grace, more and more
> people, more and more praise! So we're not giving up. How could we!
> Even though on the outside it often looks like things are falling apart
> on us, on the inside, where God is making new life, not a day goes by
> without His unfolding grace. *These hard times are small potatoes com-
> pared to the coming good times, the lavish celebration prepared for us.*
> There's far more here than meets the eye. The things we see now are
> here today, gone tomorrow. *But the things we can't see now will last for-
> ever.* For instance, we know that when these bodies of ours are taken
> down like tents and folded away, they will be replaced by resurrection
> bodies in heaven—God-made, not handmade—and we'll never have to
> relocate our "tents" again. Sometimes we can hardly wait to move—and
> so we cry out in frustration. *Compared to what's coming, living conditions
> around here seem like a stopover in an unfurnished shack, and we're tired
> of it! We've been given a glimpse of the real thing, our true home, and our
> resurrection bodies!* The Spirit of God whets our appetite by giving us a
> taste of what's ahead. *He puts a little of heaven in our hearts so that we'll
> never settle for less. (The Message).*

I hung on to Jim's ring as I read words that contain my reason to live. A
few hours later I hugged Sheri good-bye, praying that she'd feel the arms of
Jesus tonight as fatigue takes over and reality begins to seep in.

I'm now in Canada.

November 20. Day 300.

As we drove across the Peace Bridge into Fort Erie, the last place we pastored in Canada, a wave of emotion overtook my heart. The death of Dwight has magnified the irreplaceable loss of Jim. I am teetering on that cliff of despair, too tired to fight or to muster up any resolve. My body feels like it did in the days after Jim went to heaven. I've lost my appetite and I have diarrhea. My heart is heavy and lonely. Where's my courage gone?

In just a few hours, I will see my kids. Understandably, they couldn't go through another funeral, so instead of them coming to Philadelphia, we're all meeting in Canada. Curtis is flying in from California later today, and CJ and Ali are coming over this morning. We need each other.

Holy Spirit, take me to my manna before I die.

> Are not five sparrows sold for two pennies? Yet not one of them is forgotten by God. Indeed, the very hairs of your head are all numbered. Don't be afraid. You are worth more than many sparrows. (Luke 12:6–7)

Wow. How personal is my God?
I am not forgotten. I will not be afraid.
My courage is back.

November 21. Day 301.

I am staying with my parents. I woke up rested this morning and ready to do whatever I can to make my parents' sorrow a little more bearable.

I am feeling a familiar unsettledness. This time it scares me more than excites me. I feel like such a stranger in North America, but my sons would love me to be closer, and my parents have never looked so old and frail. I only want to do what Jesus wants me to do. I need Him to speak louder than my emotions.

Holy Spirit, take me to my manna…

> Therefore I tell you, *do not worry about your life . . . Who of you by worrying can add a single hour to your life?* Since you cannot do this very little thing, why do you worry about the rest? *But seek His kingdom,* and these things will be given to you as well. (Luke 12:22, 25)

I hear You, Jesus!
I will not worry about my tomorrows, nor will I be afraid!
You will unveil Your plans for me when I need to know them.
Until then, it's You I seek, not answers.

November 22. Day 302.

Curtis says he is sure Jim misses us, but that the pain of separation isn't there for him—just the longing and anticipation of the reunion to come, and for him, it won't feel like any time at all. It's comforting to think of Jim waiting for us, but I would never want him to feel the ache that we live with. For those who are left behind death is a horrible intruder, but for those who die, *death is merely a passageway to eternal life.*

Take me to my manna.

> Be dressed, ready for service and keep your lamps burning, like men waiting for their master to return from a wedding banquet, so that when he comes and knocks they can immediately open the door for him. It will be good for those servants whose master finds them watching when he comes! (Luke 12:35–36)

I am watching for You with enormous anticipation.
Jesus says that if He finds us watching, then *He will dress himself to serve and have us recline at the table, and He will come and wait on us!* (Luke 12:37.) How will I ever be able to recline and let Him do this? But this is what we're promised if we faithfully watch for His return.

My eyes are on the sky!
My ears are listening for that knock!
I can't wait to be at Your table, Lord!

November 23. Day 303.

Jesus compares the kingdom of God to a mustard seed and beads of yeast (Luke 13:18–21). How can a tiny mustard seed produce a tree that is twenty-one feet high, has roots that go down sixty-three feet, and sports branches that can be as long as seventy-two feet? Did you know that it takes twenty billion yeast cells to weigh one gram, or 1/28 of an ounce? Jesus uses perfect visuals of what our little lives are like when they are surrendered to God.

Moses was a stuttering murderer in hiding. *God used him to deliver His people from slavery.*

David was the eighth and youngest son of Jesse, who spent his days in a field with sheep. *God used him to slay a giant that terrified a nation and then made him the king.*

Agnes Gonxha Bojaxhiu was the youngest in a simple Albanian family. Her father died when she was eight, and so she was raised by a single mom. *You would know her better as Mother Teresa.*

Our God uses the smallest, the weakest, and the most unlikely to do great exploits for His glory!

Use me like a mustard seed, Jesus, and knead me into my world like yeast.

November 24. Day 304.

Curtis and I went to Jim's grave yesterday. The last time he was there it was an open hole. Now it's covered over by grass and has a marker, which he saw for the first time. We stood together for a few moments, and then I left him alone. We drove in silence all the way home.

Take me to my manna.

Jesus says, "Simply put, if you're not willing to take what is dearest to you, whether plans or people and kiss it good-bye, you can't be My disciple" (Luke 14:33, *The Message*).

Yesterday evening Uncle Henry asked me if I like Hong Kong. Although Jim and I grew to love Hong Kong, I recalled how when we first arrived, we hated everything about it. We felt assaulted by the crowds, the smells, and the noise. We longed to return to "Manana Land," the slow-paced, breathtakingly gorgeous Dominican Republic, but instead found ourselves in one of the most stressful cities on the globe. *Yet we knew that we knew* that God had called us there, so we stayed.

That's when we learned that although we may not *like* God's will, we *must* submit to it if we want to be part of God's kingdom.

> **Anyone who does not carry his cross and follow Me cannot be My disciple. (Luke 14:27)**

I am lonely. I don't like being a widow, but I must embrace God's sovereign plan if I want to be part of the kingdom of God. I must trust Him even though it makes no human sense. It's not fun having to grit my teeth and force myself to look at the sky. It's hard work to believe in what I do not see. *True joy doesn't come from how comfortable we are; it comes from knowing we're obeying Jesus in every little thing.* I've discovered that when I do that I start to see things the way Jesus does, and suddenly, I wouldn't want to be anywhere else.

Sovereign God, continue to give me the resolve of Christ so that I can continue to carry the cross You have entrusted me with.

November 25. Day 305.

Curtis is going home, and I seriously wonder whether my heart can bear the strain of another good-bye.

Take me to my manna.

The story of the lost sheep (Luke 15:1–7) will always be one of my favorites. When Jim and I told this story to kids, we loved to illustrate the joy of being found. Jim would put on "Leroy," a lion costume, and come wandering into the crowd looking for me. Using a gruff, growly voice, he'd say, "Where's Mrs. Keddy? I've lost Mrs. Keddy!," as he made his way up the center aisle. Within a few seconds the kids would all be yelling and pointing in my direction as Leroy continued to look under the pews and behind the piano. When he found me, he'd lift me right up off the ground and swing me around. As I got older and heavier, I would joke with Leroy and say, "This used to be easier, eh?" All adults in the room would laugh, and Leroy would always turn to me and say, "I love all of you, Mrs. Keddy. I'm glad I found you."

Every time we told the story of the lost sheep, I was reminded not only of how Jesus rescued me, *but of why I live.* I never want to forget that I was lost until Jesus found me! I carry inside me a hope that I am obligated to share with the world. *My sorrow must take a backseat to the task that is before me.* The Enemy would love it if my pain kept me from obeying Jesus, but there is no way that's going to happen! There are souls hanging between life and death needing me to tell them about Jesus, not just by my words, *but by how I live out this journey.*

You know what?

I have a job to do!

My heart will be just fine.

November 26. Day 306.

Yesterday I returned to the home where we all gathered the night Curtis brought Jim's body back to Canada.

I'm no longer that terrified widow sitting on the floor.

It has been a continuous discipline of speaking to my soul since those moments when we collectively declared, "It is well." God has proved that He is my strength and has taught me to lift my pain to Him so that He can use it for His glory.

Take me to my manna.

Jesus says in Luke 17:10 that when we have done what has been commanded, our response should be, "We are bondservants. We have only done our duty."

I can never take the credit for being obedient. It would be wrong to pat myself on the back for doing what I was told to do. *Whatever I do is because of Him. I stay out of the pit of despair because of His power. I look at the sky because He is the lifter of my head.*

I am a bondservant only doing her duty.

November 27. Day 307.

Whoever tries to keep his life will lose it, and whoever loses his life will preserve it. (Luke 17:33)

When the Son of Man comes, will he find faith on the earth? (Luke 18:8)

I tell you the truth; anyone who will not receive the Kingdom of God like a little child will never enter it. (Luke 17:17)

On Day 307, my soul has been reminded that God wants both an aggressive and a passive faith.

He wants me to hang on to nothing but cling fiercely to Him. He wants me to run into His arms and then be still, remembering He is God, believing that no matter what it looks like, He always has a purpose.

Jesus, I surrender.

November 28. Day 308.

Thirty years ago today was our first official date. We enjoyed a scrumptious buffet and then went to a musical. When he kissed me good night, everything within me came alive, and if we could have, we would have gotten married before sunrise. Sigh. Take me to my manna.

Peter said to Jesus, "We have left all we had to follow you." Jesus said to Peter:

> I tell you the truth, no one who has left home or wife or brothers or parents or children for the sake of the Kingdom of God will fail to receive many times as much in this age, and in the age to come, eternal life! (Luke 18:28–30).

Could there be anything more perfect for me to read on the day I will be saying another good-bye to my family and country? Seriously, the conversation between Peter and Jesus could have been between me and Jesus! I can't get over how personal my manna is each day. I could never ever deny His involvement and care over my life.

The relationship I have with Jesus is all the reward I will ever need.

I will celebrate this truth all the way back to Hong Kong.

November 30. Day 310.

Day 309 was lost in the air. Dinner and hugs were waiting for me when I returned home. I am, without a doubt, the most blessed widow on the planet. It's back to school today, and I'm sure jet lag will rear its ugliness midafternoon sometime, so I am counting on God's strength to do the impossible yet again. Take me to my manna.

A blind man knows Jesus is nearby, so he cries out until Jesus stops and gives him exactly what he wants (Luke 18:35–43).

It's so beautifully simple, isn't it? *He calls. Jesus answers.* Wouldn't it be great if every time we yelled for Jesus to do something, He did it? The reality is that we don't always get what we ask for, because *sometimes in the withholding, we receive what we really need.*

I believe with all my heart that Jesus hears my cries and knows what I want, but I'm starting to understand that however He chooses to answer is always for my eternal good.

December 1. Day 311.

After the boys left home, this was the night we always put up our Christmas tree. We'd light our candles and put on the first Christmas music of the season, and then we would celebrate in the glow of our tree. Tonight the tree will stay in its box, the candles will stay unlit, and I will long for my lover. Jesus, I'm clinging to You.

Take me to my manna.

Unlike the blind man who shouted for mercy, Zacchaeus had no idea that mercy was even an option. He was hated and friendless—until the day Jesus looked up into the sycamore tree where he was hiding and invited Himself over to his home. Zacchaeus was never the same (Luke 19:1–10).

I love that I can always count on God's mercy to pursue me and that even when I forget to call out His name, He calls out mine.

December 2. Day 312.

Jesus tells a story about a king who gives money to his servants, instructing them to put it to work until he returns. The first servant doubled his earnings and so was commended for a job well done and given ten cities to look after. The second servant increased what he was given by 50 percent, so was only given five cities. The third servant put the money in a piece of cloth, doing nothing to increase its value. The king calls him wicked and gives his money to the first servant (Luke 19:11–27).

As I read this story, I thought about how my Sovereign God has entrusted me with sorrow and has requested that I *put it to work until He returns.* I resolve to be like servant number one and invest this aloneness so that it will reap eternal dividends in the kingdom.

I will not waste what I've been given.

December 3. Day 313.

"The Lord needs it" . . . They brought it to Jesus. (Luke 19:34–35)

When Jesus speaks to me, I want my response to be just like that.
Whatever He needs, I will do.
Jesus, I'll give You whatever You want.

December 4. Day 314.

I woke up around midnight in a sweat from a terrible nightmare. Jim kept dying over and over, and no matter how hard I tried, I couldn't save him. I prayed until I fell back asleep but awakened a few hours later feeling scared and alone, so I called my precious friend Feroza. She encouraged me to remember that the same faithful God who has been with me so far will never fail me in all the days ahead.

I am desperate for my manna.

Luke 21:4 says, "Out of her poverty she gave."

Luke is writing about a poor widow who put her last two coins into the temple treasury. Those two coins were all she had to live on, yet she gave them away, and *Jesus noticed.*

I feel so depleted these days, like I have nothing left to give. I feel so spent, so empty, and so sad, yet the Holy Spirit is nudging me this morning to give out of my impoverished spirit.

I will give whatever I have left, and Jesus will notice.

December 5. Day 315.

I am feeling apprehensive about Christmas. One of Mohsina's daughters asked me if she could please help me put up the tree, so I stupidly said okay. I really don't want to do this, but Tahreem is coming over today, so it's going to happen whether I want it to or not. It will be another one of those agonizing firsts I was so hoping to avoid.

Jesus, please come near.

As I wrote that sentence, I realized it was needless request because He is right here, all the time. *And* that *is the reason why I must put up our tree.* I dare not waste an opportunity to exalt Jesus to a world that needs to know Him so badly. Again, something sorrowful has been transformed into an eternal mission. *Jesus, use my Christmas tree as a catalyst for many conversations about You!*

Take me to my manna.

Just before Jesus is betrayed and arrested, He takes His disciples to the Mount of Olives and tells them to pray so that they won't give in to the temptation that's coming. He walks a short distance away and prays to His Father.

When He comes back, His friends are sleeping. Luke writes that they were *exhausted from sorrow* (Luke 22:39–45).

I know exactly how that feels.

Jesus wakes them up because He knows that *the remedy for sorrow is prayer.*

We pray to remind our souls that it's *His* will we live and die for.

It's time to put up my Christmas tree.

December 6. Day 316.

We laughed ourselves silly as we untangled lights and strung beads in and out of the branches. We baked Christmas cookies and talked about how Jesus left heaven to come to earth. Tahreem gave me a new ornament that has a picture of Jesus lying in a manger imprinted on its surface because she thought I needed something that would always remind me that Jesus came. *Oh, how right she is.* I've decided that for as long as I am in Hong Kong, I am going to have the kids in my life help me put up the tree. It's never looked so wild, but it's perfect!

I love how God can turn sorrow into laughter.

Take me to my manna.

The last chapter of Luke has one predominant thought: each of us will experience a sovereign moment.

The two men on the road to Emmaus had a sovereign moment when Jesus broke bread with them (Luke 24:31–34).

The disciples had a sovereign moment when Jesus walked through the wall into the room where they were in hiding (Luke 24:45–49).

I believe there are sovereign moments coming for many in my world who don't yet know Jesus. Their eyes will be opened, and they will see. Their minds will be opened, and they will understand.

Those sovereign moments are coming!

They might even be around a Christmas tree.

December 7. Day 317.

The Hong Kong Board of Education refused to give me a teacher's registration number because I don't have a degree. My college diploma has always been enough, coupled with over a decade of experience and my TESL certificate, so my principal is challenging their ruling. Without this number, I cannot teach in a school. If this had happened a year ago it would have rocked my world, but now, compared to losing Jim, it's just a bump in the road that I know my Sovereign will work out in whatever way He thinks is best.

Take me to my manna.

> In the beginning was the Word, and the Word was with God, and the Word was God. (John 1:1)

Word in the Greek language means "reason," and in the Hebrew language it means "God." So for both Jews and Gentiles, the first sentence of John's Gospel was a profound revelation.

> In the beginning was the *Reason,* and the *Reason* was with God, and the *Reason* was God.

> In the beginning was *God,* and *God* was with God, and *God* was God.

Jesus is God, and Jesus is the Reason I live. He knows me and I know Him. So why would I worry even for a second about my need for a degree? Whatever happens will be just fine.

December 8. Day 318.

Andrew and his buddy heard John the Baptist call Jesus "the Lamb of God who takes away the sins of the world," so they followed Him. Jesus saw them and asked them what they wanted. Andrew said they wanted to know where He was staying, so Jesus took them to wherever home was at the time and hung out with them the rest of the day! When they left, Andrew found his brother Simon, told him they had found the Messiah, and immediately brought him to Jesus. Jesus took one look at Simon and said, "You are Simon, son of John. You will be called Peter—the rock" (John 1:35–42).

I love the progression of their journey.

They *followed* Jesus. They *hung out* with Jesus. They ran and *told someone* they had found Jesus, and then they *brought that person to Jesus* so he could see for himself!

Give me boldness to tell others that I have found the Christ! Help me to bring them to You, Jesus, so that You can call them by name and transform their lives!

December 9. Day 319.

Jesus and His family are at a wedding where the hosts have run out of wine. Mary tells Jesus, but He doesn't want to get involved. Completely ignoring Him, she tells the servants to do whatever He says! Jesus gives in to His mom and the miracles begin (John 2:1–5).

This amazing story is all about trust and obedience. Mary is asking the servants to trust Jesus, and when Jesus tells the servants to fill six stone jars with water, He's saying "trust Me." The servants obey both Mary and Jesus and are witnesses to Jesus's very first miracle. While everyone praised the bridegroom for saving the best for the last, the servants knew exactly who was responsible.

The servants didn't ask Jesus how pouring water into six stone jars could help with the wine shortage. *They just did it.*

Holy Spirit, help me to trust whatever Jesus says and then obey Him with no questions asked.

December 10. Day 320.

As the sun is rising out my window, it is setting in Canada, and Sheri and my parents are gathering together for Dwight's Canadian memorial service. Take me to my manna.

> **Now while He was in Jerusalem at the Passover Festival, many people saw the signs He was performing and believed in His name. But Jesus would not entrust Himself to them, for He knew all people. (John 2:23)**

Jesus entrusted Himself only to His Father.
His Father devised the Plan and knew the end of the Story!
Who better to trust than that?
Sovereign God, I entrust my parents and Sheri exclusively to You.

December 11. Day 321.

"A man can receive only what is given to him from heaven" (John 3:27). *This includes both joy and sorrow.*

"Jesus must become greater. I must become less" (John 3:30). *It's never about me.*

"The one who comes from heaven is above all" (John 3:31). *There is never anything to fear.*

Holy Spirit, lock this manna in my heart.

December 12. Day 322.

There is no place I'd rather be than right here worshiping Jesus.

> It's who you are and the way you live that count before God. Your worship must engage your spirit in the pursuit of truth. That's the kind of people the Father is out looking for; those who are simply and honestly themselves before Him in their worship. God is spirit. Those who worship Him must do it out of their very being, their spirits, their true selves, in adoration! (John 4:23–24, *The Message*)

Worship is sitting at His feet; trusting Him when it's hard; being overcome by His greatness; and being comforted by His sovereignty.

Jesus, I adore You.

December 13. Day 323.

I woke up with a thought.

God gives us breath to worship Him, so I dare not waste that breath on anything else!

John 4:43–54 tells the story of a royal official who asks Jesus to come and heal his dying son. Jesus tells him to go home and that his son will live. The man takes Jesus at His word and goes home to a completely healed son.

There is simply too much to lose to not *take Jesus at His word!*

Jesus says that a time is coming when all who are in their graves will hear His voice and come out. Those that have taken Him at His word will rise to live, and those who haven't will rise to be condemned (John 5:29).

I believe You. Until that day comes, I will worship You with every breath.

December 14. Day 324.

Jesus knew exactly how He was going to feed the hungry crowd, but He wanted to test Phillip, so He asked him where He could buy everyone dinner.

Although Jesus had consistently proved He always does what He says He will do, somehow Philip forgot and failed the test. He told Jesus that even if they had eight months wages, it wouldn't be enough to feed everyone! Andrew weighed in and said he'd found a little boy with a lunch. Whether he was trying to help or being sarcastic, it doesn't really matter, because it still wasn't the answer Jesus was looking for (John 6).

It's so easy to doubt and wonder, isn't it? It's very difficult to believe when something looks so impossible. Would I have smiled in expectation of what Jesus was going to do that day, or would I have been like Phillip and forgotten who asked the question?

I want to pass the test.

I want to amaze Jesus.

I want to be amazed.

Help me to believe before I see.

December 15. Day 325.

I woke up to the Brooklyn Tabernacle Choir reminding me that *Jesus is all I will ever need.* He's the beginning, the ending, and everything in between!

Jim would be forty-eight years old today. *Holy Spirit, come close to my sons. Fill their hearts with gratefulness for what has been and an expectation for what is to come. Encourage Jim's parents as they remember the birth of their son and take pride in the man he grew up to be. Put gladness in the hearts of Kathy, Myrna, and Nancy as they imagine their brother in heaven. Thank you, my Sovereign, for lending him to me for twenty-five years.*

Take me to my manna.

> I am the bread of life. Whoever comes to Me will never go hungry. Your forefathers ate manna and died, but he who feeds on Me will live forever. (John 6:35, 58, paraphrased)

Jesus, You are my life.

December 16. Day 326.

I've made a variation of Nana Elsie's spaghetti for Jim's birthday ever since we were married. Over the years the meatballs got larger, the sauce got spicier, and our waistlines got wider! Dessert was always a multilayered chocolate cake with a ridiculous amount of icing. It felt right to remember, so I invited a few friends over to celebrate his life. I think I've started another tradition.

Take me to my manna.

All God wants is for us to look at Jesus (John 6:40). It's so simple yet so hard; *but if we dare,* we will discover that He is Truth and that everything He does is for the glory of His Father.

He longs for us to simply believe and follow.

Jesus, I give You what You long for.

December 17. Day 327.

The disciples met a man who was born blind, so they asked Jesus who had sinned to cause this: the man, or his parents? *The answer Jesus gave is the answer to every "why?" ever asked.*

> This happened so that the work of God might be displayed in his life. (John 9:3)

Surrendered suffering gives the world a glimpse of God living in us. Our choice to trust Him through pain ushers in the supernatural, which nobody can deny.

> As long as it is day, we must continue to do the work of Him who sent us! (John 9:4)

When Jesus cracks the sky, any opportunity to amaze Him will be over, *so now is the time!*

Consider me Your trophy case, my Sovereign. I am honored to display Your power.

December 18. Day 328.

Jim and I were willing to do anything and go anywhere for Jesus. Although I never envisioned *anything* to include widowhood, I have to believe He did, so I pray that His work will be displayed in me so that others will be drawn to Jesus.

Take me to my manna.

Jesus heals the blind man, and all hell breaks loose. The Pharisees pitch a fit and demand to know who is responsible for this miracle. The man whose eyes have been opened tries to explain. His perception of Jesus evolves from Him being a man, to a prophet, to a man from God, to the Lord (John 9:6–38). The more questions he is asked, the more persuaded he becomes that Jesus is not like any other man. The more he reasons, the clearer things become until he finally sees Jesus for who He truly is.

One encounter with Jesus can launch us into a journey of discovery that will become our salvation.

Jesus, please walk into the lives of those who don't know you and start them on that journey! Give them one revelation after the other until they see You, call You their Lord, and worship at Your feet.

December 19. Day 329.

My sheep listen to My voice; I know them and they follow Me . . . *no one can snatch them out of My hand.* (John 10:27–28)

Is there anything else that matters?
He knows me. He loves me. He holds me.
That is exactly the reminder I needed.

December 20. Day 330.

Mary and Martha's brother was sick, so they sent word to Jesus. When Jesus heard about Lazarus, He stayed where He was for the next two days, and from what John records, there was no crisis keeping Him there. *So why would Jesus purposely hang back when His friend was in dire need?*

I think it's because Jesus knew the end of the story and that the lesson His followers would learn from His delay was invaluable.

Jesus knew Peter would deny Him, Judas would betray Him with a kiss, and the rest of His closest companions would lock themselves in a room, terrified. He also knew there was a place where sorrow and fear would be eradicated forever, and He wanted more than anything for them to share it with Him.

When Jesus arrived, Martha told Him Lazarus was dead. Jesus asked for the stone to be rolled away from the entrance of the tomb, and then He prayed:

Father, I thank You that You have heard Me. I know that You always hear Me, but I said this *for the benefit of the people standing here, that they may believe that You sent Me.* Lazarus, come out! (John 11:41–42)

Jesus didn't raise Lazarus from the dead to make his sisters happy, although I'm sure they were thrilled to their toes. *Jesus raised Lazarus from the dead so that people would see and believe.*

His chief concern was where they would spend eternity, not how happy He could make them on earth.

This is still the case. Jesus is more concerned with my soul than with my fleeting happiness on earth.

Holy Spirit, seal this truth in my heart.

December 21. Day 331.

One of my colleagues was telling me that he was taking his wife to Italy over the Christmas holiday. I encouraged him to take as many gondola rides as they had time for. He promised me he would toss the budget to the wind and enjoy this vacation like it was the last one they'd ever share!

Jim loved me like he knew we'd only have twenty-five years together. I would often come home to romance. Our little apartment would be filled with candles. He'd meet me at the door and take me to a place where nothing else mattered. *Oh, we had a great life.* Take me to my manna.

Anyone who loves their life will lose it, while anyone who hates their life in this world will keep it for eternal life. (John 12:25)

It's easy to get distracted and forget that we are strangers on a pilgrimage to where our real life will begin, especially when our life here is good.

My Father will honor the one who serves me. (John 12:26)

A few years ago I was picked up in a Mercedes-Benz and driven to a house that was built into the side of a mountain that towered over an inlet of the South China Sea. This was our view as we sat down at the long marble table for dinner. I literally had a servant on my right and another on my left. They did everything for me except chew my food. Every time I wiped my mouth and put my linen napkin down, it was replaced. My chilled water goblet was never empty. When I went to the bathroom, one of them stood outside the door. I left that night with a greater understanding of what it means to truly serve.

A servant never takes his eyes off his master. He anticipates the need before it's even expressed.

Jesus, I live to serve You, and I love You more than life and romantic afternoons.

December 22. Day 332.

Do not let your hearts be troubled. (John 14:1)

From the onset of this journey, it's been a choice. I could trust or let my heart be full of questions and rage. Just before Jim's casket was carried down the aisle to the front of the sanctuary, I turned to the rest of the family and said, *"Sing!"*

That was a conscious decision to *not let* the grief overshadow our hope.

Letting or not letting something be depends entirely on me.

I can choose to let Jesus help me, or I can choose to let self-pity make itself at home.

I choose today to guard my heart from trouble and to trust yet again.

December 23. Day 333.

In a few hours I'm flying to California to spend Christmas with my family. How on earth am I going to wake up Christmas morning without Jim beside me? I need to *let* your peace rule my heart.

Holy Spirit, please feed me.

In My Father's house are many rooms. If it were not so, I would have told you. I am going there to prepare a place for you. And if I go and prepare a place for you, I will come back and take you to be with Me that you also may be where I am. (John 14:2–3)

One day Jesus will come back for me, and all this ache and longing will be over. I choose to look at the sky and remind my soul that what I feel now is short-lived compared to what's coming!

Let's get on the plane!

December 24. Day 334.

The flight was long and uneventful. After I collected my luggage I made my way to an adjacent terminal to rendezvous with my parents and mom-in-law. There was a massive red bow on the door of my suite. Curtis was smiling, but his eyes showed me something different.

With God's help, we'll all get through this.

Take me to my manna.

In the days before Jesus died, He told his disciples:

> I will ask the Father, and He will give you *another* Counselor to be with you forever. I will not leave you as orphans. (John 14:15, 18)

Jesus assured them that they would never be alone. The Father would be sending them an invisible companion, the Holy Spirit, who would comfort and guide them. This same Holy Spirit has also come alongside me, enabling me to trust. He leads me to my manna and then helps me apply it throughout this journey to heaven.

I love You, Holy Spirit.

I can do Christmas Eve without Jim because You are with me.

December 25. Day 335.

Merry Christmas, Jimbies.

All I want for Christmas is for this to be over. I wish our love affair could have lasted a lifetime. I feel myself slipping toward that pit. *Holy Spirit, I'm desperate for Your intervention.*

> My peace I leave with you, *Do not let* your hearts be troubled and *do not be afraid.* Apart from Me you can do nothing. *Remain in My love.* I have told you this so that *My joy may be in you so that your joy may be complete.* (from John 14, 15)

I hear You, Jesus.

I'm clinging to You with all I've got.

Let's do Christmas.

8:44 p.m.

I managed to hold back the tears until after dinner. I was screaming on the inside as everyone around me talked about nothing. Without anyone noticing, I left the room and locked myself in the bathroom. All my pent-up emotions burst like a dam. Efforts to compose myself were useless. After an hour or so, my dad asked me to open the door. His skinny arms felt strong as he held me. Within a few moments, we were driving back to our hotel. The car was silent because no one felt like talking. We're all just too sad.

My heart is crushed with sorrow. I've run out of words to express this grief. I hurt for everyone. I hurt for my sons. I hurt for our parents. I hurt for Sheri. I hurt for Jim's sisters. I hurt for our friends. I hurt for me. I *have to believe* that God will use this dark time in our lives for His glory.

Sovereign God, surround us like a fortress.

December 26. Day 336.

Sleep came sometime after I watched Larry King interview Billy Graham. He talked about his sixty-one-year marriage to his best friend, Ruth. She's immobile due to severe arthritis, but he said she's still the most beautiful woman on earth.

I wanted that. I wanted to grow old together. I wanted to be one of those cute elderly couples who hold hands everywhere they go and still have that twinkle in their eyes when they look at each other.

A year ago today, we were getting on a plane to Singapore where we spent two beautiful weeks together. We talked about how thankful we were for our love and how we were looking forward to the next twenty-five years. We imagined what it would be like to be grandparents and decided we'd come back for each grandchild's birthday. Jim said he wanted to be called Gramps, and I said I'd be Nanny Sue. I never dreamt that in less than a month, it would all be over.

Jesus, I really need You! I've been swept into the undertow and need to be rescued! My hand is raised! Only You can pull me out of this! Please help me!

I felt just now as though Jim was using the words of Jesus to remind me of what is true: "You weep and mourn . . . but your grief will turn to joy. When you were giving birth to Curtis you endured great pain, but when he was born the anguish was forgotten because of the joy that followed. We had a son! It's the same now. This is a very painful time, but I will see you again and you will rejoice, and no one will take away your joy!" (from John 16:17–33.)

Sovereign God, I ask for the perseverance of Jesus to be deposited into my soul. I ask that You would enable my little family to get through this pain so we can experience the joy.

The night CJ was born, we shared the doctor with another woman in labor in the room beside me. At one point he told me that she and her baby were in distress and that an ambulance was coming to take them to a bigger hospital. We encouraged him to stay with her, promising we'd holler if we needed him, and then we went to prayer.

As we prayed for this lady and her baby, I forgot about my own pain.
That's what I must do now.
I need to pray for others who are struggling and stop thinking about my own grief.
Jesus! You have lifted me out of the deep waters and restored my soul!
Once again, You have given eternal purpose to another day.

December 27. Day 337.

Just before Jesus is taken away, He says a prayer for Himself and His disciples that I've borrowed today from John 17 and made my own:

My Heavenly Father, I want to bring You glory on earth by completing the work You have given me to do. I will continue to remember that Your strength is made perfect in my weakness, so instead of trying to be strong, I will remain in You and in Your love because apart from You I can do nothing. All I have is Yours, and all You have is mine.

I give You my sons. They belong to You. I thank You so much for their lives. I ask that You, my Sovereign God, will protect them in Jesus's name. Shield them from the Evil One so that they may have the full measure of the joy of the Lord. My prayer is not that You will take them out of the world, but that You will keep them safe from the Enemy of their souls. They are not of this world any more than I am. Sanctify them by the truth, which is Your word. I set myself apart to intercede for them.

I rejoice in all You have done and all You are going to do through my boys. In Jesus's name, I pray, Amen!

After Jesus prayed for His disciples, He prayed for those who would believe. That's us! *The good news is that His prayers are constant.* Hebrews 7:25 says, "Jesus lives to make intercession for us!"

We mean everything to Him. We are the object of His affection.

Curtis and CJ will be okay.

Jesus will make sure of it.

December 28. Day 338.

I'm alive another day to long for His return, rely on His strength, lean on His throne, rest in His peace, fall on His mercy, and marvel at His grace! Take me to my manna.

When Jesus was arrested, my friend Peter slashed off the ear of the high priest's servant. Jesus told Peter to calm down, gave the guy a new ear, and said for all to hear: "Shall I not drink the cup the Father has given me?" (John 18:11).

Jesus did not go kicking and screaming to the cross. Every answer to each question His accusers asked was *a reminder to His own soul that there was eternal purpose* to His suffering.

> My kingdom is not of this world. You are right in saying I am a king. In fact, for this reason I was born, and for this I came into the world, *to testify to the truth.* You would have no power over Me if it were not given to you from above. (John 18:36–37, John 19:11)

Jesus knew where He was from and where He was going.

Jesus knew He was here to carry out the Father's plan.

Jesus knew that nothing happened in His life that wasn't already scripted.

I want His heart to be mine. I want to remember where I'm from, where I'm going, and why I'm here, and that whatever happens along the way, whether good or bad, *He has sanctioned.*

December 29. Day 339.

None of us feel like doing anything, but we know we have to do something, so it's Nixon Library day today.

I choose to trust in my God whose ways are higher and thoughts are wiser. I lift up my brokenness, believing that He will bring eternal worth out of this pain. I send self-pity back to hell and look intently at the sky. I will represent Jesus well so that others will be persuaded to believe. Holy Spirit, come alongside me and do what You do.

Jesus said, "All of this happened so that the Scripture might be fulfilled" (John 19:24b).

Every single thing that happened surrounding the death of Jesus was written down before time began.

God *always* has a master plan with an eternal purpose.

Okay, I'm ready to go to the Nixon Library.

December 30. Day 340.

Mary Magdalene was crying because the tomb that held Jesus's body was empty. She saw a man she thought was the gardener and asked him to please tell her where they had put Jesus. He turned to her and said, "Mary"—and as soon as He spoke her name, she knew who He was (John 20:10–16).

When Jesus speaks our name, all that is wrong is suddenly right, and we see what we couldn't see before.

The disciples feared for their lives, so they hid in a room and locked the door. Jesus walked through the wall and said, "Peace be with you," and then He showed them His hands and feet (John 20:19–20).

Nothing can separate us from the love of Jesus, not even a locked door or a locked heart.

He said, "As the Father has sent me, I am sending you." And then He *breathed on them* and said, "Receive the Holy Spirit" (John 20:22). They went from hiding behind a locked door to being commissioned to be His ambassadors!

Jesus looks beyond our flaws and sees the finished product, and whatever He asks of us, He enables us to do.

I believe He *still* says our names, *still* pursues us to give us His peace, and *still* looks beyond our frailty, breathing life into our souls to use us for His glory.

Breathe on me, Jesus.

December 31. Day 341.

Our New Year's Eve tradition was to ride the Star Ferry, a boat that takes you from one side of the harbor to the other. At precisely midnight, it would stop and blow its horn. We would kiss and then stand against the railings on the side of the boat and pray for our beloved city. Tonight will mark the end of a very sad year, and the beginning of a new year that Jim won't be a part of. Take me to my manna.

I'm still fixated on the breath of God. Second Timothy 3:16 says that all Scripture is God-breathed, which is why my manna is so life-giving! In Ezekiel 37, God breathed into dry bones and raised them up to be a vast army. In Psalm 18, one breath from God's nostrils exposed the valleys of the seabed and the foundations of the earth, and the enemies were scattered and God's people saved!

> Breathe on me, Breath of God, fill me with life anew,
> That I may love what Thou dost love, and do what Thou wouldst do.
> Breathe on me, Breath of God, until my heart is pure,
> Until with Thee I will one will, to do and to endure.
> Breathe on me, Breath of God, till I am wholly Thine;
> Till all this earthly part of me glows with Thy fire divine.
> (Edwin Hatch, 1878)

January 1, 2006. Day 342.

On this first day of the New Year I resolutely declare:

On this path of widowhood I will continue to send self-pity back to hell and allow the peace of the Lord to guard my heart and mind. I will not live according to how I feel or what I see. Instead, I will believe in what I do not see and be certain of what I hope for. I will look at the sky in huge anticipation of when Jesus will come and take me to my real home.

Jesus, I can't breathe without You. I need You more than food. I can't exist without Your grace. I need You to fill me with Your perseverance and endurance. I need Your eternal encouragement. I need You to carry me. I need You to empower me. I know You will lead me and supply my every need. Use my life, hidden in Yours, to make You famous.

Take me to my manna.

In John 21, the resurrected Jesus has a beautiful conversation with Peter. He asks Peter if he loves Him, not once, but three times. The night before Jesus was crucified Peter denied knowing Jesus three times, so for each denial in his past, Jesus gives Peter a chance to proclaim his love for Him now. Peter was reinstated and commissioned to be an ambassador of the gospel of Jesus Christ.

The mercy of Jesus wipes away failures, denials, and disobedience.

The grace of God pushes us forward into His purposes, leaving our sin in a sea of forgetfulness.

Jesus, just like Peter, I run into Your mercy.

Use me in whatever way You want.

January 2. Day 343.

Yesterday morning I went to a Catholic mass. I wept as I listened to a homily about Mary, the mother of Jesus, and her unconditional yes to what God had created her to do. Mary accepted the task, taking no thought of the scandal or the danger that could result. Since the onset of this ordained path, God has shown me the kind of obedience He requires. He commands obedience which mirrors Abraham's as he held the knife over his only son, or Noah's when he built an ark even though it had never rained, or Mary's when she joyfully abandoned herself to house the very Son of God.

In Acts 1, the resurrected Jesus told His followers that they must wait for the promised Holy Spirit, who would *empower them to be His witnesses all over the world.* After He said those words, He was taken up to heaven before their very eyes. As they stood there in a bit of daze, two angels announced to them that *Jesus would one day come back in the same way He left.* They walked away, found a room in the upper part of a house, and waited for the Holy Spirit.

After three years of ministry and miracles, a crucifixion and a resurrection, there were only one hundred and twenty faithful followers in that room—*one hundred and twenty people whose lives were about to change, and whose* obedience *would turn the world upside down.*

January 3. Day 344.

Yesterday we watched the 117th Rose Bowl Parade during the worst storm Southern California has experienced in fifty years. I tried to focus on the joy it was giving my parents, who have always wanted to see the Rose Bowl in person, instead of the typhoon. A few hours into it, I leaned over to them and told them there was no hurry, but whenever they wanted to leave to let me know. They nearly leaped off the bench! Evidently they were enduring the storm for me! We maneuvered our way through moving floats to get to our vehicle, only to discover that it was blocked in and we couldn't leave. I'm sure in a few years this might be funny, but right now, not so much. Some days are just an uphill struggle, and yesterday was one of them.

But it's a new day, *filled with new mercies and new strength,* so Holy Spirit, take me to my manna.

In Acts 2, Luke records how the Holy Spirit filled the room. The one hundred and twenty began to speak in languages they had never learned, *declaring the wonders of God* to the thousands who stood on the street below. Amazed and perplexed, everyone listening wondered how this could be, so with great boldness, Peter told them the story of Jesus. *Over three thousand chose to believe in Jesus—and the first church was born.* Some of Peter's message was taken from Psalm 16:

I have set the Lord *always before me.*
Because He is at my right hand, *I will not be shaken.*
I will live in hope because You will not abandon me;
You have made known to me the paths of life;
You will fill me with *joy in Your presence,* with eternal pleasures at Your right hand!

Amen and Amen.
Day 344, here I come.

January 4. Day 345.

The early church is so appealing. Luke writes that:

All the believers were together and had everything in common. Selling their possessions and goods, *they gave to anyone who was in need.* Every day they ate together with glad and sincere hearts, praising God and enjoying the favor of all the people. And the Lord added to their numbers daily those who were being saved. (Acts 2:44–47)

Can you imagine what it would be like if we all sold our possessions to help the needy?

Poverty would be eliminated! No one would be hungry or sleeping on the street! If we lived like the early church, everyone would have a family!

If we lived like the early church, the world would take notice and want what we have.

I want the real deal.

I want to be part of a church that makes everyone on the outside want in.

January 5. Day 346.

I'm having a war with self-pity this morning. My thoughts are consumed with how Jim and I thought our lives would unfold. Allowing myself to go that place opens the door to self-pity, which leads me right to the pit of despair. That pit is like a magnet.

Everyone's loss is so huge. *Jim is irreplaceable.* We have all been left with immeasurable sorrow and sadness. I'm trying so hard to live, but my heart feels dead. Yet somehow I have to keep going. Self-pity needs to be banished back to hell, and I need to lean on the throne of my Sovereign God. I have to fix my thoughts on Jesus. I have to put my armor on and fight against the despair. I have to believe that my God will use this pain for His glory. I must look at the sky and hold unswervingly to the hope I have because of Jesus.

Holy Spirit, take me to my manna so I can do what I need to do.

In an effort to stop Peter and John from talking about Jesus, the religious bigwigs threw them in prison. Their attempts to squash the good news about Jesus were futile, because another two thousand souls chose to believe. The following day, the high priest demanded to know what power they were using to do miracles. Peter told them that it was all because of JESUS, the One they had crucified but *whom God had raised from the dead!*

> When they saw the courage of Peter and John and realized that they were unschooled, ordinary men, *they were astonished* and took note that *these men had been with Jesus.* (Acts 4:13)

Adversity served to advance the gospel.

Jail time gave Peter and John a platform to declare the truth!

The more the opposition, the more the Holy Spirit enabled them. Their courage impressed even their enemies!

Oh, this is exactly what I needed today! I want my courage to astonish everyone around me. I want them to take note that *I have been with Jesus.*

Self-pity has been thrown back to hell. I'm ready to face another day!

January 6. Day 347.

Peter and John were making such an impact for Jesus that the religious officials decided to kill them. A respected teacher of the law reasoned with the Sanhedrin that if it was truly God working through the apostles they would be powerless to stop what was happening, so it would be wise just to leave them alone. They were let go with a warning to stop talking about Jesus, and then they were flogged.

I've read that the flogging whip was called a *flagrum*. It had a short handle and generally two or three long, thick thongs, each weighted down with lead balls or mutton bones. The thongs slashed the skin, while the balls or bones made deep wounds that caused a lot of bleeding.

Now here's what grabbed my heart:

> Peter and John were flogged [with a flagrum] and left *rejoicing* . . . because they had been counted worthy of suffering disgrace for the Name. (Acts 5:41–42)

These men considered it an honor to make Jesus famous even if it meant having their backs ripped to shreds.

I rejoice that God has counted me worthy to lose much, because it has given me a platform to tell His Story.

January 7. Day 348.

I'm going home in just a few hours. I hate good-byes, but to be honest I need routine these days. Working a fifty-six-hour week is a good thing for me right now. I will miss my boys. I will miss their hugs and the laughter. I will long for them the moment they drop me off at my gate.

Take me to my manna.

As the first church grew, so did the needs. It was brought to the apostles' attention that the widows were being overlooked, so they did something about it. (I like that.) They chose seven men who were filled with the Holy Spirit, laid hands on them, and prayed, setting them apart to look after the widows (Acts 6:1–6).

There is so much to learn from the early church. Every task, whether big or small, was immersed in prayer and fueled by the power of the Holy Spirit.

Holy Spirit, I need You. I can't walk this path without You. I can't tell the story of Jesus without You.

Open my eyes to needs and empower me to do something about them. Let's go home.

January 8. Day 349.

I arrived later than expected, and I lost a day because of the time change. Deb and Sondra were waiting for me at the front doors of our building. Mohsina was in my apartment and had dinner on the table. CJ and Ali are in the air heading back to Canada, and Curtis is about to begin a new week.

Life goes on.

It feels good to be home.

January 9. Day 350.

Sovereign God, take me away.

Acts 6 and 7 contain the story of Stephen, one of the men chosen to look after the widows. Luke writes that Stephen did amazing miracles among the people, and as usual, opposition arose from the religious hierarchy, which resulted in Stephen being seized and brought before the Sanhedrin. Stephen joyfully told the story of Jesus, which made them so angry they actually gnashed their teeth, dragged him out of the city, and stoned him. "But Stephen *looked up to heaven* and saw the glory of God, and *Jesus* standing at the right hand of God!" (Acts 7:55–56).

During Stephen's *worst* moments, *he raised his eyes* above his circumstances. *Stephen looked at the sky and saw JESUS!*

As Stephen was being pelted with rocks, he prayed—*not* that the stones would stop, *not* that his accusers would be swallowed up, but that *Jesus* would receive his spirit and that their actions would not be held against them!

I will not ask for the pain to stop.

I ask only that You will take my life and be glorified!

January 10. Day 351.

After the stoning of Stephen, the church came under massive persecution. Saul, who was in charge of Stephen's execution, went from house to house dragging off Christ-followers to prison, but because the apostles were scattered everywhere, the story of Jesus spread far and wide.

When Philip was in Samaria, an angel came to him and told him to go south to a desert road. When he arrived, he saw an Ethiopian man sitting in a chariot. The Holy Spirit told Philip to go to the chariot, so he ran over and stood beside it. When he heard the Ethiopian reading the words of Isaiah, *he knew exactly why he was there.* Philip soon found himself in the chariot telling him the story of Jesus. Philip baptized him into the faith, and while he was standing in the water, the Spirit of the Lord took him miles away to Azotus (Acts 8).

I'm sure the Ethiopian and Philip told that story until the day they died!

I want to live like the apostles lived. *I want to be led by angels and given instructions by the Holy Spirit.* I want to be at the right place, at the right time, so that I never miss out on an opportunity to tell the story of Jesus. I want to be invited into the homes of those who don't understand. I want to be the one to explain the mystery of the gospel. *I want to be whisked away from one adventure to the next. I want my words to be accompanied by the miraculous, so that those around me will pay close attention to the Story of all stories.*

Sovereign God, put me beside any chariot You want.

January 11. Day 352.

I've been up since 3:15 a.m. Exhaustion equals tears, and I really need sleep. Holy Spirit, take me to my manna.

Saul, who was on a mission to destroy the church, decided to widen the net and go to Damascus. On his way there, a light from heaven enveloped him and catapulted him off his horse. While he was lying in the dirt, Jesus spoke to him: "Saul, Saul, why do you persecute Me?"

"Who are You?" asked Saul.

"I am Jesus, the one you are persecuting. Now get up and go into the city, and you will be told what to do" (Acts 9:4–5).

What a beautiful picture of the oneness we have with Jesus! He doesn't say, "Why are you persecuting My followers?" He says, "Why are you persecuting *Me?*"

When we are persecuted, so is Jesus.

When we hurt, Jesus hurts too.

When we grieve, Jesus grieves.

This is exactly why believing in Jesus is *not* a religion, but rather a *relationship*. He is the strong one, and I am the weak one. He feels *everything* I feel, including my jet lag–induced weariness, and so today *His prayers will give me the strength that I need to keep making Him famous!*

January 12. Day 353.

It was good to be reminded yesterday that Jesus and I are in this together. Whatever I feel, Jesus feels it too. Take me to my manna.

What stood out to me in Saul's conversion story was the part Ananias played. Saul was blinded after his encounter with Jesus and was taken to a house in Damascus, where he prayed and fasted for three days. He must have been terrified, but not as much as Ananias would have been when the Lord told him to go and pray for Saul to receive his sight.

> Lord, I have heard many reports about this man and all the harm he has done to Your saints in Jerusalem. And he has come here with authority from the chief priests to arrest all who call on Your name! (Acts 9:13–14)

Saul's brutality was infamous. It was at the feet of Saul that those who murdered Stephen laid their coats so they would be unhindered to throw the rocks (Acts 7:58). *What the Lord was asking of Ananias would be equivalent to asking me to go and visit Osama bin Laden.* Saul was a terrorist who felt he was doing God a favor.

The Lord told Ananias that Saul was His chosen instrument, who will carry His name to the Gentiles. Without hesitation, Ananias obeyed, and when he met Saul, he greeted him *as his brother.* He prayed for him, Saul's sight was restored, and a *terrorist was transformed into an evangelist!*

Wow, it doesn't get much better than that!

Everyone is deserving of the love and mercy of Jesus.

Jesus, bring me to a Saul.

January 13. Day 354.

Acts 10 tells a story about Jewish Peter meeting Cornelius, a God-fearing Gentile. An angel tells Cornelius to go find Peter, bring him to back to his house, and listen to all he has to say. Meanwhile, God shows Peter in a vision that nothing He has made is unclean, and while Peter's trying to wrap his mind around the unthinkable, three men show up at his door to take him to Cornelius's house. The Holy Spirit assures Peter that this is a God thing, so he goes and is the one who gets to tell the story of Jesus to a Gentile family and watch them all choose to believe.

This is not a fairy tale. This is a factual account of *the extent God will go to bring the truth to those who need to hear.* He prepared the heart of Cornelius to believe, and he prepared the heart of Peter to go.

Both men obeyed despite the strangeness of the mission, and both men's lives were changed forever.

Sovereign God, my answer to whatever You ask of me will always be a resounding yes.

January 14. Day 355.

Today marks a year. It was Friday night. We had taught all day, so we decided to just kick back and relax. We got comfy in our chair for two and had a feast of chicken karahi and rice. Jim was suffering from what we thought was indigestion. He tried every concoction we could think of, but nothing brought relief. He told me he was going to read for a while until whatever it was had passed. I went to bed but couldn't sleep. I got up a few times to check on him, and each time he told me not to worry. He thought maybe it was gastritis. He was looking pale and sweaty. I had a gut feeling he was wrong.

I googled "heart attack symptoms," and without telling him what they were symptoms of, I read them out loud and asked him if that described how he was feeling. He nodded yes while projectile vomiting across the room. I grabbed the phone and began to dial 999, Hong Kong's equivalent to 911.

When I look back, I can't believe how calm I was. I told the operator that my husband was having a heart attack; he was conscious but in terrible pain and that we needed an ambulance immediately. I told her our address in Cantonese and then hung up the phone. I felt like I was in a movie. This couldn't be happening to Jim. Maybe I was dreaming. I threw on jeans and a T-shirt and put on my shoes. I threw Jim's wallet in my purse. I knelt beside him and assured him he would be okay. I prayed.

The ambulance arrived within ten minutes. They checked his vitals and gave him oxygen. They put him on a stretcher, and we rode the elevator down ten floors to the lobby. It was almost midnight as the ambulance raced to the hospital. When we arrived, they whisked Jim away and told me to wait. I called Curtis and he said he'd be right there. I called CJ, who was an ocean away, and told him to pray.

Throughout the next few hours they did a series of tests and attempted to stabilize him. He was allowed one visitor at a time, so Curtis and I took turns. At 3:00 a.m. they moved Jim to the Cardiac ICU. The nurses asked me to leave, but I refused. Jim was shivering, so I lay beside him to try to keep him warm. At 6:00 a.m. the nurse threatened to call security if I didn't leave. I left only after she promised me that she would remember his name was Jim Keddy, not Bed 42. I told her he was my life and begged her take good care of him. When I kissed Jim good-bye, he whispered in my ear that I was his life too, and to hurry back. *I thought the worst was over, but I was so wrong.* Take me to my manna.

Peter said, "Who was I to think that I could oppose God?" (Acts 11:17).

Nothing happens unless God declares it to be, so isn't it easier just to embrace His will rather than fight it?

Sovereign God, I bow to You in complete surrender.

January 15. Day 356.

King Herod has Peter arrested and orders four soldiers to guard him. Acts 12:5 says that the church was earnestly praying for Peter. We don't know the content of their prayer, but I'm pretty sure it wasn't for his release! I'm sure their prayer was that *Jesus would be made famous.*

We're talking about the early church, who knew that following Jesus equaled persecution. *They expected to face trials. They rejoiced when they were counted worthy to suffer disgrace for the name.* Peter knew it was useless to oppose God, and that's why even though he was bound with chains and surrounded by soldiers, he was able to sleep! *Peter was trusting in his God, who brings eternal value out of pain!*

Sleeping the night before your execution is possible when you have the assurance that you belong to Jesus! Peace rules when you remember that the prison you find yourself in won't last forever. All questions cease when you know that your suffering will result in Jesus being made famous!

Perfect submission, all is at rest! I and my Savior, am happy and blest!

Watching and waiting, looking above; filled with His goodness and lost in His love!

This is my story! This is my song! Praising my Savior all the day long! ("Blessed Assurance"—Fanny Crosby, 1853)

January 16. Day 357.

I have a theory.

After the angel escorted Peter out of prison, he made his way to the house where the believers were praying. When the servant heard his voice from the other side of the door, she was so overjoyed that she forgot to let him in! She interrupted the prayer meeting to tell them that Peter was outside, and they told her she was out of her mind (Acts 12:13–15).

I've heard preachers say that the believers' astonishment was evidence of a lack of faith. These sermons always end with the listener being admonished to expect answers when they pray.

I couldn't disagree more.

Those praying saints were astonished because they were *not* praying for Peter's release; *they were praying for Jesus to be glorified through Peter's imprisonment and suffering.* I don't think their prayers had anything to do with God sending angels to break him out of prison. That's just what God decided to do. *But I do think their prayers were the reason Peter could sleep chained to prison guards.*

That's my theory, and I'm sticking to it.

Sovereign God, I will never demand anything of You. If You send an angel to rescue me I will be amazed, but I will be equally amazed at the grace and strength You give me to endure adversity.

Whatever You choose to do, I'll be okay with it. All I want is for everyone to come to know Jesus.

January 17. Day 358.

I woke up to the Brooklyn Tabernacle Choir singing a soul-strengthening, hand-clapping song about how nothing is impossible with God!

He can send angels to rescue us, or He can send the perseverance of Christ to help us endure.

He can heal our bodies or come close and fill us with a peace that makes no earthly sense.

NOTHING is impossible with our God!

Take me to my manna.

Acts 13 is an exciting read. Saul, who was now called Paul, teamed up with Barnabas, and the Holy Spirit was using them to bring the good news about Jesus to Jews and Gentiles alike. Revival erupted wherever they preached as countless hearts were opened to the Truth. This of course riled up the local religious sect, who stirred up persecution and kicked them out of their territory, so the boys shook the dust from their sandals and moved on to the next city. They were *filled* with joy and the Holy Spirit because they *knew* they were fulfilling God's purpose for them in their generation.

Sovereign God, that's all I ask for.

I want to serve Your *purpose in my generation.*

Help me to show them that nothing is impossible *with You.*

January 18. Day 359.

As I made my early morning tea, the Brooklyn Tabernacle Choir serenaded my soul with a love song to Jesus. When I opened God's Word, they began to sing about the reward that is certain for the faithful. It did my soul good to be reminded that *what we do for Jesus is never in vain.* Doing something for Jesus is often equated to selling all our possessions and moving to Africa. *We usually don't think of it in terms of crucifying our flesh, rejoicing in our suffering, trusting God in the darkness, and keeping our eyes on the sky.*

Whatever we do for Jesus is never in vain. I like that a lot.

Take me to my manna.

Acts 14:22 says, "We must go through many hardships to enter the kingdom of God."

It doesn't say *we might.* It says *we must.*

We run from suffering, yet I know in my spirit that what Paul said is as true now as it was then. The eternal necessity of suffering is all through God's Word. In Acts 14 some Jews stirred up the Gentiles against Paul and Barnabas, but instead of this dynamic duo making a quick exit, *they lengthened their stay and continued to tell the story of Jesus,* which led to Paul being stoned and dragged out of the city. When they left him for dead, he got up and walked *right back into the city* and *continued where he left off!* Suffering spurred Paul on. When they went to Derbe to encourage the church to remain true to the faith, Paul *never once complained* about his suffering; in fact, it was the exact opposite! *He rejoiced in it because Jesus was being made famous.*

We *must* go through many hardships to enter the kingdom of God!

We *must* remain true!

We *must* look at the sky and long for His return, because *what we do for Jesus is never, ever in vain!*

January 19. Day 360.

My CD alarm clock didn't work today! Thankfully my internal clock woke me up, but my soul missed my morning song. The sky is still inky black. That's how my heart feels sometimes on this path. No song and a very dark sky. But those are the moments when I can choose to lift up my heart *regardless of how I feel* and declare:

When I am weak—You are strong!

I trust You though I do not understand.

To hell with self-pity!

I read once that Amy Carmichael did not stop reading God's Word each day until something grabbed her heart. That's what I did this morning. I read and read, and suddenly there it was in Acts 16.

Paul and his companions were trying to go to the province of Asia to share the news about Jesus, but they were stopped by the Holy Spirit. They decided to go another way, and this time the Spirit of Jesus stopped them again, so they left and went to Troas. It was here, during the night, that God gave Paul a vision of a man begging him to come to Macedonia and so that's what they did.

When we truly only want what only God wants, then we can be sure that He will get us to where He wants us!

I never need to worry about what's next.

My triune God has all of my steps already charted and won't let me make a mistake.

The sun is shining ever so slightly. The black sky has turned a deep blue, and I hear a song in my heart.

January 20. Day 361.

What would I do without the Brooklyn Tabernacle Choir? They were with Jim and I for every adventure, and now they are my closest companions on this ordained path. Their music sets the tone of my day and always lifts my eyes to the sky. *Thank you, Brooklyn Tabernacle Choir, for being God's voice to me every single day.*

Take me to my manna.

Paul and Silas were arrested, falsely accused, stripped, beaten, flogged, imprisoned, put in chains, and left in the darkness to rot . . . *and this was after they had obeyed God and gone to Macedonia!*

They didn't ask why.

They never demanded an explanation.

Instead, they sang, they prayed, and Jesus was glorified!

God sent an earthquake that shook the foundations of the prison and threw open the doors. The jailer woke up and was ready to kill himself because he was sure all his prisoners would be gone, but Paul stopped him, reassuring him that everyone was still there. He fell on his knees asking how he could be saved, and Paul and Silas got to tell him the story of their Jesus, and he and his entire family chose to believe! (Acts 16:25–34).

Does God use suffering? Do floggings and chains have eternal worth? *YES!* An entire family came to know Jesus because Paul and Silas chose to worship God despite their pain. *Our reaction to adversity can persuade those around us that the Jesus we serve is real.*

I have a lot to live for.

January 21. Day 362.

I had dinner last night with a friend who was passing through Hong Kong on her way to Thailand. A few years ago she worked here, and while she looked for an apartment, she lived with us. After a quick hello, she asked me how I get out of bed every morning. She told me that she's never met a couple more one or more in love than Jim and me. She said that she and her husband were working toward that kind of relationship, so her question was sincere: *"How do you get out of bed every morning?"*

I told her that every second is a miracle. I told her that I continuously *choose* to rest in God's sovereignty and believe with all my heart that God will give my pain eternal worth. I told her that my war is with self-pity, and that many times a day I have to send it back to hell and remind my soul to trust. I told her I look at the sky in expectation of when Jesus will crack the skies to take me home, but until that moment comes, I live to make Him famous.

Take me to my manna.

> He Himself gives all men life and breath and everything else. He determines the times set for them and the exact places where they should live. *For in Him we live and move and have our being.* (Acts 17:25–28)

This is how I got out of bed today; this is how I'll get out of bed tomorrow and in all the tomorrows to come!

January 22. Day 363.

Look to the Lord and His strength; seek His face always. (Psalm 105:4)

Jim use to say to me, "Look at His face, Subies. Do you see any worry there?" It's so true. *There is not even a hint of worry or sadness.* All I see is assurance, peace, and love. So here I sit, looking at His face.

Holy Spirit, carry me to my manna.

Everywhere Paul went, he had a twofold mission. He was either persuading people to believe in Jesus or encouraging those who were already believers to endure till the end. No matter what opposition was thrown his way, *he never stopped telling the Story.*

And because of his obedience, the name of Jesus was made famous.

That's all I want.

January 23. Day 364.

I love You, my Sovereign God! Every morning You turn my eyes to the sky and fill my heart with purpose. Holy Spirit, take me to my manna.

> And now, compelled by the Spirit, I am going to Jerusalem, not knowing what will happen to me there. I only know that in every city the Holy Spirit warns me that prison and hardships are facing me. *However, I*

consider my life worth nothing to me, if only I may finish the race and com-
plete the task the Lord Jesus has given me, which is the task of testifying
to the gospel of God's grace. (Acts 20:23–24)

Paul was saying good-bye to Ephesus and walking headfirst into sorrow, but he knew that *beyond* that was an eternal glory that he couldn't even begin to imagine. The only thing Paul was concerned about was finishing the race and completing the task Jesus had given him to do. Suffering didn't detour him. People's opinions didn't matter. *He lived to tell the story of Jesus.*

So do I.

January 24. Day 365.

Paul's companions knew that Jerusalem meant danger, and because they loved Paul they tried to change his mind, but *Paul would not be dissuaded.*

> Why are you weeping and breaking my heart? I'm ready not only to
> be bound, but also to die for the name of the Lord Jesus. (Acts 21:13)

A year ago today I asked Jim if during his week in the hospital he'd ever thought he was going to die. He told me he hadn't. Then he looked at me and said, "I'm not afraid to die, though. I'm ready. I can't wait to see what's ahead."

Jim lived for God's will to be done and for God's purposes to be fulfilled in his life. He'd been telling me since we were dating that his last breath would come when he had accomplished his purpose here on earth.

Every follower of Jesus should live that way.

Whatever You want, Jesus, is okay with me.

January 25. Day 366.

One year.

I woke up with a promise that Jesus dropped into my spirit the week of Jim's heart attack: *"I will plant your feet on the ground. I will lift your head."*

I clung to that promise for the seven days Jim was in the hospital. I would whisper it to myself as I rode the elevator up to Jim's ward and during the taxi ride home. I had forgotten all about it until this morning. I realize only now that God was preparing me for the journey I was about to embark upon.

Throughout this past year, my Sovereign God has indeed planted my feet on the ground and lifted my head. He has proven to me that His strength is made perfect in my weakness; that His grace is enough; and that joy does not depend on my circumstances. He has taught me that my pain can have eternal worth if I lift it up to Him.

I have embraced the truth that He has put me on this path and that Jim "had to get out so that others could get in." Daily Jesus lifts my eyes to the sky and puts an anticipation in my heart for *that day* when I will finally see His face and have every tear wiped away.

In a few hours I will be boarding a plane to London, England, to speak at a conference. They asked me to talk about what to do when you're faced with adversity. My prayer is that every hurting heart will be encouraged *to believe in what they do not see, trust though they don't understand, and choose to look at the sky.* As Jim so perfectly said in one of his last messages, "The day will come when we will see Him, and we'll fall at His feet . . . and our little voices and tiny lives will be caught up into that chorus that is Him. One voice; one song; one joy of joys: Him."

Year two, here I come.

EPILOGUE

At the time of publishing, it has been nearly a decade since Jim's homegoing, and every day continues to be a miracle.

I returned to Canada in the spring of 2007 because God told me to, but that, my friends, is another book.

My precious Jim, my brother Dwight, and both my parents have moved to heaven, leaving me here on earth to prove daily that God's strength really is made perfect in our weakness. Although this world labels me a widow and an orphan, I am part of the Body of Christ, which is immeasurable and so beautiful it takes my breath away.

I still miss my Jim and long for his hand to be in mine, but I am living proof that with God nothing is impossible. *All questions have been silenced by a peace that only God can give.* My heart is filled with joy because I know Jesus and Jesus knows me.

I'm on His mat, going down His mountain, held by His arms, laughing with The One who makes it possible to *truly live*, not just exist.

DEALING WITH GRIEF, GODS WAY.

1. Embrace God's sovereignty.

God's first step in the grieving process is to recognize that He is in control. Surrendering all your questions ushers in His supernatural peace.

2. Continuously choose to trust.

The choice to trust God is not a onetime deal. It is a constant, conscious decision to trust that His ways are always going to be higher than yours. With every breath, you choose. With every choice comes strength to choose again.

3. Remember that this is not all there is.

Our time here on earth is but a pilgrimage to the real life to come. The trials, the sorrow, and the pain are light and momentary compared to the uncontainable joy that awaits us in heaven! When you look at things in the light of eternity, the mountain becomes a hill and the climb is doable. Always look at the sky in anticipation of that day when your faith will be made sight!

4. Realize that suffering is valuable.

Suffering pushes us into the arms of Jesus! It reminds us that we can't do this journey without Him.

Suffering teaches us that we can't go by how we feel or by what we see. We must believe in what we hope for and be certain of what we do not see because without faith, it is impossible to please God. Emotions are not reliable, but Jesus is. Stand on God's Word and hold on to His promises, because they will never fail.

Suffering purifies us. James says that the testing of our faith develops perseverance, and that perseverance must finish its work so that we will be mature and complete, not lacking anything (James 1:3–4).

Suffering showcases God's attributes! When we are weak; He is strong. We have this treasure in jars of clay to show that this all-surpassing power comes from God and not us (2 Corinthians 4:7).

Suffering makes us homesick for heaven. It lifts our eyes to the sky and puts a longing in our hearts for the day when all wrong will be right and all sorrow will be erased.

Suffering advances the gospel. Those who have suffered can comfort with the comfort with which God has comforted them. (2 Corinthians 1:4). When I talk to a widow and tell her Jesus will never leave her, she believes me, because I have proved it to be true. When others who don't know Jesus look at me and see a twinkle in my eye and a bright smile on my face, they ask why, and I get to tell them.

5. Find someone to love.

Don't wait for someone to love you; you find someone to bless and encourage. The less you think about your own pain, the lighter your heart will feel. There is always a hurting heart that could use a hug or a pot of soup. Open your heart and your home to the lonely, and your despair will evaporate as the joy of the Lord takes over and gives eternal value to your pain.

Acknowledgments

Curtis and CJ, you keep Jim alive in how you phrase a sentence, how you laugh, and how you live. I know every mom thinks they have the best sons, but they are simply wrong, because I do. Amy and Ali, you are much more than my daughters-in-law. You are my friends and my sisters. You have filled my arms with grandchildren and our home with life.

Along with my family, there are countless friends on both sides of the ocean who have never stopped walking this journey with me. God has used you to help put me back together. You've called me, fed me, employed me, and pushed me forward when I got stuck. You've cried with me, laughed with me, and reminded me that life is too short to ever go near the pit. You've let me cook for you, and you've cooked feasts for me. We've flown above the clouds and through typhoons. Your arms have steadied me, protected me, and held me. Your prayers have saved me and propelled me to say yes to my God when everything in me wanted to say no.

To my precious family and my faithful friends, thank you. . . . I love you with all of my heart.

There's a conversation in *The Lord of the Rings*, in which Pippen laments to the great Gandalf that he didn't think it would end this way. Gandalf replies "End? No, the journey doesn't end here. Death is just another path, one that we all must take. The grey rain-curtain of this world rolls back, and all turns to silver glass, and then you see it." When Pippen wonders aloud what exactly he will see, Gandalf says "white shores, and beyond, a far green country under a swift sunrise," to which Pippen concludes:

"Well, that isn't so bad."

It won't be long until we all see what we long for.

Until then, we have a job to do so that everyone will have that unshakable hope.

Contact the Author:

Sue Keddy is a passionate communicator, who lives to make the love of Jesus famous.

E-mail: lookathesky@gmail.com
Twitter: @keddysue